The Long Gilded Age

AMERICAN BUSINESS, POLITICS, AND SOCIETY

Series editors
Andrew Wender Cohen, Pamela Walker Laird,
Mark H. Rose, and Elizabeth Tandy Shermer

Books in the series American Business, Politics, and Society explore the
relationships over time between governmental institutions and the creation
and performance of markets, firms, and industries large and small. The central
theme of this series is that politics, law, and public policy—understood broadly to
embrace not only lawmaking but also the structuring presence of governmental
institutions—has been fundamental to the evolution of American business
from the colonial era to the present. The series aims to explore, in particular,
developments that have enduring consequences.

A complete list of books in the series is available from the publisher.

THE LONG GILDED AGE

AMERICAN CAPITALISM *and the* LESSONS
of a NEW WORLD ORDER

LEON FINK

PENN

UNIVERSITY OF PENNSYLVANIA PRESS

PHILADELPHIA

Published by
University of Pennsylvania Press
Philadelphia, Pennsylvania 19104-4112
www.upenn.edu/pennpress

Printed in the United States of America on acid-free paper
1 3 5 7 9 10 8 6 4 2

Library of Congress Cataloging-in-Publication Data
Fink, Leon, 1948–
   The long Gilded Age : American capitalism and the lessons of a new world order /
Leon Fink.—1st ed.
      p.   cm.—(American business, politics, and society)
   Includes bibliographical references and index.
   ISBN 978-0-8122-4688-9 (hardcover : alk. paper)
   1. United States—History—1865–1921. 2. Capitalism—United States—History—19th
century. 3. Capitalism—United States—History—20th century. 4. Labor—United
States—History—19th century. 5. Labor—United States—History—20th century.
6. Globalization—History—19th century. 7. Globalization—History—20th century. I. Title.
II. Series: American business, politics, and society.
E661.F54   2015
973.8—dc23   2014029614

To Nina, Naila, and Julius: A new world is ever being born.

Contents

Introduction   1

Chapter 1. The American Ideology   12

Chapter 2. Great Strikes Revisited   34

Chapter 3. The University and Industrial Reform   63

Chapter 4. Labor's Search for Legitimacy   90

Chapter 5. Coming of Age in Internationalist Times   120

Epilogue   148

Notes   155

Index   195

Acknowledgments   205

Introduction

One way or another, after 1875, there was growing
skepticism about the effectiveness of the autonomous and
self-correcting market economy, Adam Smith's famous
"hidden hand," without some assistance from state and
public authority. The hand was becoming visible in all sorts
of ways.

—E. J. Hobsbawm, *The Age of Empire, 1875–1914*

The Long Gilded Age encompasses a set of discrete but overlapping essays
with three main themes. The first is that the arrangements and institutions
that we now take for granted in American economic life depended, in fact,
on a thick set of *political* ideas that were intensely fought over for decades
before being consolidated in the opening years of the previous century. The
second is that the question of *workers' power* within industry lay at the
center of many of these conflicts. Finally, and perhaps most provocatively,
I argue for the *internationalism* of the processes at work across the prewar
era. In particular, I hope to demonstrate that American outcomes offered
but one set of variants within a worldwide confrontation between the capitalist marketplace and those determined to transform it according to
socially defined ends, that American labor radicals and reformers were
themselves intensely aware of the larger menu of historical and political
possibilities of their age, and that the legacy of this earlier era of globalization offers possibilities yet to be fully tested in our own era, one famously
baptized by President George H. W. Bush in 1990 as a *new world order*.[1]

My contribution adds but a new twist to a mountain of judgments
previously proffered upon a time period that itself is regularly open to
vigorous debate about its duration and very name. Classically divided into
two segments, the Gilded Age and Progressive Era, as these years recede
ever farther from the present, insiders have commonly lumped the two

together into one un-poetic amalgam called the GAPE. Both names, we quickly note, convey invidious distinctions rare to the appellations of other aggregates of time (compare "Jacksonian" or "Civil War era" or even "Roaring Twenties" or "Long 1960s"). Typically, the Gilded Age (named after the 1873 novel by Mark Twain and Charles Dudley Warner) pejoratively conjures up a period of unbridled urban-industrial expansion, government corruption, labor conflict, and recurrent depression from 1877 to roughly 1900. The Progressive Era, on the other hand, self-named by some of its own reform-minded champions, is likely to summon up more positive associations as an attempt by a variety of actors across the first two decades of the twentieth century (stopping just before or after U.S. engagement in World War I depending on the interpreter) to reckon with the very excesses of the Gilded Age.

To be sure, historians themselves have never been happy with such simplistic dichotomization. Just as one can locate no shortage of creative reformers in the Gilded Age, the Progressive Era also rings with scandal, corruption, and economic mayhem. Attempting to get beyond historical moralizing, a few scholars have famously ventured forth with more integrative conceptual tags for this period of national development, such as "the search for order," "organizational society," "age of modernization," or, most recently, "new spirits." With a more global view (and stopping at the watershed of the Great War), the masterful Eric Hobsbawm similarly unified the period in Marxian metaphor as "the age of empire."

Personally, and for the interpretive emphasis of this volume, I like playing off the very *judgmentalism* inherent in the original categories. Within reason (that is, the standards of evidence-gathering and sifting that we assign to the historical craft), we look to history to understand our own place in time. That quest inevitably puts the questions asked of the past at the changing beck and call of the historian's own times. We want to know what happened because it *mattered* in determining not only who we are but who we might have been—and thus what we can make of our own world. For that reason I currently prefer the option of "The Long Gilded Age" for the entire GAPE (for convenience, let's round the years to 1880–1920). Critically inquisitive (if still inevitably somewhat pejorative), the phrase usefully refocuses attention on bursting social inequalities as well as the political management of industrial capitalism across a crucial and formative period of the nation's development.

As regularly pointed out in U.S. history textbooks, the physical changes of the country in this period were stupendous and world-shaking. Carl Degler emphasized in what he called the "age of the economic revolution" that the rise of industry not only transformed how and where Americans lived but, by creating a near-unquenchable demand for labor, repeopled America with an industrial workforce drawn from the far corners of the globe. By 1890 the annual value of manufactured goods overtook the sum of agricultural commodities for the first time in American history, and within five years, the nation ranked fourth as of 1860 had become the world's supreme industrial power. Likely the most tangible sign of the application of machine power to domestic and world trade was the railway grid: by 1890 U.S. trackage surpassed that of all Europe, including Russia.[2]

To distinguish the turn-of-the-twentieth-century material changes from an earlier dynamic unleashed by textile manufactory and steam power in late eighteenth-century Britain, economic historians generally associate the Gilded Age with a "second industrial revolution." Beginning with the Bessemer steel process, famously adopted by Andrew Carnegie in the mid-1870s, a leap in industrial productivity and consolidation depended on new technologies, including electricity, chemical engineering, as well as communications applications like the telegraph and radio. Bigness was both cause and effect of industrialization. By 1910, corporate consolidation had produced the Sugar Trust, the Beef Trust, the Steel Trust, the Oil Trust, and the Money Trust; alongside Carnegie, meat-packers Gustavus Swift and Philip Armour, railroad giant J. J. Hill, oil tycoon John D. Rockefeller, and mythical investment banker J. P. Morgan had become household names.[3] The science-and-technology base of American business preeminence by the early twentieth century equally depended on a new knowledge economy, manifest in a spreading network of research universities.

Geographically, the behemoth of the economic revolution was the industrial city: over one hundred cities grew by 100 percent or more in the decade of the 1880s alone, and by 1890 Chicago and Philadelphia had joined New York City as centers of more than a million residents. Whereas little more than a tenth of Americans lived in cities of more than 50,000 people in 1850, the "urban" population became a majority, as documented by the 1920 census. America's urban-industrial revolution also entailed its own demographic upheaval. By 1910, immigrant workers—increasingly from southern and eastern Europe—dominated the labor force in coal and copper mining, iron and steel, construction, oil refining, as well as once proudly Yankee cotton textiles: as Herbert Gutman (with Ira Berlin) definitively concluded about the industrial landscape: "most American workers were immigrants or the children of immigrants."[4]

The material and technological changes of the era, dramatic as they were, have inclined us mistakenly to think of the Long Gilded Age as one where business, science, and economic interests mattered more than politics or ideas. Indeed, it is not uncommon to teach the GAPE as one where politics and culture (read, the Progressive Era) are struggling to "catch up with" economic and social change. Yet, this is surely a crude rendering of the inherent mutual dependence of the economic and political realms. As I hope to demonstrate in several of the succeeding essays, *the law* (as a reflection of both legislative and judicial processes) *mattered a great deal* in fashioning the peculiarities of American capitalism.

And nowhere, I suggest, was the particularism of American political development more in play than in the area of workplace relations between labor and management. Workers themselves, drawing at once on republican traditions of citizen action and on the yearnings of those yet to taste full citizenship rights, first took the initiative to demand a place at the economic table. Audaciously, the Knights of Labor used both the ballot box and the boycott to push for union recognition and the eight-hour day. The skilled trades and industrial unions like the mineworkers in the American Federation of Labor (AFL) likewise rebelled against wage cuts and the abuse of union representatives. Altogether, an era of titanic clashes in major industries including the railroads, coal, and steel as well as local strikes in manufacturing, urban transit, and construction placed the Labor Question (i.e., just what role should workers have in America's new industrial economy?) front and center in political campaigns, legislative corridors, church pulpits, as well as social science scholarship.

Finally, I have become ever more aware of the provincialism of all nationally-confined chronological frameworks. This volume thus also self-consciously adds to a larger move by American historians (indeed, a move often made earlier by those outside U.S. history and especially by those writing about earlier periods) to see beyond national borders as well to situate what happens within those borders in a broader context or, as it is often now called, an America-in-the-world approach. This impulse was first formalized in the *La Pietra Report* issued in 2000 by the Organization of American Historians Project on Internationalizing the Study of American

History: "If historians have often treated the nation as self-contained and undifferentiated, it is increasingly clear that this assumption is true in neither the present nor the past. . . . Both the nation and the other historical phenomena we examine must be resituated in larger contexts because the movements of people, money, knowledge, and things are not contained by single political units."[5]

Although it might be argued that *any* period of American history can benefit from a combination of comparative and transnational insights, the bona fides for the turn-of-the-century period are particularly compelling. More than ever before in its history, the U.S. economy was tethered to international forces, and the long-distance interactions—whether economic, political, or cultural—would not return to a similar state of intensity until our own times. A prior, mid-century transportation revolution—encompassing railroads, steamships, and construction of the Suez Canal—set the stage for a dizzying period of global movement, both human and commercial. By the late 1880s, for example, steamships were ferrying the majority of the world's trade, and their plunging prices facilitated a new, mass steerage class of travelers. By 1914, Europe was importing more than three-quarters of its butter and wheat, and nearly half its meat—with the latter two products effectively fueling the North American farm economy.[6] Altogether, global trade as a share of global wealth would not reach its 1913 summit until 1970.

But the globe-trotting influences extended beyond the material and corporeal. As historian Thomas Bender has summarized, the global depressions of the 1870s and 1890s led many to question inherited economic orthodoxies. Like Daniel Rodgers before him, Bender points to the rise of an "awareness of the social," or an environmental approach to the community's welfare, that echoed among both academic and public policy elites.[6] Politically, it was a tendency that stretched from circles around the Catholic Church on the right to a reformed "new liberalism" of the center to out-and-out socialist revolutionism on the far left. Altogether, as British historian Charles Emmerson summed up the pre-World War I moment: "A world economy is interconnected as never before by flows of money, trade, and people, and by the unprecedented spread of new, distance-destroying technologies. A global society, perhaps even a global moral consciousness, is emerging as a result."[8] A political phrase-maker, indeed, might well have characterized the era a new world order.

One might have expected labor historians—particularly those post-1960s "new labor historians" who added demography, migration, as well

as race and gender dimensions to the study of their working-class subjects
—to have earlier extended the geographic boundaries of their field. But, I
think there are at least two reasons why the transnational move in this
arena generally proved no more advanced than in most other subfields of
American history.[9] For one, new labor historians were, in fact, consciously
resisting a putatively comparative framework that seemed to answer the
important questions about the working class before they were asked: the
American Exceptionalism Argument. As I summarized in a previous work,
"One of the favorite tasks of American historians has been to explain why
the United States, alone among the nations of the western world, passed
through the industrial revolution without the establishment of a class consciousness and an independent working-class political movement."[10] Not
surprisingly, the verdict of this older comparative tradition, most commonly associated with Werner Sombart's 1906 *Why Is There No Socialism
in America?* thesis, did not appeal politically to a generation of historians
looking for embers of insurgency under native soil.[11] Beyond ideology,
moreover, the method of the comparative approach favored by sociologists
and political scientists, proved geographically as well as historically stilted.
Whatever the focus—cheap land, the cult of individualism, early mass
suffrage, a heterogeneous labor force, the federal separation of powers,
application of brute force, etc.—exceptionalist arguments assumed the
autonomy of action within the individual nation-state. In short, they
assumed that what happened (politically) in Germany, England, and/or the
U.S. *stayed* there, as irreducible functions of particular in-country configu-
rations of power, ideology, and the like. In the end, once a new generation
of social historians in Europe as well as America cast doubt on the ideal-
typical "class-conscious" proletariat of classic Marxism—that is, it didn't
seem to exist anywhere—they also inadvertently undermined the motive
for large-scale comparative work.[12]

Aside from fending off a stultifying "internationalist" model of
working-class development on the Left, the New Labor Historians had
additional reasons, at once personal and political, to stress the *indigenous*
nature of American labor and radical developments. Undoubtedly, the
McCarthyism of the early 1950s cast a shadow of illegitimacy and conspiracy on any radical political project that was assigned a *foreign* origin, let
alone sustained international inspiration. But there was something more.
As intellectual historian David S. Brown emphasizes, the immigrant (and
especially Jewish-immigrant) children who first advanced the new history

"from below" were sensitive to *their own* distance from the American political heartland, and hence eager to bridge the gap. The University of Wisconsin at Madison, in particular, with deep roots in the nation's progressive past, helped a new generation of students, including many "red diaper babies" from New York Jewish families, to redefine the central themes of American history around the democratic yearnings of ordinary working people. Not surprisingly, two journals closely tied to an emergent New Left scholarship—*Studies on the Left* (1959) and *Radical America* (1967)—emerged from Madison.

My own beloved adviser, Herbert Gutman, exemplified this trend. Raised in Queens in a radical Yiddish-speaking household, his pursuit of the American working-class experience, begun at Columbia University (where he completed an M.A. under Richard Hofstadter in 1950), did not catch fire until he transferred to Madison for his Ph.D. "The Madison years," he would later recall, "made me understand that all my left politics had not prepared me to understand America west (or even east) of the Hudson River. Not in the slightest."[13]

For Gutman, as for a spreading host of New Labor Historians, the American industrial landscape itself thus proved a sufficiently broad and complex tableau to understand both the origins of Gilded Age labor conflicts as well as the *source of ideological opposition* (commonly identified with American "labor republicanism") to the power of anti-democratic elites. These skillful social historians, of course, painstakingly documented the role of immigration in U.S. class formation, and they were not unmindful of the contributions of foreign-born socialists and anarchists in American-centered struggles. Yet, waging their own intellectual war against a consensus-minded generation of scholars who had preceded them, they focused on the *domestic* roots of popular resistance and rebellion. As James R. Green explained in a preface to his influential study of early twentieth-century radicalism in the Southwest, "One of the most important objectives of this study is to describe the forgotten men and women who made the movement such a strong indigenous expression of socialism."[14]

Politically, of course, the valence of nationalism/internationalism has shifted in the last few decades rather remarkably across the political spectrum. Pressed by multinational investment interests, nationalist walls of tariff protection, immigration restrictions, and, alas, labor standards as well, have all tumbled. Much weakened, the U.S. labor movement (together with the progressive wing of the Democratic Party to which it attaches itself), desperate for alternatives, generally embraces internationalist cooperation and even global labor standard-setting as a response to the competitive "race to the bottom." A purely nationalist and populist discourse is now far more common on the political Right than the political Left.[15] At the same time—and hastened by the "liberation" of formerly Communist state economies into the global capitalist marketplace—competitive pressures on European regimes have also narrowed the differences in labor and social welfare policies among the very countries whose relatively buoyant Social Democracy had once seemed to distinguish them from the free market American Exception.

However ambiguous the result from a political point of view, the current moment is a most auspicious one for rethinking American labor history through a more internationalist lens. By widening the camera angle spatially, we not only gain access to a comparative range of outcomes among contemporary national actors, but also can better zero in on the historical what, when, and why that made the U.S. record peculiar (if not outright exceptional). As suggested above, historians of all fields are helping to shape the contours of a more capacious transnational or comparatively internationalist history. My approach here tends to slither between transnationalist (how historical forces at any given moment crossed and/or superseded single-country boundaries) and comparative (how similar challenges received distinct treatment in different nation-states) analysis. What I hope I have kept consistent, however, is a "grounded globalism," that is, attention to specific context at discrete moments in time.[16]

This, at least, is my charge in the following set of essays. I say "essays" in the disparate plural rather than "book" in the unified singular, because it is a more accurate account of the genesis of the project. I spent an initial period of work combing through both older and newer historiography in labor, business, and political history looking for entry points that might prove at once productive and provocative in reexamining the distinctiveness of American institutional development. Based on my own tastes and tests of significance, I ended up with five research inquests that each took on a life of its own. While all the essays relate to central themes of American labor and working-class history—strikes, industrial relations, labor law and the state, radical and reform thought, political movements—they do so in new and perhaps unexpected ways. Each chapter, moreover, engages the "world" theme by a collective different angle; they focus, in turn, on ideas, action, institutions, policy, and political movement culture. In their very selectivity, of course, the essays inevitably slight other major themes of the period. Fortunately, readers will find excellent, and more pointed treatment of such subjects as race, gender, immigration, and imperial exploits elsewhere.[17]

Societies, like individual souls, do not live by bread (or material reproduction) alone. Rather, they are sustained by belief systems backed up by a legal framework. In Chapter 1 I argue that the concept of "free labor"—vouchsafed by Union victory in the Civil War—has served as a key pillar of both modern-day labor law and social stability. Although the source of continuous contest among competing social groups, American freedom at the workplace, as crucially adjudicated by the Supreme Court, has overwhelmingly tilted towards individual property rights at the expense of larger community standards. What this means in practice for the labor movement and the larger political culture, I try to illustrate by comparison with France, a society whose dedication to "liberty" was also sealed in revolutionary sacrifice.

Another sort of sacrifice, this one demanded of the thousands of men and women involved in the great Gilded Age strikes, beckons in Chapter 2. Here, we can observe the contest over the nature and limits of American freedom played out in real time. In reconsidering a decade of iconic conflicts—Homestead in 1892, Pullman in 1894, and the anthracite coal strike of 1902—I choose to focus on the strategic choices taken and not taken by the leaders on all three sides: business, labor, and the state. What were their motives? What were their options? What difference did it make? Based on comparative analysis with Great Britain, I suggest that the strike outcomes themselves helped define what social scientists came to think of as American Exceptionalism or the weakness of a U.S. working-class presence. While emphasizing the historical forces of agency and contingency, I also present a broadly revisionist view of all three battles based in part on reframing Andrew Carnegie as an ambivalent Scot, recasting Eugene V. Debs as an unnecessary martyr, and reevaluating conservative miners' leader John L. Mitchell and Republican Party boss Mark Hanna as unsung but at least partially worthy working-class heroes.

Chapter 3 steps back from the immediate industrial battlegrounds to explore the genesis of labor reform thought that became applied to the conflicts of the period. The subject confronts us with one of the classic sets of actors regularly identified with the Progressive Era: "middle-class" intellectuals. How did a generation of new social science professionals, in particular, respond to an era of class conflict, urban poverty, and mass immigration? In his monumental *Atlantic Crossings*, Daniel T. Rodgers makes the case for an Atlantic-wide world of reformers and public officials, eager to rebuild the city and modernize the countryside according to an international policy playbook. Supplementing Rodgers's analysis with particular attention to labor issues, I compare and contrast the sources of what might be called "radical reform" ideas in the U.S. with those in Britain and Germany. I suggest that among the most positive and unique aspects of American development was the rise of the research university, best represented in the social science fields by the "engaged" scholarship of labor economist Richard T. Ely and his colleagues and students at the University of Wisconsin. For an extended moment, I argue, the Wisconsin Experiment acted out the pragmatic, cosmopolitan and "social democratic" promise of an American progressivism otherwise and all too soon given over to technocratic elitism.

In Chapter 4, I turn to legal and legislative chambers, where the labor movement and its middle-class allies as well as its antagonists worked out the institutional pathways of American industrial relations from the era of the Knights of Labor through the heyday of the American Federation of Labor. One question, I suggest, always bedeviled organized labor and its sympathizers: the question of legitimacy. Why, in short, could labor unionism not gain a surer foothold in American law and public life until the 1930s or, for that matter, even until today? Again, I suggest that a wider field of vision treating divergent development across societies resting on a common-law legal heritage (thus encompassing the UK, Canada, and especially the territories of Australia and New Zealand, or what the British, due to their global juxtaposition, call the Antipodes) offers new insight. Essentially, I suggest, the door of industrial jurisprudence in the English-speaking world was open, at least for some time, to a number of variations. For lesser-skilled, more easily replaced industrial workers—whose ranks in the U.S. were overwhelmingly composed of new immigrants—some support from the state proved essential to assure them a place at the bargaining table with their employers. Despite considerable internal debate and discussion, however, the dominant AFL-defined labor movement opted for a relatively anti-statist "British model." when it might have been better served by the examples of Australia and New Zealand that combined state-sanctioned systems of union recognition with industrial arbitration of disputes.

Another form of Long Gilded Age internationalism is represented by the construction of the Socialist Party of America. As a political ideology drawing explicitly from European roots and as a social movement originally defined by its varied immigrant advocates, socialism carried both the promise and the peril of its inherently transnational presence. In Chapter 5 I try to recover the spirit behind the "golden age" of American socialism. Its very un-American-ness, I insinuate (contra much recent labor history scholarship), was part of the appeal of socialist doctrines to a young generation itching to taste the forbidden fruits of a wider world. Just as the post-adolescent American upper class ventured on its grand tour and new urban émigrés explored the thrills of Coney Island, so did other means of travel, both figurative and literal, summon those eager to break with Victorian norms. From social democracy to revolutionary syndicalism, anarchism to socialist feminism, and radical secularism to Christian socialism—the insurgent political tendencies of the age all beckoned in accents from across the globe. And a generation bred by this unspoken era of globalization—of study, travel, immigration, as well as international political solidarities—tried to take full advantage.

Finally, in a brief Epilogue, I make an effort to connect the Long Gilded Age to the American labor history that succeeded it. *The Long Gilded Age*'s subtitle speaks of the "lessons" of its time period. By that word, I mean to include at once the morals drawn, for good or ill, by Gilded Age contemporaries, and those that, looking back, we learn by considering events over a longer stretch of time. Where, in particular, do we see points of continuity, or perhaps even a second chance to come at old problems with new insights? To be sure, we live in a very different world from the one described in these essays. Yet, the urge to understand, and by understanding renew, continues. What, then besides world wars, devastating depressions, and a loss of confidence separate the promise of their times from our own?

Chapter 1

The American Ideology

The world has never had a good definition of the word
liberty, and the American people, just now, are much in
want of one. We all declare for liberty; but in using the same
word we do not all mean the same thing.
—Abraham Lincoln, 1864

Had Alexis de Tocqueville, miraculously, been able to revisit France and
America a scant thirty years after his death in 1859, he might have been
tempted to dramatically invert his principal judgments on the two nations.
For Tocqueville, self-constituted civic organizations (*associations* in his
vocabulary) figured centrally in distinguishing a buoyant democracy from
the twinned specters of suffocating absolutism and excessive individualism.
On the one hand, the ubiquity of such agents, commonly labeled the "spirit
of volunteerism," provided for Tocqueville in *Democracy in America* (1835,
1840) the lodestone of America's social promise.[1] On the other hand, as
he argued in *The Old Regime and the Revolution* (1856), an all-powerful,
centralized state—reflected in the LeChapelier Law of 1791 banning guilds
and other intermediary bodies—snuffed out the lifeblood of liberal democracy in France. "For Tocqueville," as historian Richard Swedberg summarizes, "the tragedy of the French Revolution was that it inspired freedom
but that people had no idea how to go about creating a free society."[2]

And yet, by the late nineteenth century, the French state, while never
abandoning its characteristic long reach, had moved markedly away from
the suffocating control characteristic of both its absolutist and revolutionary heritage. By the time of the February 1848 Revolution, conservative
republicans like Tocqueville were already beginning to positively reappraise

worker associations as a possible brace against socialist statism. Over the ensuing decades, a combination of republican and labor/socialist reformers did, in fact, restore an associative dynamic to the body politic. Among the key departures affecting working people were the 1864 law abolishing the crime of "coalition," the 1884 law legalizing trade unions and associations, an 1892 law facilitating conciliation and arbitration, and the Labor Code of 1910 that officially recognized a legal realm for collective bargaining and trade union action.[3]

Still in place today, France's institutional recognition of Tocqueville's vaunted intermediary bodies has no parallel in American democracy. Except for business combination through the agency of incorporation, Americans in the industrial era found it more and more difficult under the prevailing laws to "join together" to advance their common economic interest. In particular this was the case for organized workers. Although union membership was generally recognized in principle after Massachusetts Judge Lemuel Shaw's *Commonwealth v. Hunt* decision of 1842, in practice such bodies experienced multiple, often crippling, obstacles. By the late nineteenth century, the American national state had yet to adopt the socially interventionist powers of its tricolor counterpart, but neither was it any longer directed by the balance of civic interests that had once impressed Tocqueville. To be sure, Tocqueville himself had early on warned Americans of the inequalities sure to develop within a "manufacturing aristocracy," but the warning had fallen largely on deaf ears.[4] By 1900, few observers would have doubted which country had more succumbed to extreme individualism.[5]

How and why had the "free society" that enjoyed such a head start come up so short so soon? The question begs further inquiry. This chapter examines the issue through the gap between formal political ideals and lived experience, as centered on working people and their characteristic institutional voice, the labor union. With a continuing nod to the European, and especially the French contrast, it seeks to identify, in a cultural as well as legal-institutional sense, the obstacles that working people have encountered in securing and expanding their share of the American promise.

When asked what he thought about Western civilization, Gandhi reportedly quipped, "it would be a good idea." A late nineteenth-century American trade unionist might have said the same thing about "free labor." Initially associated with positive images of opportunity, progress, and liberation, the concept had since become identified with arbitrary dismissals, anti-strike injunctions, and a general loss of control at work that for many workers amounted to what they called "wage slavery." A common-core conviction, it turned out, only awkwardly covered a developing industrial landscape. How to balance the inheritance of the free-labor ideal with the reality of capitalist economic development at the end of the nineteenth century posed a special challenge to the American labor movement.

Workers in Gilded Age America confronted what we might call the free-labor "double paradox." The first paradox spoke to the ambivalence of the republican heritage. On the one hand, a legacy of freedoms and rights stemming from the Revolutionary era, an economy of relative labor scarcity, and the Civil War's extirpation of slavery surrounded the nation-state and its history in a positive or at least hopeful hue for most working people. Much earlier than in Europe, both physically coerced entry into labor and criminal sanctions for leaving it were eradicated among the nominally "free" population.[6] The Civil War itself confirmed the free-labor order. Beginning with Lincoln's rejection of the terms of the Dred Scott case of 1857, a new, national definition of freedom (encapsulated in the Civil War amendments to the Constitution) replaced a patchwork of regional variations, each with its own set of limitations on the basis of age and citizenship status as well as gender and race.

Yet, the very regime that destroyed the South's slavocracy also enhanced individual rights at the expense of community norms long vouchsafed by resort to common law precedent. Historian William J. Novak thus speaks of the very "invention of American constitutional law" tied to a "legal centralization of state power" that ultimately defined "a wholly new political philosophy" focused on a "radical reconstruction of individual rights."[7] In particular, the newly-created constitutional protections of "due process," "equal protection," and "rights of citizens of the United States" would buttress one aspect of free-labor doctrine—the employer's "freedom of contract"—while simultaneously threatening organized workers' collective field of action. The upshot was that nearly every attempt by unions to organize or mobilize workers in the era appealed back to nationalist, "free-labor" principles, while at the same time declaiming against immediate conditions that had grown out of the soil nurtured by those very same principles. As historian Christopher Tomlins suggests, the Civil War toppled one "constellation of un/freedom" only to replace it with a new one.[8]

There was a second layer of irony and complexity to the Gilded Age discourse of free labor. The workers who made the claim on the national free-labor heritage included many who were not even American citizens—and many more only recently so. Herbert Gutman first highlighted this point, noting in one of his influential essays how two Scottish American immigrants—railroad detective Allan Pinkerton and Braidwood, Illinois miners leader Daniel M'Lachlan—made different uses of the same political inheritance. As Gutman noted about another immigrant, New Jersey labor editor Joseph P. McDonnell, who had served as Irish secretary of the Marxist First International before emigrating in the early 1870s, "his rhetoric was bathed in working-class republican ideology[,] saturated by it."[9] On at least two counts, then, we are left to wonder about the hold, and meaning, of free labor ideology in the culture at large.

One colorful, yet not untypical, story illustrates the simultaneously unifying yet divisive nature of free-labor borrowings in the Gilded Age. As Thomas G. Andrews documents in *Killing for Coal*, the original promise of the West was signaled by the path-breaking railroad engineer and coal owner Williiam J. Palmer, who in the early 1870s identified the mountain regions as a refuge from the "foreign swarms" on the Eastern seaboard, who could be filtered out and prepared "by a gradual process for coming to the inner temple of Americanism out in Colorado, where Republican institutions will be maintained in pristine purity." By the 1890s, however, the coal miners themselves had tailored Palmer's message to their own immediate and increasingly desperate situation. Facing wage cuts and the overwhelming power of the Colorado Fuel and Iron Company amid a bitter national strike in 1894, some two thousand miners marched "behind American flags and brass bands." In the same spirit, a state United Mine Workers organizer rebuked operators for "having taken from [the colliers] their best blood and their American privilege of earning an honest livelihood." The strikers, he insisted, "stood by the Declaration of Independence" and its guarantee of "life, liberty and the pursuit of happiness." At a moment of extreme peril, a workers' community comprising twenty-nine nationality groups thus found common cause in rights they attributed to the American Revolution. Explained one anonymous orator, "Patriots assembled on the Boston Commons . . . and dared [the British] to oppress them longer, and I say to you that they were men from every civilized land . . . and they raised that flag and said 'under that flag we will be free men or under that flag you may bury our dead bodies.' That flag, gentlemen, waves still.'" When their strike was ultimately defeated by a combination of injunctions and strikebreakers, union leaders proclaimed that "Liberty crushed to earth will rise again."[10]

How did it come to pass that the same discursive system of political and economic "liberty" could at once unite the post-Civil War nation and also bitterly divide it on class lines? Historian Eric Foner offers a convincing explanation. Business, economists, and leading newspapers, he suggests, jumped on an "emergent market definition of economic freedom," emphasizing the benefits of marketplace logic, the laborer's "juridical freedom" and the "idea of contract."[11] Already by the mid-nineteenth century, employment relations, as regulated by the states, were regularly subsumed into the hierarchical discourse of master-and-servant relationships[12] The trend took on enhanced meaning beginning with Stephen J. Field's famous dissent in the *Slaughter-House* cases in 1873, which identified the Fourteenth Amendment as a guarantor of individual freedom of contract, calling it a basic "right of free labor." Infringements on just this "right" soon became the basis for the manifold legal injunctions against strikes and boycotts. As if "contract rights" were not enough, moreover, business-friendly exponents of the "science" of social Darwinism like William Graham Sumner equally helped to explain social inequality and sanction the success of the successful.[13]

An enduring, early twentieth-century addition to the employers' lexicon of free labor arrived with the concept of the "right-to-work." In one of the first uses of the phrase, muckraking journalist Ray Stannard Baker took up the cudgels for the estimated 17,000 men who defied union orders and threats to continue work during the 1902 anthracite strike (see Chapter 2). As Baker quoted a nonstriking mining engineer: "I have a right to work when I like, for what I like, and for whom I like." It was an attitude, quickly surrounded by legal restrictions on picketing, that helped turn back labor's first great industrial surge, and it was soon re-outfitted as the "American Plan" to safeguard the open shop post-World War I and regularly redeployed thereafter.[14]

Workers, as Foner (like Herbert Gutman before him) recognized, equally "spoke the language of free labor." Yet, it is perhaps more exact to say that Labor spoke *multiple dialects* of that language. As late as the 1860s, a self-consciously free-labor advocate like President Abraham Lincoln could imagine the industrial system as one where a "prudent, penniless beginner in the world labors for wages awhile, saves a surplus with which to buy tools or land for himself; then labors on his own account another while, and at length hires another new beginner to help him." Yet, within a decade, the unmistakable evidence of industrial hierarchy—most evident in the expansion of mines and

railroads—belied such optimistic scenarios. Already by 1870, as confirmed by
the census enumeration, two-thirds of those engaged in the marketplace were
hirelings.[15] Many critics saw the dawning system of industrial capitalism as
one of systemic, liberty-denying oppression. Their central argument, repeatedly made by leaders and publicists within the late nineteenth-century labor
movement, closely aligned a budding working-class identity with the strident
free-labor versus slavery theme of the Civil War. Precisely because of the
"immediate reality" of slavery, the economic dependence of wage earners lent
"special power" to a sense that wage work was less than free.[16]

Perhaps the clearest exposition of the wage-system-as-slavery critique
in America came from Boston machinist and eight-hour reformer Ira
Steward. How much, he rhetorically asked, was "the anti-slavery idea"
worth, "without the power to exercise it"? Given the conditions of industrial employment, there was little "free" about free labor. "The laborer's
commodity," he elaborated, "perishes every day beyond the possibility of
recovery. He must sell today's labor today, or never." Only by interrupt-
ing the social and political power of the employer (in Steward's mind via
the legislated shorter day) could freedom be *restored* to the individual
laborer.[17]

The wage-slavery argument, linking as it did the legacies of yeoman
democracy and abolitionist thought, demanded social alternatives. So it was
that the mass movements of the late nineteenth century slid easily (as in
the case of the Knights of Labor) into talk of the "abolition of the wages
system," or (as in the case of the People's Party) a demand for "industrial
freedom" that required the structural dismantling of a society of "tramps
and millionaires."[18] Sounding a stark contradiction between individual
political liberty and industrial employment, Knights leader George E.
McNeill proclaimed, "We declare an inevitable and irresistible conflict
between the wage-system of labor and the republican system of government."[19] In each case these radical reformers looked to a combination of
group self-activity (whether through labor unions, farmers' alliances, and/
or producer cooperatives) and ameliorative legislation to create, as the preamble to the Knights' constitution put it in 1885, a necessary "check . . .
upon unjust accumulation, and the power for evil of aggregated wealth."[20]
Committed to a republican commonwealth in which self-governing citizens
would, through the power of the franchise, keep monopoly power and
exploitation at bay, the Knights of Labor and their allies disdained individual liberty of contract doctrine as a tool of "wage slavery."[21]

Despite such rhetorical swagger, in practice the nineteenth-century labor movement regularly jockeyed between conciliatory and even individual strategies of advancement within the wage system versus more systemic attacks on the putative source of their oppression. Partly it was a matter of varied and evolving calculations of group interest. For decades many of the most skilled workers, for example, as represented by self-styled "respectable" craft unions, continued to subscribe to the tenets of what others now viewed as free-labor mythology. The railroad brotherhoods were perhaps the quintessential representatives of this perspective. "Sobriety, Benevolence, and Industry" proclaimed the masthead of the Brotherhood of Locomotive Firemen. Even in the aftermath of the great railroad riots of 1877 in which he took no part, the young Eugene V. Debs, editor of the *Locomotive Firemen's Magazine*, could still describe the railroad corporation as "the architect of progress" and anticipate a harmonious relationship with local banker and regional railroad owner William Riley McKeen.[22]

Soon, economic concentration and deteriorating conditions of work forced railwaymen, via their brotherhoods, to revise their beliefs.[23] The contracts to which the skilled railroaders subscribed were thus but the follow-up stage to the earlier practice among artisans and craft workers of setting their own standards of wages and hours and enforcing such standards unilaterally (not by negotiation or contract with the boss) through the closed shop. As mechanization took command and the autonomous conditions of craft control weakened, skilled workers clung to job control, as historian David Montgomery most assiduously demonstrated, through negotiated trade agreements.[24]

Interestingly, it was the appeal to individual character—and in particular the safeguarding of one's "manliness," the repository of traditional artisan virtue—that in many cases brought craft workers to the battlements of the era's Great Upheaval. Reflecting on the trials of the Knights of Labor amid the Gould Strike of 1885, Debs displayed a newly minted radical social critique in an editorial entitled, "Art Thou a Man?," in which he defended the rights inherent in a worker's manhood against the power of monopoly.[25] In important respects, the erosion of earlier free-labor idealism seems to have been sparked by male worker fears of dependency, linked at once to economic change and to a gender shift in the marketplace. As Alice Kessler-Harris has elaborated, women's employment—whether forced or voluntary—posed a cultural problem: "just as men's free labor was predicated on their capacity to support a family, so women's was assumed to

sustain the family labor of men. . . . For women's wage work to threaten
the male's capacity to be free was a problem just as it was a problem if
women's wage work undermined the capacity of either men or women to
be effective family members."[26] At best, therefore, women's discretionary
income might supplement the male breadwinner's earnings.[27] The control
and autonomy that had once clearly separated at least the skilled craftsman
from the dependency of slaves, women, and lowly laborers was, for many,
now under siege. In such circumstances, resort to the male breadwinner
ideal—sometimes in a defensive and politically conservative way—defined
the arena of grievance more powerfully than mere economic arguments. It
was on such a basis, for example, that craft unions commonly excluded
women members and that railway brotherhoods long established separate
seniority lists and other mechanisms of exclusion aimed at African American workers.[28]

Beyond a sometimes confusing resort to a cross-class political inheritance, workers' ambivalence about the free-labor marketplace was also conceptual. What *was* the wage-system, exactly? And, more to the point, what
were its most egregious, unacceptable features? The fact is, beneath the
arguments of both free-labor market critics like Ira Steward and apologists
like Supreme Court Justice Stephen A. Field beckoned a wide, and messier,
territory of workaday experience. The issue recalls the French textile trade
in the late eighteenth and early nineteenth centuries. As historian William
Reddy noted more generally about the English and French artisan trades in
these years, the "catastrophes" that generally befell them "resembled hardly
at all what the effects of a free market would look like. . . . No market for
labor was ever created in either of these countries. In this crucial sense the
market system failed to appear."[29] As a result, two illusions developed
within the new nineteenth-century market culture: "that gain was the basic
human motive and that unregulated competition brought maximum progress." This dual set of assumptions was rather quickly accepted as normative by both defenders of advancing industrial capitalism and their
opponents. Yet reality on the ground, at least in the French textile industry,
did not square with its ideological categorization. Even as the antagonists
gravitated across the nineteenth century toward a common embrace of a
"market model" of human motivation and behavior, the result, Reddy
argues, left both contemporaries and historians with an "extremely over-
simplified view" of contemporary material conditions and labor relations
as actually experienced.[30]

Like the French textile trade, Gilded Age industrial employment was also riddled with "deformations" of market culture—or what we might synonymously label free-labor culture within the competitive wage system. Indeed, across the spectrum of industrial employment, it is hard to find a sector that did *not* combine a significant amount of coercion, subterfuge, or other extra-economic sanctions with competitive free-labor competition for jobs and wages. Similarly, it was often these very deformations rather than the secular logic of the wage-system itself that most readily drew the ire of American workers.

Some of the most common—and notorious—cases of deformation derived from the practice of contract labor. A clear warning signal arrived with the near-decade-long construction of the transcontinental railroad. Completed four years after the triumph of the "free-labor" North in the Civil War, the railroad vouchsafed the strength of the Union, but on the backs of two equally exploited, if unequally cursed, groups of immigrant stoop laborers: the Irish working from the East and the Chinese working from the West. In 1863 alone, nearly 100,000 Irish laborers accepted pacts with a combination of U.S. military and emigration society recruiters for steamship tickets. Among those not immediately outfitted in Union uniforms, few escaped either the steamship or the holding pens at New York City's Castle Garden without signing a labor contract. Beginning in 1864, the federal government (concerned with the drain of manpower into the army) itself promised for the first time to enforce labor contracts made on foreign soil. Almost immediately, employers took advantage of the situation to break strikes with directly imported laborers.[31]

The confinement of the Chinese was yet more conspicuous, and notorious. In the midst of devastating Chinese civil wars across the 1850s and 1860s, a combination of forced (or "coolie") labor and the lure of voluntary, cheap steerage fares on steamship routes from Hong Kong to San Francisco accounted for a huge surge of labor migrants on long-term contracts bound for the railroad camps. The Hui-Kuan, aka the Chinese Six Companies, acted as effective padrones over the immigrant workforce, setting up contracts and effectively enforcing them on worker and railroad alike. In any case, the combination of high death rates, low wages, and constraining contracts (the so-called credit-ticket system) easily opened the Chinese labor experiment to charges of "slavery," which, combined with racist stereotypes, quickly led to campaigns to exclude the Chinese from competition with "white" workers as well as to forbid their further entry into the country altogether. From such origins of ethnic marginalization emerged one of the sorriest chapters of American labor history, one in which even the generally egalitarian Knights of Labor joined with a vengeance.

The switch from a campaign against *importation* of Chinese, along with other contract laborers, to one against Chinese immigration tout court developed only in stages, and with substantial misgivings within the organized labor community. Throughout the 1860s, for example, William Sylvis, iron molders' and National Labor Union president and leader of the national campaign against contract labor, insisted that the imported workers "should not be spurned and treated as enemies," since "they are only the dupes of the wily agents." Even as Dennis Kearney made Chinese exclusion a touchstone of the broader-based Workingmen's Party platform in California—and as other powerful figures like Maine's Sen. James G. Blaine proclaimed the incompatibility of the "man who must have beef and bread, and would prefer beer" and the "man who can live on rice"—most of organized labor held back, limiting their policy prescriptions to a ban on all foreign laborers under contract. Typical, for a time, were the reported remarks of New York Central Labor Union President Robert Blissert: "He did not think it right to forbid any of God's creatures from coming to America. What [he] opposed was the Importation of Slaves." Alas, by 1880, fearing the arrival of a mass exodus from the "powder keg atmosphere" of San Francisco, even labor radicals like Detroit's Richard Trevellick and Chicago's Albert Parsons had succumbed to the anti-Chinese fever.[32]

Related to the sins of contract labor for men was the notorious subcontracting system associated with the heavily female garment "sweatshop." A chain of subcontracting—with each link in the chain determined to squeeze a profit from the barest margins of productivity—accounted for the sense of exploitation associated with sweating. In abominable conditions, women toiled, as turn-of-the-century journalist Eva McDonald Valesh reported, "under a cunningly devised slavery, until death mercifully sets them free." Indeed, from the turn of the century, the distinctive structure of the urban garment shop—in particular the centrality of the contractor in relation to an immigrant labor force—evoked initial parallels to the critique of "coolieism" on the West Coast. Most important, public blame for such un-American practice for a time swung precariously between employers and workers themselves. Concerns about new immigrant cleanliness, criminality, and health threatened to downgrade the status of Jews as a whole on the contemporary "evolutionary ladder." In 1905, the commissioner general of immigration thus generically condemned Jewish immigrants as "decrepit men and women."[33]

What saved the Jews the opprobrium visited on the Chinese was the deflection of the discourse of immigrant "degeneracy" to one of environmental degradation. In the case of the Russian Jews, a host of agents—German Jews, middle-class public-health and reform advocates, as well as the contemporary labor movement—effectively identified industrial capitalism (as exemplified by the sweatshop), not race, as the culprit. In the ensuing discourse of factory inspection, as championed by the International Ladies' Garment Workers' Union, the "modern" factory was contrasted to the sweatshop as a means to improve sanitation, eliminate degrading homework, and lift the overall cultural profile of the immigrant community. In the factory, or "model shop" as articulated by the industry's union-management Joint Board of Sanitary Control after 1910, "the boss remained, but healthy male workers earned a family wage, while enjoying a host of comforts and conveniences. . . . Where the sweatshop enfeebled, the model shop cured." Restore the working-class family's "independence"—as effected by the male provider—the argument suggested, and the wolf of unfreedom could be kept at the door. It is worth noting that the "sweatshop debate" helped to cut short a more systemic discussion of the iniquities of free labor and the free contract. With proper control—in particular a place for unions in the negotiation of wages and conditions—workers, it seemed, could transform the sweatshop from Exhibit A of capitalistic iniquity into "a correctable problem of poor management."[34]

After intense lobbying by the Knights of Labor and other labor reformers, Congress first systematically grappled with the problem of contract labor in the 1885 Foran Act, which specified fines on labor importers as well as immediate deportation of all workers brought to America under contract. Yet the act proved to be riddled with contradictions inherent in free-labor thought itself. Reflecting an all-out skepticism toward labor recruitment, the law voided "all contracts" to import foreign workers, making no distinction between voluntary and involuntary service. Absent a work contract, however, the would-be immigrant laborer arriving at Castle Garden faced a bind: how could he prove he would not become a public charge (another grounds for deportation)? Parsing legislative intent, the courts tended to create their own, highly racialized distinctions between "ignorant" or "coerced" migrants and individuals who had clearly come on their own, informed volition. What one government investigator called a "curious contradiction" in immigration law was only fitfully resolved by subsequent legislation specifically targeting the immigrant padrone (or labor contractor) for prosecution and exempting skilled workers recruited to fill designated industrial needs.[35] By emphasizing the moral depravity of the padrone preying on helpless (especially Italian) child laborers, moreover, the administrators of the Foran Act slowly turned it away from its original intent. From "a critique of the doctrine of voluntary contract," argues historian Gunther Peck, it became "an instrument of its ideological defense." Meanwhile, the problem of immigrant contract labor waned on its own. Free immigration itself proved quite plentiful (at least until drastic immigration restriction in 1924), and corporate personnel managers replaced padrones in supplying industry with a tractable labor force.[36]

A similar preoccupation—at least among middle-class labor reformers—with immoral recruitment and hiring practices focused on female domestic workers. In New York City, for example, as historian Vanessa H. May has documented, Frances Kellor and the National Municipal League focused particularly on "tenement" employment agencies, effectively unregulated family-based enterprises, which served as go-betweens to "respectable" middle-class households. These unscrupulous agents, reformers alleged, lured young immigrant and African American arrivals to the city with offers of employment, at once charging the domestics exorbitant fees and exposing their employers to a "class of diseased, paupers, criminals, and degenerates." A 1904 employment agency law, by setting licensing fees and "business-like" standards on the industry, sought to drive the small-fry recruiters out of business; the law, alas, did nothing for the wages and working conditions of domestic workers themselves.[37]

From the perspective of Gilded Age workers, the most noxious form of labor contracting probably derived from the employment of prisoners to compete with or supplant free labor in the marketplace. Characteristic of the sensibility of the time was the 1869 plank of the National Labor Reform Party, pairing the demand for abolition of the importation of "a servile race"—that is, immigrant contract labor—with abolition of the "system of contract labor in our prisons."[38] The latter issue came with longer roots. As early as the "Auburn system" in the 1820s, New York and other states employed convicts in numerous trades both for reasons of economy and therapeutic self-discipline. Fearing direct competition from such enterprise, mechanics gathered in protest as early as the 1830s and forced the New

York state legislature to set various limits on the prison trades.[39] Given wartime strains on the state budget, New York again loosened its regulations in the 1860s—a pattern for other cash-poor states that would reach its most notorious expression in the South's "convict lease" system. Here, a prison population that was becoming overwhelmingly black was systematically rented out to private employers on railroads, mines, and plantations with little public supervision or monitoring of exploding casualty rates.[40]

In the North, use of Sing Sing laborers to try to break the iron molders' union turned the issue into organized labor's cause célèbre in the immediate post-Civil War years. Not surprisingly, when the labor movement generally revived in the 1880s, curtailing convict labor again turned up near the top of its political agenda. In the original 1878 preamble to its constitution (and continuing across several constitutional revisions) the Knights of Labor declared its intent "to abolish the system of letting out by contract the labor of convicts in our prisons and reformatory institutions."[41] Anti-convict labor laws spread across the northern industrial belt in the 1880s and 1890s. Long resistant to such pressures, even the southern states formally responded to reform campaigns after the turn of the century. By 1928, Alabama, the last holdout, had legally foresworn convict leasing, even as direct public employment—as in roadside chain gangs—developed in its stead.[42]

Unfortunately, the gap between state penal-reform codes and the reality on the ground persisted for decades. Heartrending historical accounts of the brutalities enacted in forced labor camps—a "neo-slavery" applied to over one hundred thousand workers, many simply arrested for vagrancy, from the 1870s until World War II—provide the starkest proof of the limits of statutes left on their own.[43] Green Cottenham, for example, a son of Alabama ex-slaves, was charged and convicted of vagrancy in 1908, then remanded to a Birmingham coal mine under the charge of the Tennessee Coal, Iron & Railroad Company; there, in the company of "more than a thousand other black men," he was "chained inside a long wooden barrack at night and required to spend nearly every waking hour digging and loading coal."[44] Brutally and baldly coerced labor thus served in the South as a constant threat to hold over the heads of the poorest of free laborers. Not surprisingly, given the notoriety of the issue at the time, the Knights of Labor identified abolition of convict lease among its fifteen prime "objectives" in 1878. Notably, however, the Knights' convict labor plank was only one of several demands that honed in on what we might consider 'distortions' of the labor market. A call for mechanics' lien legislation (giving workers a priority over other creditors in employer debt settlements) struck at employers' asymmetrical power in workplace relationships. "Abolishment" of the "contract system" on public works projects aimed at once for transparency in municipal and state hiring. Finally, dual demands for an end to child labor in workshops, mines, and factories on the one hand and "equal pay for equal work" for both sexes on the other represented further blows for market *neutrality*—that is, a marketplace that provided an equal playing field for all adult workers.[45]

For years after the Knights' era, it is worth noting that what workers took to be *extra*-market coercions employed by employers occupied a prime spot in fueling labor rage and protests. Prime examples were the grievances against coal companies for practicing short-weighing or imposing scrip and company store systems or other forms of wage theft on their employees.[46] Similarly, various studies have noted the flashpoint of struggle occasioned by a variety of directly coercive practices ranging from what appeared to be arbitrary layoffs and dismissals to the use of private police forces to control of access to company property to the denial of bathroom breaks on the job.[47] Even as the master and servant laws that compelled a young female textile worker to a twelve-month confinement in the mill may have been breached (at least in the statutes of the free states) by mid-century, the underlying principle of coercion, notes David Montgomery, continually "reappeared in court decisions" and was reinforced as well by "draconic vagrancy laws that made it a crime not to have a job."[48] All such abuses were grist for the mill of labor reformers, but in exposing them workers themselves were inclined to single out contractual coercion as an *illegitimate exception* to free labor *norms*.

But, was not such scrupulous attention to marketplace abuses at odds, at least philosophically, with an out-and-out rejection of the free-labor contract altogether, as sounded in the rhetoric of labor radicals like Ira Steward and George McNeill? In short, even if the workers (by legislation or self-action as in the building of cooperatives) accomplished all fifteen of the Knights of Labor's official objectives of 1878, or even their 1885 expanded list of twenty-two demands, would they not still be operating, at least primarily, within a wage system of labor? When push came to shove, therefore, abstractions like "wage labor," "free labor," and "free contract" paled in significance to the *actual* pushing and shoving on the ground that determined how such concepts affected real men and women. It is a point that demands concrete illustration.

In her recent revaluation of the conflicts leading up to the Great Southwest Strike of 1886, historian Theresa A. Case presents labor mobilization
as an example of robust, grassroots republicanism that for a limited time
united an otherwise disparate railroad workforce. Union organizers initially
overcame a significant black-white racial division (and determination to
preserve their privileged status on the part of white workers) as well as
internal hierarchies among both shopmen and the running trades. All the
more impressive, then, that resistance to the recession-era wage cuts of Jay
Gould could weld the men on a network of southwestern roads (including
the Wabash, the Missouri, Kansas, and Texas, and Missouri Pacific lines)
into effective fighting units across 1885 and 1886 under the aegis of the
Knights of Labor, and particularly the Martin Irons-led District 101.[49]

Yet, as Case indicates, the labor forces that did battle against Gould's
railroad empire also seized on threats of the potential employment of Chinese and convict workers to burnish the movement's free-labor message.
The actual presence of these allegedly "unfree" competitors was rather min-
imal. Still, the Central Pacific Railroad had turned to Chinese laborers in
the 1860s, some Texas newspapers had proposed using them as a goad to
spur the efficiency of emancipated slaves, and Gould had replaced striking
coal miners with Chinese in an 1874 dispute. Amid rising fears, moreover,
the wives of railwaymen in Texas had in several instances boycotted Chinese
laundries because they competed with white washerwomen. Similarly, while
most Texas and Arkansas convicts were overwhelmingly leased to farms
and plantations, the railroads also hired a trickle of white prisoners for odd
jobs.[50]

In the circumstances of spreading wage and job cuts and a manipulative
and cunning management from afar, however, the "dread of dependence"
was palpable for both the laboring and small merchant class of the region.
So it was that the strikers, white and black, initially enjoyed strong support
from the local press and elected officials of surrounding communities. In
Sedalia, Missouri, center of strike strategy, the workers formed their own
guard unit to protect idled railroad property, and in Parsons, Kansas, the
local paper found nothing wrong with union men keeping would-be strikebreaking " 'tramps' away from the shops."[51] In both March and September
1885, Knights of Labor mobilizations brought the Gould railway network
to heel: in both cases railroad management sat down with labor representatives, withdrew cuts, and rehired fired union stalwarts for what appeared to
be an extended commitment to industrial peace. The same period witnessed

a gathering independent labor politics in communities around the railroad region. Altogether, the workers' actions bespoke a most buoyant expansion of free labor ideals: "these men conceived of "free labor" as at once economic, cultural, and political—freedom meant dignity, stability, a fair return for labor, a producer's claim on the workplace itself, and the opportunity to provide for families and to be public actors as worker citizens."[52]

Yet the constraints on the free-labor express soon came to the fore. When Gould's general manager, R. M. Hoxie, turned away from arbitration and openly dared the Knights to break a court injunction imposed on actions against a road in receivership, he punctured the broad but shallow base behind the industrial upheaval. As court orders cleared strikers from shops and workhouses, the skilled railway brotherhoods deserted striking trainmen and shopmen. Then, when Gould himself avoided a face-to-face encounter with General Master Workman Terence Powderly in March 1886, the union forces faced a cruel dilemma: back off or up the ante of confrontation by means of a wider walkout and sympathy actions. When Martin Irons and the District 101 leadership chose the latter option, they split not only the earlier cross-class regional coalition behind the strikers but the Knights of Labor as a whole. Violent seizures of trains, armed exchanges with strikebreakers and company detectives, and ultimate resort to the state militia in Ft. Worth, Parsons, and East St. Louis punctuated a month of industrial turmoil that ended in a crushing defeat of the union forces.[53] Though the railroad upheavals left an opening for new, biracial, pre-populist political coalitions across the region, they left scant legacy of workplace organization.[54]

In the end, the violence of the Southwest Strike exposed the contradiction between "free labor" as interpreted by workers themselves and "freedom of contract" as interpreted by the courts. By the midpoint of the southwestern railway strikes, the courts were interpreting even peaceful efforts to curtail strikebreaking as a threat to the freedom of contract and had responded to requests for injunctive relief beyond an initial focus on roads that were bankrupt and under the supervision of federal judges. There was, in short, nothing logically "inherent" about the expanded power of the judiciary: up to 1886, courts had been more self-restrictive in their interventions; beginning with the Southwest Strike, they became much more sympathetic to employer complainants.[55]

There is no denying the tensions that Gilded Age workers experienced with the *application* of free-labor doctrines to labor-management relations.

Still, it was not just the justices who embraced the "sanctity" of the employment contract. Organized labor, too, for the most part did not reject but rather embraced the labor contract as a vessel of influence in the labor market. In its view, the legalism of contracts needed only to be extended to the *group* rather than *individual* rights of employees. As union-friendly legal giant Louis Brandeis explained three years before his appointment to the Supreme Court: "The employee must have as much power and as much freedom in making a contract with the employer as the employer has in making a contract with him, and for that purpose it is necessary that employees should be bound together in some union; because the individual employee is ordinarily helpless against the employer."[56] Whatever its specific terms, the contract explicitly conferred union recognition, the crux of legitimacy. That it served just that purpose was all too apparent, for example, to Charles Francis Adams, president of the Union Pacific Railroad. In earlier philosophical musings, Adams had allowed that there needed to be some adjustments to allow the "representative, republican system of government" to catch up to the "corporate industrial system," and he even accepted a role for government in tempering railroad monopolies and unfair market competition. By 1891, however, he was notably bristling about the countervailing power and "excessive regulation" that railroad unionists had brought to bear on his business by substituting collective bargaining for the individual employment contract.[57]

The coal industry proved the prime site for the development of what historian David Brody has called "the logic of workplace contractualism"; nowhere else were the "jealously held prerogatives of American management so constrained by contractually defined job rights." As early as the 1860s, Pennsylvania anthracite miners had shrewdly embraced "market unionism," calculatingly using work stoppages to reduce the coal supply and thus drive up prices. The movement notched a major breakthrough with the first "joint conference" in the bituminous fields in 1897 that established competitive wage scales across differentiated regions (except for the unions' Achilles heel of West Virginia). It was precisely the contract system—at least when sustained by a militant rank and file—whom a latter-day Wobbly credited for turning "plain, humble, submissive [creatures] into . . . men."[58]

Perhaps the other most famous embrace of the labor contract and market unionism—this at the other end of the industrial hierarchy from coal miners—occurred among turn-of-the-century garment workers. In New

York City the predominantly female shirtwaist strike of 1909 (or "Uprising of the Twenty Thousand") combined with an industry-wide Cloakmakers' strike the following year produced the Protocol of Peace—rationalizing a chaotic industry with standardized wages, hours, and working conditions, and ultimately corralling the larger manufacturers into a deal akin to those hatched by the mineworkers. Gaining a more stable and efficient labor force in exchange for higher wages, the major clothing manufacturers for an extended period bought into a system that historian Colin Gordon calls "regulatory unionism," a system that contemporary labor journalist Benjamin Stolberg defined as "a sort of joint industrial syndicate of boss and worker."[59]

Finally, there was likely no more thorough—or inventive—labor adaptation of free-market principles than that of American merchant seamen, as reflected in their venerable leader Andrew Furuseth and his signature accomplishment, the Merchant Seamen's Act of 1915 (aka La Follette Act). The "unfreedom" of the seamen—in particular, their lack of the right to quit during the course of a contract as well as their susceptibility to physical punishment by ship captains—propelled the public face of the desired maritime labor reforms. But here was a case where workers skipped nimbly from throwing off the last vestiges of industrial "vassalage" to a favored place within the global wage system, and all in the name of "free labor."

To elaborate, for decades, U.S. seamen watched their numbers on the high seas plummet as merchants (including American ones) took advantage of less-regulated and lower-waged foreign-flag vessels through which to deliver international commerce. In the name of human rights (thus most famously ending criminal punishments for desertion), the La Follette Act consciously aimed to "free" maritime workers worldwide from the grip of segmented coercive national labor markets by applying its provisions to any ship of whatever flag that docked in a U.S. port. By its provisions, any sailor (of whatever nationality) could quit his ship in port and demand half-wages through U.S. courts while he sought his next contract on board a ship presumably paying the highest prevailing rates for maritime labor. As union advocates figured it, if "sea labor," like any other commodity, were allowed to float—freed from draconian penalties against desertion—at market price, then all would-be employers worldwide would have to pay that price. "The remedy," argued the Sailors' Union in 1914, "is to set free the economic laws governing wages."[60] Yet, by way of remedy, a removal of the desertion penalty on U.S. ships alone would not do the trick. With average

U.S. sailor wages nearly $40/month compared to British rates at $20–25, Swedes at $17 and Chinese at $7–9, restricted U.S.-only regulations would likely utterly drive U.S. ships from the sea.[61] Apply the new standards to *foreign* ships—what one La Follette bill partisan called a "free seas" principle—and you could expect a gradual convergence of *all* sea wages at a higher rate.[62] However mixed the returns (the subject necessarily of another study) from what was appropriately conceived at the time as a "radical" piece of legislation, the point here is that organized workers themselves were making their own confident, if selective, use of market-oriented thinking.

One way to read free-labor ideology in the Long Gilded Age, then, might be in the frame of what Eric Hobsbawm called "learning of the rules of the game." Long-established notions of a "fair wage" were transformed as workers "recognized the nature of the trade cycle and increasingly demanded "what the traffic would bear."[63] The era began with widespread suspicion of and desperate search for alternatives to the rapidly emerging wage system of labor, as arbitrated at once by market conditions and the coercive hand of employers. Over time, by this reading, labor accepted the inevitable, giving up a direct challenge to market and managerial hegemony in favor of incremental gains, registered by the most skilled or at least well-organized sectors of the working class.

Yet, in approaching the subject from the "bottom up," or at least through the eyes of contemporary labor actors, such a functionalist scenario seems inadequate. Workers as well as capitalists were experimenting in these years with the exercise of various kinds of leverage or checks and balances over the operations of labor-management relations and the larger social welfare. Free wage labor, per se, may have been largely accepted early on as a given by all parties, but that admission settled little that was significant for workers' lives. First, relations in the labor marketplace were often strained and complicated by manifest manipulations and unfreedoms—viz. contract labor, convict labor, company stores, and so on. Second, the "voluntary contract" at the essence of free labor might or might not serve and advance the workers' own welfare (and indeed collective power), depending on the political and economic context in which it was invoked. Contractual discipline could effectively shackle or liberate working people, depending on the context. Freedom, we might say, was in the hand as well as the eye of the beholder. In the name of freedom, then, late nineteenth-century

Americans were regularly fighting about power and economic security. The latter themes have remained well-nigh permanent issues (if eventually deprived of the soul-stirring force attached to the freedom concept). When contemporaries—ranging from industrialists and conservative jurists to trade unionists and socialist agitators—declared the system of "free labor" to be at risk from the hands of one antagonist or another, they were engaging a peculiarly American intellectual and political argument.[64]

But might we not venture farther by way of assessment? All nations, Benedict Anderson has famously argued, construct their identity around an "imagined community" "conceived as a deep, horizontal comradeship."[65] Benedict's younger sibling Perry Anderson adds a darker tinge to the evaluation of such projects by resurrecting an older concept of national mystification. Just as Marx and Engels in *The German Ideology* identified, in the writings of Hegel and Feuerbach, a false idealism that masked the true economic relations of society, Perry Anderson dissects an "Indian ideology," wherein Hindu chauvinism and even vestigial caste thinking masquerade as universalism within outwardly secular, universalist, and even socialist ideals.[66] Given the chapter's argument thus far, it is perhaps no great leap to reach for an equivalent "American ideology." As a far-reaching distortion of social reality that nevertheless enjoys a strong grip on the national political and intellectual imagination, American free labor seems nicely to fill the bill. At once emancipatory in relation to individual economic rights and choices (at least at a formal level), it has simultaneously helped to narrow the options for communal and collective national standards.

At least from the comparative historical perspective with which we began, "freedom" in America has been asked to carry an awfully heavy load. In France, for example, at about the same time as the creation of the American constitutional order of individual rights, even the bourgeois leaders of the political center, were being pushed to adopt a comparatively expansive set of national welfare measures. It was a battle, as one historian has put it, "between liberty and obligation," in which (at least as compared to the U.S.) there was substantial cultural capital on the side of the second proposition.[67] In fairness, the forces pushing for social "solidarism"—a term that became something of a mantra for expanding state functions in the Third Republic (1870–1940)—did not all emanate from the ideological left. A perceived demographic crisis buttressing "pronatalist" support for family welfare, Catholic social doctrines, and a "social defense" to ward off socialist revolution all played a role.[68] To put it perhaps too crudely,

"Fraternité" and "Égalité" in the French revolutionary inheritance helped to balance the cultural resonance of "Liberté."

Curiously, one factor consistently cited as a buttress to French welfarism also possessed strong American bona fides. The eminent social historian Philip Nord especially credits the voluntarist associations and mutual-aid associations—including Masonic lodges and trade unions—for building a culture of "republican idealism" encompassing "human solidarity" and ultimately the infrastructure of state-based welfarism.[69] The American nineteenth century, of course, did not lack for either fraternalism or larger mutualist, self-help networks. The Knights of Labor, for example, both imitated and overlapped with the lodge structure spread across the surrounding social landscape. As an early twentieth-century account put it, "Class consciousness, American style . . . expressed itself through the characteristic medium of social clubs and secret orders. The native technique of reform is, first of all, to demand three raps and a high sign."[70] Yet, somehow, in ways still inadequately explored by historians, the mutualist path in the U.S. gave way less to state than to private, commercially oriented institutions.[71]

The paradox attending American free labor comes more clearly into view. We see at once how it remained a broad-based ideal in a nation politically attentive to freedoms precisely because so much coercion, double-dealing, and subterfuge still existed in the employment relationship. Campaigns to eliminate "distortions" clouding fair-dealing in a marketplace of buyers and sellers of labor—whether it be unfair competition from convicts, duplicitous weighing of coal, or coercive checks on the right-to-quit affecting seamen and contract laborers—attracted sure-fire attention from organized labor and the larger public. Second, identification with "free labor" status served American workers, however imperfectly, as a badge of common interest and identity. Encompassing diverse occupations, skill, and income levels that otherwise experienced quite specific, sometimes even internally conflicting grievances, America's free laborers also bridged diverse ethnic and racial groups. Moreover, the pride in free-labor identity made it a harbor for new immigrants (even noncitizens) as well as a potent political stick to wave at class enemies as would-be tyrants who would deprive Americans of their birthright of freedom: this was our source of "deep, horizontal comradeship."

At the same time, however, the labor movement paid a price for trusting so ardently to its own version of Freedom Road. Not only did its industrial and political antagonists lay continuous claim to alternate interpretations of the same ideals. In addition, the ranks of the "unfree" (be they African Americans, convicts, Chinese, new immigrants, women, or whoever next appeared as a most haplessly exploited labor force) too easily served as a scapegoat for the strains confronting free laborers. Early in the century, such a distorted sense of victimhood had notably distanced white workers from black slaves.[72] Whether the ideal of free labor proved an expansive or collapsing category would be repeatedly tested, regularly pitting contract rights associated with both an individualist ideology and property owner-ship interest against the right of association and value of solidarity embraced by organized labor. In 1935, W. E. B. Du Bois similarly posited an enduring conflict between "abolition—democracy based on freedom, intelligence and power for all men" and "[a system of] industry for private profit directed by an autocracy determined at any price to amass wealth and power."[73] It was a conflict Tocqueville and other early democratic ideal-ists had not foreseen. Moreover, and perhaps this was the most telling point, in the U.S., unlike France, the group sense (or what French historian William H. Sewell, Jr., calls the "corporate idiom") was never so robust as to effectively balance individual property rights in the affairs of state.[74] Thus, however compelling—and perhaps even politically necessary—a component it was as part of a social movement in a nation bound by an eighteenth-century constitutional framework, the free-labor doctrine exposed a deep problem confronting the American working people: free-dom was not enough.

Chapter 2

Great Strikes Revisited

A strike is one thing, and we know what a strike is; but armed private mercenaries are another, and they are a thing which in this effete old country we emphatically would not tolerate. . . . Mr. Andrew Carnegie has preached to us upon "Triumphant Democracy," he has lectured us upon the rights and duties of wealth. . . . It is indeed a wholesome piece of satire.

—*St. James Gazette*, 1892

The popular image of America's era of titanic industrial conflicts has become all too tidy. Invocation of the labor battles of the Long Gilded Age typically triggers one of two sets of related dismissals (at least in my college classroom). The first takes comfort in historical distance. The bad old days of the Gilded Age, encompassing social Darwinism, robber barons, and a rough and sometimes tragic encounter between a new class of industrial workers and utterly rapacious business owners, ultimately gave way to a less primitive, more "modernized" set of employment relations and thus has little bearing on present-day concerns. Alternatively, the second disabling reaction derives from the all-too-close parallels between the older period's central themes and our own. For some, especially on the political Left, the turn-of-the-century conflicts provide little more than an overt demonstration of capitalist class exploitation and determination to crush the system's challengers that remains very much in place today. For these students, the forms and locales of exploitation may have changed, but the essential outcomes remain the same: the good guys get clobbered and our country is the worse off for it. Simply counter-posing the hard-hearted coldness of Gilded Age villains like capitalists Henry Clay Frick and George F. Baer to the hard-working immigrant steelworkers at Homestead or idealists like railroad leader Eugene Debs, however, risks turning the era into extended melodrama in which it is easy to take sides but hard to see why the details still matter.

To avoid this conceptual pitfall, this chapter offers a a renewed inquest into three major moments of Gilded Age industrial unrest: the Homestead lockout of 1892, the Pullman boycott and strike of 1894, and the anthracite strike of 1902. All three events were suffused with prime aspects of what many have considered immoveable and overwhelming obstacles facing the American labor movement—determinedly anti-union employers; a polyglot, often ethnically divided workforce, and ready resort to public authority (in the form of the militia, public officials, or courts) to curtail the conflict. Yet, my rereading of this decade of confrontation suggests more open-ended possibilities in real time than is assumed in subsequent consideration of the events by historians. Moreover, it is in keeping with the suggestion of recent business and legal scholars that politics as much as "economic and technological constraints" conditioned the American variant of industrial capitalism that rose to twentieth-century dominance.[1] In particular, labor historians can learn much from a renewed emphasis on the role of elites and the ideology of anti-unionism over the course of modern American history.[2]

The argument here equally emphasizes the role of contingency as invoked by historian Richard White: in short, "things did not have to be this way."[3] Unexpected outcomes, to be sure, are not the same as random ones. Social actors have choices, but not free choices: they are constrained by various material (economic), political, as well as cultural limits of their surroundings. In the selective reconstruction that follows, therefore, I hope to identify both larger *patterns of development* and pivotal actors who *in the context of their times* might have moved history in a different direction.

Among the latter, consider the following facts. Andrew Carnegie lived to regret his actions in the case of the Homestead Steel strike. American Railway Union leader Eugene V. Debs knew the odds were long in the case of a nationwide boycott of Pullman sleeping cars. George Pullman himself won that battle but lost the war behind his vision of a well-ordered company town. Attorney General Richard T. Olney, who effectively hounded Debs to prison, tried later to do penance for his hard-line position. Ideologically pure railroad owner George F. Baer made a public fool of himself in the anthracite strike of 1902, while both self-seeking union leader John Mitchell and financial plutocrat J. P. Morgan emerged from the same conflict cloaked in civic-mindedness. Turning a biblical injunction into a question, we might well ask, "How are the mighty fallen?" and equally, How do the fallen sometimes do good?[4] The vicissitudes of triumph and tragedy are surely among the most compelling themes of historical narrative; as such it pays us to peer farther into events too long taken for granted.

One basic question, of course, is what set off these strikes? At least in a superficial way, we can quickly answer that question by pointing to a larger pattern in the proximate *cause* of American strikes. Practically every confrontation of the era has the same immediate trigger: a significant wage cut. What is more, this material sacrifice, regularly imposed in hard times, in every case is interpreted as an attack on worker rights if not more generally on human dignity and freedom. The pattern begins well before our period. The first "turnouts" among the young women textile workers at the Lowell mills in 1834 were responses to 15 percent wage cuts that had also been accompanied by *increases* in boarding-house rents. The Lynn shoeworkers' strike, begun on Washington's birthday in 1860 and the largest such action to that date, was initiated to restore rates that had been slashed three years before. Likewise, the tumultuous mass strikes of 1877 began when Baltimore and Ohio workers rebelled against a wage cut piled on a wage cut.[5]

Every downturn, let alone panic and depression, it seems, induced the same dynamic. At Homestead in 1892, union refusal of a reduction in tonnage rates set Andrew Carnegie on a course to lock out the company's union men. In the same year, Coeur d'Alene, Idaho, coal miners walked out over a wage cut and increase in work hours. Famously, in the midst of depression conditions in 1894, George Pullman cut wages for the factory workers who built his sleeping cars an average of 25 percent, without any corresponding reduction in company housing rents.[6] Distress among the anthracite miners boiled over in 1900 around the more indirect attack on workers' income from the "infamous system of dockage."[7] In November 1909, some twenty thousand mostly Yiddish-speaking young women sparked an eleven-week strike over cuts in the piece-rate offered by inside contractors; the following year a walkout by a mere sixteen of their counterparts over another piece-rate cut at Chicago's mammoth Hart, Schaffner, and Marx factory soon coalesced into a strike of 40,000 operatives.[8] Finally, when textile workers in Lawrence, Massachusetts, learned in 1912 that employers had responded to state shorter hours legislation (reducing hours for women and children only from 56 to 54 per week) by eliminating the extra two hours' pay, they too set off a walkout of more than 20,000 workers in what would subsequently become known as the Bread and Roses strike.[9] Indeed, in the annals of the era, the wave of May Day, 1886, eight-hour strikes stand out as worker initiatives *not* begun in response to employer wage cuts, though there is a caveat even to this exception: just as in the subsequent Lawrence Strike, many struck employers prompted walkouts by refusing worker demands to receive the same wage (previously figured on a ten-hour schedule) for the shortened workday.

In a boom-bust economy, conflicting imperatives, it seems, set employers and workers bitterly against each other. Employers, in particular, facing declining revenues and desperately clinging to property rights arguments (explored in Chapter 1) as well as their bottom lines, long appeared clueless in adopting any policy other than wage cuts, despite their disruptive social and political after-effects.[10] By the onset of the Great Depression, however, a new pattern seemed to emerge. Negative public reaction and labor upheavals as a result of wage-cutting—the old pattern we have observed from 1860 to 1912 (and which continued through the 1920/21 downturn)—appeared finally to take a behavioral toll on the nation's business leaders. While hesitating to cut wages, beleaguered depression industries instead cut work hours, and then eliminated jobs altogether.[11]

In more recent times, other options continue to prevail over the incendiary wage cuts of the Long Gilded Age. Perhaps it was not until conservative anger at public-sector workers (highlighted by the air traffic controllers' strike in 1981) that the catchphrase "fire their asses" caught up to real-world managerial practices.[12] In any case, selective layoffs and job cuts have regularly replaced the favored Gilded Age remedy to employer economic stress. If not exactly an "out of sight, out of mind" solution, reduction of the workforce tends to render the victims comparatively invisible, even as those spared a pink slip are effectively reminded to think again before upsetting corporate decorum. Even public-sector employers, faced with few options amid the recent Great Recession, have notably tried to avoid naked wage cuts in favor of "furloughs," or mandatory days off.

Yet, knowing what "triggered' Gilded Age unrest does little to explain how it developed or ended. For that, we must summon up some of the main characters. Given their power in the era, and the fact that in most labor-management conflicts they usually played with a winning hand, I want to look first, in each case, at labor's opponents. Then I will circle back in selective reconsideration of the pro-labor forces of the day.

In the figures of Carnegie and Pullman, we have prime specimens of the class that has been popularly memorialized as either "Robber Barons" or "Captains of Industry," but in either case as prototypes of American anti-unionism. Yet, they were also rather complex figures. In particular, as key contributors to the distinctiveness of the American industrial order, they seem sometimes to be grappling as much with the ghosts of British or European pasts as concrete American realities.

Carnegie, of course, was the protagonist of the Homestead Strike of 1892, a fateful standoff between one of the biggest corporations and the most powerful union of the Gilded Age. When the Amalgamated Association of Iron and Steel Workers (AAISW) together with an aroused local citizenry proved unable to withstand a combination of lockout, importation of Pinkertons to protect strikebreakers, and ultimate application of state militia, unionism took a toll beyond the immediate casualties of nine dead and eleven wounded. In the steel industry, declining wages and yellow-dog contracts requiring a binding non-union pledge subsequently became the norm. Overvaluing its remaining resources, the Amalgamated made a final, fateful decision to confront the newly formed U.S. Steel monolith in 1901, a decision ending in crushing defeat.[13] Once the last steel lodge in the country dissolved in 1903, Big Steel inoculated itself from trade unionism for the next thirty-four years.[14]

Moreover, despite Carnegie's calculated self-removal to his Scottish castle and delegation of authority to his business lieutenant Henry Clay Frick during the Homestead events, a clear chain of authority set the fateful events in motion. Like the Boston Associates who a half century before had created the spindle city of Lowell out of Merrimack River farmland, Carnegie had within a decade turned a village of a few hundred residents into an industrial center of 8,000 people mainly occupied making steel plate (much of it for the U.S. navy) with the nation's largest rolling mill. It was Carnegie who first negotiated a "sliding scale" (geared to the market price of a key component in the manufacturing process) with the Amalgamated in 1889, then, deciding to go entirely non-union, provoked a strike by stockpiling plates, fencing in the plant, insisting on a reduction in tonnage rates, contracting with the Pinkertons to recruit a substitute labor force, then calling for military intervention and ultimately encouraging the most draconian legal penalties against the strikers.[15] Indeed, John McLuckie, the twice-elected burgess (mayor) of Homestead, fled the state rather than face charges of murder, conspiracy, and treason for opposing the Pinkertons; a once-proud skilled worker, his pro-union stand cost him his job, his home, and his marriage.[16] There is thus ample evidence to finger Carnegie as the "intellectual" author of the Homestead tragedy, while leaving Frick—who would survive an assassination attempt by anarchist Alexander Berkman at the end of the strike— to serve as the fall guy.

Yet, we are also left to reconcile Carnegie's onerous role as industrial autocrat with his philanthropical acts both before and after the strike. Of course, his philanthropy, as perhaps most famously associated with his endowment of public libraries, could be chalked up to liberal guilt or worse. From the beginning there is a touch of defensiveness in "The Gospel of Wealth" (Carnegie's famous 1889 essay). "While the law [of competition] may be hard for the individual," Carnegie insisted, "it is best for the race." Yet, he allowed that the concentration of wealth in a few hands (like his own) would likely be accepted in a free society only so long as the rich treat it as a "sacred trust."[17] In addition, gift-giving could prove quite strategic: Carnegie himself was finalizing plans for the Carnegie Library of Homestead —arriving in town with "a Pullman-car-full of guests"—just two months before he locked out his employees. The Homestead historian thus does not have to reach far to contextualize such acts within the framework of behavioral "social deception" as explained by anthropologist Marcel Mauss, that "the transaction itself is based on obligation and economic self-interest" in furtherance of social hierarchy.[18]

Still, there were aspects of the man that seem to point to less predictable behavioral patterns. Outwardly confident and even boisterously sure of himself, Carnegie likely could not easily dissociate the grievances of Homestead workers from his own past as the son of a failed Scottish handloom weaver and grandson of a proud Chartist activist in the working-class movement for radical democratic reform that swept British industrial districts for a decade after 1838. Escape from the class system is thus a central theme behind the soaring rhetoric of his *Triumphant Democracy* (1886). Notably, it is not entrepreneurship, technology, or even hard work which, for Carnegie, account for the American Republic's triumphal "rush" past the "old nations of the world [that] creep on at a snail's pace." Rather, with universal suffrage and free public education, "the people are not emasculated by being made to feel that their own country decrees their inferiority, and holds them unworthy of privileges accorded to others." Freed from a "social system which ranks them beneath an arrogant class of drones," Carnegie anticipates Israel Zangwell's melting-pot, where "children of Russian and German serfs, of Irish evicted tenants, Scottish crofters, and other victims of feudal tyranny are transmuted into republican Americans."[19] Carnegie's career was self-consciously steeped in the ideals of both social and political independence. It is thus no accident that when, at eighteen, having just graduated from four years of service as a telegraph messenger to become private secretary to Pennsylvania Railroad owner Tom Scott, Carnegie would look around at his adopted country and exclaim (in correspondence to a British uncle), "We have the Charter."[20]

Even as a profit-seeking American industrialist, therefore, Carnegie was in some significant respects still tethered to the democratic concerns of the British liberal tradition. Regularly spending half of each year in the UK (historian A. S. Eisenstadt labels him the quintessential "Pan-Anglian"), Carnegie cultivated close ties with the "radical-liberal" wing of the Liberal Party, including an early friendship with writer-editor John Morley that led him into the inner circle of reform-oriented statesmen in the age of William Gladstone, Liberal leader and four-time prime minister from the late 1860s through the mid-1890s.[21] By the mid-1880s, Carnegie was helping to finance a syndicate of Liberal newspapers: pushing vociferously for Irish Home Rule and land reform, abolition of the House of Lords, and manhood suffrage. "Carnegie's Radicalism" (according to biographer Joseph Wall) proved a frequent source of embarrassment to party leader Gladstone, with whom he maintained a generally cordial relationship.[22]

Yet, on specifically labor-related issues, Carnegie's British commitments across the 1880s and early 1890s are unclear. Among his close associates, Morley in 1891 bitterly opposed an eight hour bill for miners, while other friends like Charles Dilke and John Burns were strong labor advocates. On the very eve of his September 1891 departure to America to deal with the expiring Homestead contract, Carnegie hedged on the question of hours legislation: internationally competitive industries like steel, he suggested, could not practically conform to restrictive regulation, yet he allowed that "we shall have more and more occasion for the State to legislate on behalf of the workers."[23] Perhaps most surprising was Carnegie's £100 contribution to the campaign of Scottish socialist Keir Hardie, elected the first independent Labour MP (with de facto Liberal support) at West Ham South in 1892: was he expressing sympathies for Hardie's social-democratic principles or merely patronizing a fellow Scot?[24] Whatever the competing, sometimes contradictory pulls on his political sympathies, Carnegie surely bore witness to the contemporary tensions between an older, individualist liberal-radicalism and a New Liberalism that tied citizenship in an industrial society to state-aided worker welfare and trade union protections.

In retrospect, one aspect of Carnegie's thought, evident in his own discourse, seems to have facilitated a confrontational stance with his American workforce. If he was a spread-eagled American patriot, Carnegie was also an Anglo American cultural chauvinist. Thus, even as he idealistically allowed for immigrants from other stock to remake themselves in the American setting, he betrayed no doubt as to which bloodline made up the "noble strain" (how odd a phrase for a radical anti-monarchist) of cultural inheritance. His sufferance of an obstreperous unionized workforce— particularly one heavy with unreconstructed ethnic outsiders—was noticeably limited. At his Edgar Thomson works in 1891, he readily assented to both Frick and Schwab's denigration of workers' recalcitrance as "nothing more than a drunken Hungarian spree" and anticipation of "another attack by the Huns tonight."[25] As lesser citizens, expressions from the vast ranks of unskilled, immigrant labor might be more easily dismissed. As Carnegie asserted on his way to Homestead in 1891, they "lack the necessary qualities: educational, physical, and moral. The common laborer is a common labourer because he is common."[26]

In any event, Carnegie's reckoning with the carnage and disfavor of the Homestead event proved an uneasy one. He was pilloried on both sides of the Atlantic by erstwhile allies. His home-country *Edinburgh Dispatch* sneered that "neither our capitalists nor our labourers have any inclination to imitate the methods which prevail in the land of "Triumphant Democracy,'" while the *St. Louis Post-Dispatch* judged that "America can well spare Mr. Carnegie. Ten thousand Carnegie Public Libraries would not compensate the country for the direct evils resulting from the Homestead lockout."[27] Depressed and secluded in the immediate aftermath of the violence, Carnegie returned to Homestead in January 1893, where he attempted publicly to bury the lockout and its aftermath as a kind of "horrid dream." While rhetorically still supporting Frick's moves, he loudly whispered at least a retrospective dissent from the decision to send in the strikebreakers, an event he glossed in a private message to Morley as "that Homestead Blunder."[28] Growing tensions dating from the strike between Frick and Carnegie would lead the former to resign his chairmanship in 1899, with Charles Schwab stepping into the breach.[29] Echoing Carnegie's

own post-strike whisperings, Schwab, forty years later, would similarly
regret his role in the Pinkerton affair, while offering a hypothetical tactical
alternative:

> At Homestead, had I been running affairs, I would have called the
> men in and told it was impossible to meet their terms. I would have
> told them we would simply close down until the justice of our posi-
> tion had been demonstrated—even if we had to close down for ever.
> But I would have told them that nobody else would be given their
> jobs. . . . There is nothing a worker resents more than to see some
> man taking his job. A factory can be closed down, its chimneys
> smokeless, waiting for the worker to come back to his job, and all
> will be peaceful. But the moment workers are imported, and the
> striker sees his own place usurped, there is bound to be trouble.[30]

Though there was never a direct mea culpa from Carnegie, we nevertheless witness some post-Homestead alterations in his thought and behavior.
On the labor front, while taking advantage of lowered wage scales conse-
quent to the decimation of the Amalgamated, he effectively cut workers'
living costs, with lowered rents at company housing and new low-interest
mortgage loans as well as cut rates on coal and gas supplies.[31]In addition,
Carnegie made much of what he considered a personal reconciliation with
Homestead Strike martyr John McLuckie. When family friend and art historian, John C. Van Dyke, accidentally stumbled on an indigent McLuckie
in Mexico's Baja California in 1900, Carnegie, acting anonymously through
Van Dyke, offered whatever money he needed "to put him on his feet
again." McLuckie declined the offer, insisting that he would make it on his
own, and within months, Van Dyke found him again, now securely
employed at the Sonora Railway and happily remarried to a Mexican
woman. When Van Dyke then told McLuckie that the previous monetary
offer had come from Carnegie, McLuckie reportedly replied, "Well, that
was damned white of Andy, wasn't it?" The compliment so moved Carnegie
that in a memoir penned in 1906, he gushed that he "knew McLuckie well
as a good fellow" and that he "would rather risk that verdict of McLuckie's
as a passport to Paradise than all the theological dogmas invented by
man."[32]

Aside from guilt offerings, however, perhaps the nearest hint of a
change of heart towards trade unionism lay in Carnegie's post-millennium

connection to the AFL-friendly National Civic Federation (NCF): in 1908, Carnegie was not only its biggest financial backer but also contributed specifically to the defense of AFL president Samuel Gompers from contempt of court charges in the pivotal Buck's Stove and Range case.[33]

Meanwhile, Carnegie increasingly turned his public advocacy to international affairs. Whereas he had happily supported a U.S. naval buildup (which also happened to rely on armored plate from his mills) and also joined the rush to "free Cuba" in 1898, Carnegie soon after refurbished his liberal, anti-imperialist principles in adamant opposition to the Philippines campaign. Opposing "distant possessions" (except where a colony could be expected to "produce Americans" as in Hawaii), Carnegie asked defiantly, "Are we to exchange Triumphant Democracy for Triumphant Despotism?"[34] (Secretary of State Hay countered by pointing out the contradiction of Carnegie's anti-interventionist stance regarding Filipinos and his treatment of striking workers at Homestead.) For a time Carnegie's anti-imperialism extended even to possible political collaboration with the Republican's archenemy William Jennings Bryan. Though never consummated as a political alliance, Carnegie later supported Secretary of State Bryan's earnest efforts (in the Wilson Administration) at arranging international arbitration treaties. His last commitment, what he called his greatest, was the establishment of the Carnegie Endowment for International Peace in 1910. As in his early simple faith in American democracy and free enterprise, Carnegie convinced himself that a series of international treaties and peace conferences were truly delivering world peace under international law by 1914. True to form, he died in 1919 still possessed of great hopes for the League of Nations.[35]

Never a deep thinker but rather an impressive doer, Carnegie was a man caught between different worlds of time and place. Living effectively as a bi-national, he regularly projected the idealism and worldly success that he attached to his American experience back onto the forms of mid-nineteenth-century British radical democracy. For decades he could thus remain a radical-liberal in Britain while adopting conservative Republican loyalties in the United States. Yet, the times caught up with him at both ends. By the 1890s British liberals, pushed by the rise of a politicized labor movement, were coming to grips with the consequences of the manhood suffrage principle that stood at the root of Carnegie's own Chartist-inspired political faith. For all his forward-looking projections, Carnegie himself could not quite make the move of many of his British contemporaries towards a New Liberalism for the industrial age. Rather, with his simple faith in democracy-equals-opportunity-for-all shattered by labor conflict, he turned to the bromides of international peace and reconciliation as an alternate site of idealization. In Carnegie's case, however, the democratic ideal effectively stopped at the factory gate.

Even as many contemporaries (not to mention latter-day historians) on both sides of the Atlantic criticized and second-guessed Carnegie for his actions in 1892, there has been decidedly less second-guessing of organized labor's decision-making there—and for good reason. Basically, both contemporaries and historians see little that the AAISW and its allies could have done to avert the disaster that befell it once Carnegie and his minions determined to operate non-union. Aside from the strategic opening to a less-skilled workforce enhanced by the shift to open-hearth steelmaking, Carnegie could play two decisive political cards in the Homestead showdown. Each of them, moreover, would figure repeatedly in defining a "weak-labor" American exceptionalist path for the next forty years.

The first was the employer's ability to summon police power to put down a workers' uprising and proceed, behind the security curtain, to restart production with a non-union workforce including a corps of strikebreakers imported from outside the local community. The sway of Carnegie and Frick over Democratic governor Robert Pattison and county Republican boss Christopher Magee proved critical in the governor's decision to dispatch 8,500 National Guard troops to Homestead, thereby displacing effective control over events heretofore exercised by Burgess McLuckie and a disciplined strike Advisory Committee headed by steelworker Hugh O'Donnell. As O'Donnell immediately acknowledged following the governor's decision, "We can't fight the state of Pennsylvania, and even if we could, we cannot fight the United States government."[36] Once the militia, bivouacked on company property and prepared to reopen the works at the company's bidding, intervened, the confrontation was over.

It is worth noting that unlike many other American industrial disputes, Homestead was not a case of a fatally divided or poorly led workforce. Though hierarchies of skill, ethnicity (especially Old Immigrant versus East European), and race (African Americans in significant numbers first arrived at Homestead only in the aftermath of the 1892 strike) certainly existed within both the union and local community, a remarkable cross-ethnic (and cross-gender) solidarity had held up throughout the siege. Yet, everything changed with the arrival of the militia. Chicago's *Arbeiter-Zeitung* compared the situation unfavorably to Bismarck's threatened use of force against the Ruhr miners. As a self-identified "Homesteader" rhetorically asked in its German-language pages, "What is the difference between the state's soldiers and the Pinkertons?"[37]

The second (and often concurrent) resort of employers for help from the state was to the courts. In this case, Carnegie Steel's chief counsel, Philander C. Knox, who would later serve the federal government as attorney general and secretary of state, proved a zealous litigant. As historian Paul Krause summarizes, "many of the Homestead workers, unable to raise sufficient funds for bail, were incarcerated for extended periods, and a number of those who had helped lead the sympathy strike at Duquesne also received prison sentences." In a more controversial move, Knox collaborated with Chief Justice Edward Paxson of the Pennsylvania Supreme Court to charge thirty-three members of the Advisory Committee with no less than a charge of treason, based on a Civil War-era statute aimed at discouraging those who would attack the state. Though the treason indictments were ultimately withdrawn, the union's resources and a good bit of its public legitimacy had been shattered by the legal onslaught.[38]

The degree to which the "political" landscape mattered at Homestead (and other big industrial centers) in the Long Gilded Age is perhaps best suggested by the outcomes once that landscape changed in the 1930s. The political maturation of the steel region's immigrant working-class utterly changed the odds. When the CIO Steel Workers Organizing Committee opened its campaign in July 1936, the state police escorted their chief, lieutenant governor and UMWA secretary-treasurer Thomas Kennedy, into Homestead to be the main speaker, and "filtered through the crowd as insurance against interference by company-dominated municipal police."[39] Before long, mighty U.S. Steel (heir to the Carnegie empire) would come to terms with the union. This was the New Deal alliance between the Democratic Party and organized labor in action.

Given what we know now about the circumstances of the 1890s, could any acts on the workers' part have turned the tide at Homestead in a more favorable direction? It is unlikely. At a funeral service for one victim of the July 6 battle with the Pinkertons, local Methodist minister J. J. McIlyar insisted that "arbitration" might have resolved the dispute, but instead violence was "brought about by one man [Frick], who is less respected by the laboring people than any other employer in the country."[40] The one pressure point that is perhaps more visible in retrospect than to contemporaries was the ambivalence of Carnegie himself. He visibly suffered, though more in Britain than in the United States, for the loss of reputation among liberal-radical circles that had proved an important point of his political identity. Had Homestead workers (and/or other American labor leaders) at the time appealed directly to the likes of Keir Hardie or John Burns—or even William Gladstone—to intervene with their friend Carnegie, might they have bought time for a process of conciliation to which Rev. McIlyar appealed?

To posit international solidarity action on the part of a grassroots movement in the 1890s, of course, risks conviction for historical anachronism. It is true that across the industrial lands of Euro-America, one looks hard for examples that Homestead or other steelworkers could have been expected to copy with any positive effect. Decades earlier, it is true, the abolitionist movement had operated across borders in safekeeping runaway slaves, but the lesson there for the labor movement would have involved a major imaginative leap.[41] If one looked beyond landed to maritime occupations, however, there was indeed a serious move afoot to harness the power of workers operating across national boundaries. Out of necessity (due to the recruitment of their workmates across national boundaries), seafarer and dockworker unions, who formed the core of the British "New Unionist" upsurge of the late 1880s and 1890s, were experimenting with transnational actions: as early as 1896 they would create a pan-European organization and by 1911 carry off a partially successful trans-Atlantic strike.[42] Whether workers outside the incipient seafarer-dockworker alliance took notice of such pioneering attempts at labor internationalism is an un-researched question. One thing seems certain. Left to their own resources, the strikers' fate—without an apparent way to turn "Homestead" into a national or even international issue—was sealed.

Next to Carnegie, perhaps no industrialist is more associated with the combustibility of the Gilded Age than George Pullman. Like Carnegie's Homestead, Pullman's giant sleeping-car factory rose from bare farmland almost overnight. From 1881 to 1884 the town of Pullman grew from a population of 4 to 8,513.[43] Unlike Carnegie's steel plants and almost every other American industrial setting, however, the rise of Pullman town was also stamped with a vision of company-planned social order and harmony. Just as famously, that "paternal" vision blew up in the Pullman strike and boycott of 1894. In a nutshell, when the company (along with the general economy) entered a profound slump in 1893 and Pullman drastically slashed wages without cutting rents of his tenants, his workers, newly organized into the fledgling American Railway Union (ARU), struck and soon secured the support of ARU president Eugene V. Debs for a nationwide boycott of trains bearing Pullman cars. When every move to uncouple sleeping cars led to the dismissal of the offending workers, the ARU called out all its members and allies on the offending railroad lines. The stage was thus set for a massive confrontation between the union and the nation's railroad owners united under the General Managers' Association. Alas for the workers, the railroads received immediate support in squashing the strike from the federal government, as directed by President Cleveland's attorney general Richard Olney, himself a longtime railway attorney and director. After securing injunctions against the strikers with a pioneering (not to mention unanticipated and legally dubious) invocation of the Sherman Antitrust Act, Olney, over the objections of both state and local officials, sent federal troops under General Nelson A. Miles to Chicago to restore order. Over July 6 and 7, U.S. deputy marshals and state militia (ordered into action in Illinois, California, Iowa, and Michigan as well) shot and killed an estimated 13 railroad "rioters" and wounded 57 others in the Chicago area alone.[44] For violating previous injunctions and additionally charged with conspiracy to subvert the U.S. government, indictments leading to arrest and ultimate conviction were issued against Debs and three other ARU leaders on July 10. With further prosecutions of hundreds of other strikers, the Pullman strike—and with it the ARU—was crushed. Following guilty verdicts for contempt of court sustained by the U.S. Supreme Court in May 1895, Debs would serve six months in the county jail in Woodstock, Illinois.[45] Not long after he emerged, Debs declared that a new struggle—this for a socialist transformation of the American state—would be needed to defend the most basic of workers' rights.[46]

Classic "exceptionalist" themes echo throughout the Pullman narrative. The obdurate capitalist owner, the fiercely anti-labor federal government backed both by a pliant judiciary and armed might, and a heroic but doomed effort of organized workers to swim against the tides of constituted authority and middle-class opinion. Yet, how set and foreordained were the options and outcomes?

A brief review of key players in the Pullman events reveals some gaping holes in the picture of an a priori "American" opposition to a vibrant

workers' movement. George Pullman's company town, in its very establishment, defied any principle of "shared governance" with its workers. Yet,
Pullman, however unyielding, can be seen as a Progressive reformer of a
peculiar type. If no pan-Anglian like Carnegie, he too was reacting to an
image of the wretchedness of urban conditions for the masses in Britain
and on the Continent that could only be remedied by systematic social
planning. As early as the 1870s, Pullman took an interest in the "model
tenement movement," believing that clean and healthy living conditions
served not only as a good in themselves but as a measurable spur to worker
productivity. A contemporary French observer commented on Pullman's
dedication to the "Anglo-Saxon idea, that exterior respectability aids true
self-respect."[47] Perhaps the quirkiest aspect of Pullman's reformism (was
this American provincialism or rather transnational over-exposure?) was
his dedication to a purely *commercial*, profit-based model for all his environmental innovations. As his biographers attest, he apparently disdained
the *European*-style paternalism associated with otherwise-similar company
towns in Guise, France; Krupp's factory works at Essen, Germany; and Sir
Titus Salt's model village of Saltaire in Yorkshire.[48] To Pullman's mind,
sentimental or merely "philanthropic" gestures of social welfare were likely
to prove ineffectual and short-lived; rather, he staked his claim to environmental uplift on a "hard-headed bottom-line mentality" that beautiful
surroundings could pay for themselves and thus prove the urban-
developmental rule rather than the exception.[49]

For Pullman, labor unions represented poisoned fruit in urban
working-class surroundings. Like his image of the healthy city, his dark
view of the unions derived initially from Charles Reade's British novel, *Put
Yourself in His Place* (1870), which, according to the testimony of Reade's
daughter, Pullman "read and reread."[50] A less-gifted realist in the style of
Dickens, Reade conjured up the industrial city of Hillsborough (a stand-in
for Sheffield), "perhaps the most hideous town in creation. Houses seem
to have battled in the air, and stuck wherever they tumbled down dead out
of the melee. But, worst of all, the city is pockmarked with public-houses,
and bristles with high round chimneys." (Not for nothing did Pullman ban
saloons in Pullman town.) Yet, as the novel's protagonist, workman-
inventor Henry Little discovers, what stands in the way of progress in Hillsborough is not just the ignorance and selfishness of industrialists but the
mean-spirited corruption of trade unionists. (As his biographer discovered,
for nearly a decade prior to fashioning this novel, Reade had been clipping

newspaper articles on strikes and trade unions under the heading "the dirty oligarchy."[51]) Progress can prevail, the novel suggests, only so long as fair-minded employers and aspiring workers are freed from outside political entanglements. In the harsh reality of the urban jungle, Pullman apprehended, it was imperative that the well-intentioned entrepreneur stick to his guns. In uncommonly combining the role of paternalistic social planning with an undying faith in market mechanisms, Pullman thus sketched a form of "American Exceptionalism" that was also a direct response to European example.

Like Carnegie, Pullman won the round with his worker foes, but (again like Carnegie) he did not get off (to badly pun) scot-free. The crushing of the strike and imprisonment of Debs put the industrialist and key political supporters in a bad public light. The resulting strike commission authorized by a pressured President Cleveland proved caustic in its assessment of the paternalistic treatment of the workers at Pullman and effectively spanked the industry by calling for an impartial railroad commission, trade union recognition, and even compulsory arbitration in the settlement of future disputes.[52] The boycott and strike also left the whole concept of the company town with a bad name. By 1894, the state's supreme court stripped the Pullman Company of its ownership rights over town property, ending the vision with which it was conceived. Pullman himself died of a heart attack in 1897, never regaining his public stature, and seeking eternal shelter from potential depredations of ex-Pullman rioters in one of the most secure tombs ever constructed.[53]

The law-and-order forces at Pullman include at least two other figures who superficially fit the mold of corporate lackeys. Both General Nelson Miles and Attorney General Olney played important coercive roles in relation to the striking workers. As western field commander of the U.S. army, Miles had helped subdue Chief Joseph and Geronimo before closing in on the Sioux and securing Sitting Bull's arrest in 1890. By outward measure, his supervision, as major general, regular army of the federal government's occupying forces in the Chicago region seems the perfect embodiment of what Richard Slotkin described as the transfer of the "myth of the frontier" onto the industrial landscape.[54]

On more than one occasion, however, Miles's very military professionalism also raised a cautionary flag in the use of unbridled force. Even as an Indian-fighter, he proved something of a moderate. Although he had insisted on incarceration of Sitting Bull as a symbol of pacification, Miles was outraged by the war-lust of the cavalry's attack at Wounded Knee, which he labeled an "abominable criminal blunder and a horrible massacre of women and children." Miles was initially even more skeptical about the army's role in pacifying strikers. At the beginning of July 1894, he counseled an over-eager President Cleveland that conditions "did not yet warrant federal troops," and when overruled by Olney and pressed into action, he drew the ire of his superiors by demanding specific instructions as to if and when his men should "fire upon a riotous mass of citizenry." The wife of Secretary of State Walter Gresham noted at the time that Miles had "contempt" for George Pullman and openly sympathized "with the masses."[55] In the course of strike-related confrontations, Miles would be repeatedly criticized from on high for not sufficiently massing his troops and not responding quickly enough to taunts from surrounding crowds. In short, frontier logic did not spread automatically to urban law enforcement (or apparently even convince some of its key frontier players).

Olney more easily fits the mantle of aggressive corporate tool. He was certainly well-trained for the part. Son of a New England banker and heir to a woolen factory family legacy, he graduated from Brown University and then Harvard Law School before marrying the daughter of an ex-Supreme Court justice and becoming his associate. By 1889 Olney was serving as general counsel of the CB&Q, a western railroad (afflicted by a major strike in 1888) formed from Boston capital. Historian Richard White thus captures Olney as "intellectually . . . not subtle; he was often erratic . . . but always practical and always bold"; for good measure, adds White, he was "a tyrant" who "quite literally hated infants and small animals." Olney, by such a reading, served as an appropriate symbol of the corporation-run state, or as White again pungently summarizes: "While Debs was organizing railroad workers, and while the Populists and other antimonopolists were organizing western states, the railroads were organizing the cabinet and the federal bureaucracy."[56] Given all his associations, we might well expect Olney to share the view of other railroad executives like John W. Kendrick, general manager of the Northern Pacific, for whom the Pullman dispute ultimately tested "whether the roads shall be absolutely controlled by the labor element, or by the managers and the owners."[57] In keeping with such expectations, in the months prior to the Pullman boycott, Olney had energetically prosecuted the Commonwealers advancing on Washington to demand jobs—using the pretext of federal receivership quickly responding to appeals from federal judges to send in the army to halt trains carrying these unemployed activists.[58] Olney, more than anyone else in government, pushed President Cleveland to take an immediate, hard line against the boycotters. "From the announcement of the boycott in late June to the collapse of the strike in mid-July," biographer Gerald G. Eggert writes, "Olney's primary objective was to crush the strike."[59]

Yet, even Olney felt the constraint of both politics and the law (and perhaps a deeper personal morality as well) in advancing a one-sided resolution of industrial disputes. Although he apparently felt no compunction in prosecuting those (like Debs and the Commonwealers) who would use force—i.e. intimidating strikebreakers, seizing trains, etc.—in pursuit of their cause, he otherwise balked at bald corporate power. It is thus worth noting that he had exercised forbearance in the use of federal power during Debs's successful direction of the Great Northern strike in 1893.[60] Moreover, only two months after Debs's July 1894 arraignment, Olney showed both cunning and restraint in intervening on the side of the Brotherhood of Railway Trainmen (a craft union that had publicly opposed the ARU's boycott) when the Philadelphia and Reading Railroad, taking advantage of its receivership, demanded of BRT members that they resign from the union or be fired.[61] The findings of the U.S. Strike Commission—which Cleveland had appointed amidst mounting outrage from labor advocates within the Democratic Party—of company manipulation in the recruitment of federal marshals struck a further nerve in the self-righteous attorney general. Soon, he joined the commissioners in condemning the extrajudicial role of the railway corporations, and he surprised many of his peers not only in reaffirming labor's right to organize but also in supporting the commission's call for compulsory arbitration of selected disputes. A series of ameliorative railroad labor measures (including the right to join a union and voluntary arbitration), for which Olney gave his insistent support, were ultimately secured in 1898 as the Erdman Act. A most telling comment on the shakeup of thinking in the period was that of CB&Q owner Charles Elliott Perkins: "I do not understand what has come over Olney."[62]

Though pilloried in much of the mainstream press at the time as a labor tyrant ("King Debs" ran the famous *Harper's Weekly* cartoon of July 14, 1894) threatening the nation's commerce, ARU leader Eugene V. Debs has generally been treated sympathetically by historians as a democratic leader victimized by arbitrary corporate power. Yet, given the stakes of the Pullman conflict and its outcome—particularly the end of sustained industrial unionism on the railroads and further setback to the larger popular anti-monopoly movement—it is worth asking if Debs & Co., within the context of his core beliefs and the opportunities of the times, might have acted differently or left any significant cards unplayed. The question is raised because Debs's public profile post-Pullman—that is, as "martyred"strike-leader-turned-valiant-but-always-losing socialist icon—diverges so dramatically from the profile pre-Pullman.

Debs, after all, had demonstrated nothing less than organizational genius in fashioning the ARU in June 1893. Across twenty years, he had worked his way up into the high counsels of the proudly conservative Brotherhood of Locomotive Firemen, only to witness the futility of even coordinated action among the several brotherhoods in the Burlington strike of 1888. Already by 1890, he was appealing to a larger "spirit of fraternity" that he witnessed across the land, and the ARU—open to all railway workers, regardless of craft or service (though in accord with brotherhood practice still white-only)—proved the initial vehicle of his grand vision.[63] Boldly, the fledgling ARU soon challenged James J. Hill's Great Northern Railway, shutting down the road across the West while nimbly side-stepping trains with mail cars so as not to provoke governmental retaliation. When Debs (to Hill's surprise) accepted a Minnesota state arbitration process, the ARU walked away with the recovery of their lost wages as well as a skyrocketing national membership.[64]

Given the shrewdness with which he had previously conducted his union business, why did Debs risk it all on spreading strikes in the midst of mass unemployment? He had already seen the injunction used to devastating effect in the Burlington strike, and he had witnessed Attorney General Olney's lightning legal strikes against the Commonwealers on railroads in receivership. He knew that the employers' General Managers' Association was itching to reverse the early momentum of the ARU. And he knew that he could not count on solidarity from the railroad brotherhoods who resented their upstart rival. Meanwhile, though growing increasingly physically desperate, the striking ARU members in Pullman town were collecting manifold political support. They not only commanded the sympathy and active support of the mayor, the governor, and major newspapers but a new cross-class coalition demanding arbitration and other Pullman Company compromises. Institutionalized in the Civic Federation of Chicago (later the National Civic Federation), this reform movement (featuring Chicago banker, world's fair organizer, and by 1900 Secretary of the Treasury Lyman

Gage alongside settlement house leader Jane Addams) ultimately failed to dissuade George Pullman from his confrontational, and to their minds disastrous, course.[65] (Addams herself would be left to ruminate darkly on the event—condemning both sides for descending to the use of force—in a long-unpublished essay she entitled "A Modern Lear."[66])

Soon, the conflict slipped altogether out of local hands. By most unfortunate timing, the ARU's first annual convention convened in Chicago a month into the strike and amidst growing cries for help from Pullman residents. As historian Nick Salvatore indicates, Debs initially hesitated but then succumbed to a tide of militant resistance that he had himself helped to generate. It is true that Debs tried to reinvent his Great Northern success by premising direct action on two attempts to prod Pullman towards arbitration, but the last-minute maneuvers went nowhere. In the end, Debs's calculus of hesitation seems to have been swamped by an instinct for justice. Contradicting his own tactical message, his convention address thus summoned the delegates to a defense of their most basic rights and self-dignity: "When men accept degrading conditions and wear collars and fetters without resistance, when a man surrenders his honest convictions, his loyalty to principle, he ceases to be a man."[67]

Such rhetoric is not the stuff of strategic half-measures. Had Debs more forthrightly stood up to the ARU delegates, might he have averted an all-out war with the nation's railroads (and ultimately the U.S. government) by *localizing* the conflict (i.e., limiting the shutdown to Chicago), *boycotting more selectively* (e.g.,, no mailcars), or selecting another half-measure of solidarity like miners' leader John Mitchell would use in 1902? If so, he might have ultimately linked a mass industrial base of organized transportation workers with that of miners, and maritime workers to form an American version of the Triple Alliance that defined British labor's powerful public presence prior to World War I. Instead, outside the mines and big-city garment shops, American labor emerged more beaten than unbowed from what Graham Adams called the "age of industrial violence."[68] More than Homestead, Pullman is a case where the materials and choices available might have been assembled differently to quite different effects. Moreover, if individual decisions could be so decisive, why do we (as historians) continue to rely on more secular explanations, as if the drift of history were more akin to geological shifts than the moral will of individuals?

Among the major industrial struggles of the Long Gilded Age, the anthracite strike of 1902 broke the mold in at least three critical respects. First, organized workers won a signal, if provisional, victory over one of the most powerful and anti-union employer groups in the country. Second, at a crucial moment in the confrontation, the workers *had the U.S. government decidedly on their side*. Finally, as economist and labor historian Selig Perlman noted, it was the first time in American history when a disruptive strike went on for months "without being condemned as a revolutionary menace."[69] What were the roots of such structural and political exceptionalism? And why were the gains of 1902 so seemingly fleeting?

A thumbnail sketch of events leading to the 1902 strike quickly centers on a few key players. Textbooks regularly cite the stereotypical villain of the story, leading coal owner George F. Baer who stood adamantly against unionization in the anthracite range and uttered one of the most notorious apologias for corporate rule on record. Pressed by a religious sympathizer for the workers, Baer exploded: "The rights and interests of the laboring man will be protected and cared for—not by the labor agitators, but by the Christian men to whom God in His infinite wisdom has given the control of the property interests of the country, and upon the successful Management of which so much depends."[70] In this conflict, however, not only would Baer not have his way, but also his viewpoint proved an embarrassment to the class with which he associated. By the turn of the century, Baer and the large railroad owners who had been used to running the geographically compact anthracite region of northeastern Pennsylvania since the collapse of contract miner organization in the mid-1870s faced an upheaval from below that they could no longer control.

Overcoming brutal repression as well as once-profound internal divisions of both skill and ethnicity, and fresh from a breakthrough agreement in multi-state bituminous fields in 1897, the United Mine Workers of America, led by John Mitchell, had remarkably called out an estimated 97 percent of the anthracite workforce on strike for recognition and a wage increase in mid-September, 1900. The owners, moreover, after refusing Mitchell's invitation to a joint conference and/or arbitration, faced not only an assertive rank-and-file fired by the organizing talents of Mary "Mother" Jones but strong outside political pressure. With much of the heating oil on the East Coast derived from anthracite, an extended strike raised fears of widespread suffering and with it a threat to the rosy reelection call to "stand pat" and enjoy a "full dinner pail" by President McKinley and his campaign organizer, Ohio senator Mark Hanna. Soon Hanna had reached out to J. P. Morgan, chief investor in the anthracite railroads, to broker a labor "truce," as both owners and union leadership agreed to a 10 percent raise and no recriminations in an informal settlement that stopped short of recognition or a signed agreement.

It was precisely expiration of the 1900 truce that precipitated a new strike in May 1902. Again, Mitchell called on the intervention of Hanna, who now served as head of the industrial committee of the increasingly influential National Civic Federation. As the strike stretched on through the summer and into fall, and as Baer and the key owners dug in their heels, Hanna (again in close collaboration with Mitchell) appealed to two outside figures—President Theodore Roosevelt and J. P. Morgan (acting through his "right-hand man" George Perkins)—to break the impasse. A difficult decision faced Mitchell midway through the arduous five-month conflict. Learning of the growing desperation of their anthracite brethren, bituminous locals of the union demanded a special convention to take up a call for an industry-wide strike, albeit in violation of their own contracts. Fearing that his whole collaborative strategy was about to come undone, Mitchell upped the ante on all his partners. On the one hand, Mitchell vanquished union militants (even giving NCF agents carte blanche access to spread its moderate message among bituminous locals) with a full-throated convention appeal for a budgetary appropriation and strike-supporting "assessment" of members rather than a sympathy strike.[71] On the other hand—fending off a proposal from Perkins and NCF chairman Ralph M. Easley—he refused to send the strikers back to work while a committee appointed by Hanna appealed to Morgan for a compromise solution.[72]

In short, Mitchell (unlike Debs in the Pullman Strike) played both ends against the middle. Ultimately, fears of worker militancy and potential political recrimination forced President Roosevelt's hand. The essence of an agreement, including binding arbitration by a presidential commission, was finally hammered out between Morgan and Secretary of War Elihu Root (who also happened to serve as general counsel to J. P. Morgan and Company) on board the financier's yacht *Corsair III*. Even as the owners' representatives argued that they could not negotiate with a "set of outlaws" who should be treated to a show of military force, Morgan himself secured their acquiescence to the arbitration agreement.[73]

A final settlement, announced to the public in March 1903 granted working miners an additional 10 percent raise while cutting the normal workday from ten to nine hours. Although it included no trade agreement, a board of conciliation (with elected representatives from designated mining districts) to oversee implementation of the award brought the union as close to de facto recognition in anthracite as it was to secure until World War I.[74] All in all there is good reason to credit the general public reaction of the time that the strike represented a significant union victory. In the Eastern European mining communities, the strike settlement touched off jubilant celebration. Labeling Mitchell a "second Napoleon of labor," the editors of the area Polish, Lithuanian, Slovak, and Ukrainian newspapers jointly proclaimed that the "embodiment of everything that is pure, just, right and sublime is John Mitchell"; for decades many communities celebrated Mitchell Day.[75] Only a few years after the event, former miner and state mine inspector Andrew Roy justifiably called Mitchell's campaign "the best managed of any strike that ever occurred in the United States."[76]

In the annals of the larger "class settlement" of the Gilded Age, the figures of both Mitchell and Hanna (and perhaps Morgan as well) likely deserve closer attention than they have received.[77] A former child laborer in the mines, Mitchell assumed his union presidency at age twenty-nine, only a year before taking on the whole anthracite industry in 1900. One writer aptly describes him as "ministerial in mien, like a parson more than a labor leader, and philosophically a moderate, two traits which endeared him to the press and to Mark Hanna."[78] A native of Braidwood, Illinois, Mitchell's ideological moderation was likely bred from his experience with joint labor-management cooperation in the bituminous industry. There, a state of constant overproduction and resulting wild fluctuations in price among small operators had led many operators to look to the union as a welcome enforcer of competitive standards across a diverse region. In 1897, the sweeping Joint Agreement (including the eight-hour day, dues checkoff, and differential rates depending on conditions) throughout the Central Competitive Field followed a remarkably peaceful strike that reflected not only the miners' collective power but also the owners' implicit recognition of the union as a necessary stabilizing agent for the industry.[79]

Yet, Mitchell was forced to reckon with more adverse circumstances in the anthracite fields. Already sure of their market grip on the mines, the railroad owners wanted no meddling from the union. For that reason the owners, beginning in the 1870s imported a southern and eastern European immigrant labor surplus, while also creating a myriad of wage policies that worked against a commonality of experience among the workers.[80] Indeed, before the uprising at the turn of the century, union organizers were openly dismissive of their chances in anthracite. A protectionist defensiveness towards the new immigrants was evident in 1889 legislation that established certification rights for miners—forcing even experienced immigrant miners to serve two years in a "helper" position in Pennsylvania collieries before accessing the industry's higher paying "contract" positions.[81] In addition a union-sponsored tax (3 cents/day) was imposed on employers of unnaturalized workers, to be deducted from the offending workers' pay. For years, therefore, the union likely accomplished more for anthracite miners in Harrisburg than in the coal region itself. As late as 1896–97, Schuylkill district president John Fahy all but abandoned a grassroots campaign in favor of a modest legislative agenda to abolish company stores and gain semi-monthly pay.[82]

Though Mitchell's own instincts as union leader were hardly those of a rabble-rouser, he skillfully rode the rising militancy among the anthracite rank and file to maximum public effect. Throughout the five-month stoppage in 1902, Mitchell played a double game. While insisting to his middle-class allies like Hanna that he was trying to keep a lid on an all-out suspension of work and publicly opposing moves toward sympathetic action from the bituminous fields, Mitchell was also whipping up the energies of the workers' fiercest partisans. He wrote Mother Jones in the early days of the strike, "I have every reason to believe that the strike will be made general and permanent. I am of the opinion that this will be the fiercest struggle in which we have yet engaged. It will be a fight to the end, and our organization will either achieve a great triumph or it will be completely annihilated."[83]

Yet, in addition to industrial agitation, Mitchell carried the miners' fight to the political terrain. Undoubtedly, his most valuable political weapon lay in his relationship with Sen. Mark Hanna and, for a time, a larger business-labor bloc around the National Civic Federation. Hanna, as much as anyone the instigator of national Republican Party dominance from the election of McKinley in 1896 to Franklin Roosevelt in 1932, was eager to cultivate working-class voters and not averse to dealing with trade unions. As a Cleveland-based businessman who married into a coal and iron fortune, his own companies had regularly treated with unions when few other local producers were doing so.[84] Moreover, he regularly remembered with regret his role in summoning the militia to put down an unruly strike by Massillon miners in 1876 (in the ensuing trial the attorney who successfully defended the radical miners was young William McKinley, who would later fashion two remarkably pro-labor terms as governor before setting out to run for president, with Hanna's help, in 1896).[85] Indeed, so cooperative had the relations of Hanna & Co.'s bituminous mines and Great Lakes shipping companies become with both Daniel Keefe's longshoremen's union and the UMWA that they played a pivotal role in Hanna's election (by the legislature) to the U.S. Senate in 1898.[86] Not surprisingly, as effective chairman of President McKinley's reelection campaign in 1900, it was Hanna who took the lead in heading off an anthracite confrontation before the election.

Only weeks after the 1900 election, Hanna made another important connection to the labor leaders—this time as head of the Industrial Department of the National Civic Federation (NCF). Growing from its Chicago roots, the NCF had "gone national" in 1900 under the direction of reform journalist Ralph Easley, as aided by a marquee list of business and labor leaders, the former encompassing Carnegie, financier August Belmont, Jr., and Morgan partner G. W. Perkins, the latter including AFL president Samuel Gompers as well as Mitchell and Keefe.[87] When President Roosevelt in 1902 finally secured the acceptance by the employers of the coal arbitration commission, he appropriately credited a political rival who was no personal friend: "Well, Uncle Mark's work has borne fruit."[88] And, for a brief period, Hanna and the NCF did indeed seem to be contributing to a significant turn in American industrial relations: by November 1903 they had reportedly helped secure nearly one hundred trade agreements.[89] Altogether, it was an entente geared toward keeping American industry safely "corporate," while cutting at least the strongest unions in on the deal. The dealmaking, indeed, was personal as well as political: for years Perkins paid one-third of Mitchell's $8,000 salary as a division head of the NCF.[90]

Yet, Hanna's illness and death in early 1904 marked a turning point for the NCF in both momentum and direction. While the Federation's previous focus on trade agreements drifted to other subjects, the more virulently anti-union "open shop" message of the National Association of Manufacturers (NAM), led by Indianapolis industrialist David M. Parry after 1902, soon challenged the NCF's influence in key business quarters.[91]It was an ironic turn, since Hanna and other Republican operatives had helped coax the NAM into being in 1895–96 largely as an adjunct to the McKinley campaign. Now the NAM—alongside other employer allies like the National Metal Trades Association, the National Founders' Association, the American Anti-Boycott Association, and the Citizens' Industrial Association of America—led the charge against any contractual conciliation with the trade unions. Quickly, both Mitchell and Hanna were forced on the defensive by Parry's slashing attacks on the AFL as a "fountainhead . . . which breeds boycotters, picketers and Socialists."[92] Mitchell himself, facing illness and declining membership rolls, was pushed out of his UMWA presidency in 1908; though he subsequently took an administrative position in the NCF, he never again wielded the influence he had as a union leader.[93]

How much should be made of the Mitchell-Hanna entente in American business and political life? Was the government-labor-management collaboration it witnessed merely a momentary opportunistic conjuncture of interests or did it presage a larger possibility of tripartite social peace? One contemporary who thought the latter was influential Progressive reformer Herbert Croly. Better known as author of *The Promise of American Life* (1909) and co-founder of *The New Republic* with Walter Lippmann and Walter Weyl (1914), Croly accepted a contract from Hanna's son in 1911 to write the biography, *Marcus Alonzo Hanna: His Life and Work* (1912). Croly's sympathetic account of a subject he knew was commonly denounced as the "living embodiment of a greedy, brutalized and remorseless plutocracy," perhaps not surprisingly, did not go over well at the time.[94] Notwithstanding its possible taint from the pecuniary considerations of the author, the work repays attention for the very way that Croly adapts Hanna to serve the needs of a high-Progressive moment.[95]

Having only recently sketched his own call for a pragmatic, experimental state that would smooth class tensions by way of government regulation, Croly treated Hanna as a representative of "pioneer politics" and "pioneer economics"—a system that admittedly did not in itself make for "social fair play"—whose common sense and decent instincts nevertheless carried him towards genuine reform impulses.[96] Among those impulses, none was more important than Hanna's grudging sympathy for worker dignity in the form of trade unionism and the need for peaceful settlement of industrial disputes (objectives that Croly had also accented in his *Promise of American Life*).[97] As Croly quotes Hanna in a 1902 Chatauqua speech, "The natural tendency in this country, ay, and in the world over, has been the selfish appropriation of the larger share by capital. . . . If labor had some grievance and each laborer in his individual capacity went to his employer and asked for consideration, how much would be shown to him? Not much. Therefore, when they banded together in an organization for their own benefit which would give them the power, if necessary, to demand a remedy, I say organized labor was justified." To the end of his life, Croly argues, Hanna

beseeched the employer class to (in Croly's words) "establish a foundation
for joint action and mutual good-will by conferring with unionized laborers
and their representatives and entering into agreements with them."[98]

It is only implicit in the Hanna biography, but Croly likely also bore in
mind the special influence Hanna had been able to exercise on the single
most powerful American business figure at the turn of the century, J. P.
Morgan. In three critical moments of labor-management conflict—the
anthracite strike of 1900, the strike against U.S. Steel in 1901, and the
anthracite strike of 1902—Hanna had prevailed on the financial titan with
a logic (however self-interested) of at least moderate accommodation to the
forces of organized labor. In the middle case (which we have not examined
here), Morgan himself tried to call off a system-wide war by extending
collective bargaining contracts at already unionized mills, still a significant
proportion of the industry. Multiple commentaries point to an utterly bun-
gled response by the AAISW leadership to the Hanna-NCF intervention
that for a time had the support of both Morgan and AFL leader Samuel
Gompers. A botched strike erased the union from existence, completing the
demolition process begun at Homestead. Yet, as in the Pullman boycott,
not just raw power but timing and tactics mattered.[99]

Might Morgan himself have served any further moderating role in American industrial relations? Between 1902 and his death in 1913, he seems to
have retired from that particular limelight. His daughter Anne Morgan, however, famously intervened (along with Alva Belmont) as part of a Women's
Trade Union League delegation in support of New York City's women shirtwaist strikers in 1910. At the time, an intimate friend of the family told a
reporter, "Mr. Morgan naturally has very different views from Anne, but he
is a broad-minded man and respects his daughter for thinking and acting for
herself. . . . The story that he had angrily sworn to disinherit her for her
avowed sympathy for the strikers is absolutely false."[100]

By the time he was eulogizing Hanna, Croly and his left-progressive
friends had already given up on the NCF and purely voluntary good-will
gestures between labor and management. As he recognized, class conflict
("ill-feeling and mutual suspicion") had only "increased during the past
ten years." Near the end of his 500-page biography, Croly thus laid the
template for a different set of measures: "The results which Mr. Hanna
hoped to accomplish informally by the agency of a private organization
backed by public opinion evidently demand a more powerful and authori-
tative engine of the social will—one which he himself might have been loath

to call into action."[101] In short, in the progressive view, the voluntaristic era of Hanna, Gompers, and the NCF was over; it was time for decisive governmental action to restore fairness and equality at the workplace.

Is there a unifying thread to our analysis of the Gilded Age-Progressive Era series of great industrial conflicts? In the introduction to *American Labor Struggles*, a valuable treatment of ten great strikes (including Homestead, Pullman, and Anthracite 1902) published in 1936, Samuel Yellen summarizes: "Certain conditions . . . become unbearable to the workers in an industry; they organize, they strike, often they strike a second time to defend their organization. Certain forces are brought to bear upon them by employers, by the government, by social agencies, even by other labor organizations. They resist these forces successfully and win, or they succumb to them and lose. The story is simple enough." Perhaps not so simple, however, is an assessment of those "forces" that helped to make or break the workers' struggles. Repeatedly, in these contests, we see not only raw tests of workplace-centered power but also complicated agendas of morality, authority and legitimacy. Carnegie and Frick could prevail—there was never much doubt—at Homestead, but would the terms of such victory be acceptable to the voting, investing, and consuming public? Pullman, likewise, could beat back a national ARU mobilization, but only by sacrificing his own treasured version of serene, paternal governance. An unlikely alliance of John Mitchell and Mark Hanna, on the other hand, proved that restrictions could indeed be placed on one-sided corporate control of a basic industry. The facts on the ground suggest that as of 1902 no one rule of thumb, and no clear model of industrial relations, had yet fastened itself on the American workplace.

The impact of contingencies examined here is further highlighted in comparative perspective. Not only were the new unions (i.e., organizations of semiskilled and unskilled industrial workers) crucial to the takeoff of labor parties in Britain and Australia, but their counterparts in the United States (particularly the ARU and UMWA) also showed considerable aptitude for independent political action. Indeed, as historian Robin Archer suggests, a movement towards a labor party (evidenced in Gompers's defeat by UMWA president John McBride in 1894 and formation of a labor-populist party in Illinois that same year) might well have won official AFL backing (in line with Australian developments) had not the ARU been so thoroughly crushed by the end of the Pullman strike.[102]

Yet, even if we rule out as too far-fetched the emergence of a U.S. labor party in these years, other historical contingencies surely still beckoned. By way of prime example, the role of collective bargaining, and thus a real workers' stake in the corporate liberal order, was still up for grabs even after the eclipse of producerist-republican movements. Just what a more robust, longer-lived Mitchell-Hanna axis might have accomplished is hard to say. Yet, had the agreements reached by 1904 in the printing industry, building trades, machine tool industry, bituminous mining, and some railroads been supplemented by additional sectors in coal, steel, and rail, might not pre-World War I progressivism have taken on a decidedly more social-democratic hue? At the very least, the NCF turn away from collective bargaining toward top-down corporate welfarism (so definitive of American industrial relations by the 1920s) might have been averted. The signs, in short, point to an unrecognized fork in the road *within* the formation historian James Weinstein in 1968 summarily dismissed as "corporate liberalism."[103]

Given the circumstances, therefore, historians should pause before declaring with confidence why and when organized labor ended up as a peculiarly weak force in the American polity. Only on further consideration of the conflicts during the decades of the 1890s and 1900s are we likely to appreciate a potentially pivotal turn in American history. Employers, after all, looked back at the Gilded Age strikes and learned something from them about how to treat workers in the midst of economic depression. Reformers, like Croly, equally tried to assemble the elements of an American version of social democracy from the elements at hand in a conflicted culture. By the 1930s, the labor movement as well applied the lessons of prior setbacks—organizing with the same energy at the ballot-box as at the workplace. If we probe the past for its (sometimes buried) openings, might we not find a window still of use for own day?

Chapter 3

The University and Industrial Reform

Scholarship for the sake of the scholar simply is refined
selfishness. Scholarship for the sake of the state and the
people is refined patriotism.

—Thomas Chamberlin, University of
Wisconsin president, 1890

America's labor wars enjoyed a long reach. It was, assuredly, not just the
combatants themselves—the Carnegies, Pullmans, and Morgans on one
side, the Powderlys, Gomperses, and Debses on the other—or even the
intervening political class of Cleveland, Hanna, Roosevelt, et al., who played
a role in responding to an era of social strife. A few extraordinary men and
women of letters also influenced the action of their times. Among them
was labor economist Richard T. Ely, who arrived at the University of Wisconsin in 1892. Indeed, for an extended period, Ely was acknowledged by
people of many shades of reform and revolutionary thought—including
many who disagreed with him—as *the* American authority on radical social
change.

A few examples suffice to convey the range of these contacts. The editor
of the San Francisco socialist paper *Truth* addressed Ely in 1883 as "the
only man of your class (the professional, the capitalistic) . . . who has ever
written on this subject that did not lose his head. . . . If you are not a
socialist at heart I am very badly mistaken, and if you are not a Socialist
you are the most cold-blooded social anatomist in existence."[1] Similarly,
labor editor and socialist-anarchist Joseph Labadie offered the professor the
fervent appeal of a more rough-hewn intellect: "Men in your station in the
world generally know very little of the *real* condition of the people. You

may read about them, but you do not *see* them and *feel* them, and therefore we expect very little from them. Once in a while a man like yourself may see the terrible conflict that is surely coming, and feeling that there possibly is some wrong in the industrial world will interest himself in inquiring into the cause."[2] For the same reason, British Fabian leader Sidney Webb, beginning an extended correspondence, sought a conversation "as to the progress and prospect of the Socialist idea in America."[3] At the same time, Knights General Master Workman Terence Powderly also appealed to Ely for assistance in drafting a legislative agenda for "independent labor" forces.[4] Further afield, Women's Christian Temperance Union (WCTU) leader Frances Willard, while urging Ely to write a textbook for children "that treats the Golden Rule in action," exulted, "I rejoice every time I see your name in the papers, for I know it means a stirring up of people's dry bones on the subjects concerning which they so badly need to be stirred in order to relieve them from chronic rheumatism of the mind."[5]

Who was this man Ely and how did he and other university-based academics come to figure in the political culture of their day? In this chapter, I want to revisit the social class we might call the American *intelligentsia* and especially its relation to the labor movement and the state apparatus as allied forces for change during the Long Gilded Age. In keeping with the emphasis on political culture and contingency emphasized respectively in Chapters 1 and 2, I suggest that American higher education, and particularly the public research university, provided a way-station in this period for innovative and progressive policy discussions on the subject of labor rights and worker welfare. Just how such an opportunity might open and close I illustrate with reference to events surrounding one exemplary institution, the University of Wisconsin. Intriguingly, it is an example at once of the expansive assimilation of internationalist and cosmopolitan influences on the one hand, and of the limits of a place-based, time-sensitive political order on the other.

The university focus adds at least two new dimensions to our understanding of "progressive" reforms. First, the very founding of crucial graduate programs in the late nineteenth century adds heft to an integrated periodization of the period, transcending the classic Gilded Age/Progressive Era divisions. Second, it suggests that the "politics" of universities (and especially the public research universities) were crucial to the trajectory of contemporary policy making, even as these same institutions also provided the stepping stones for a latter-day America's economic and technological preeminence. In this second sense, moreover, both the strength and liabilities of the university as a social actor come into view.

Across the Western world, the decades of America's Long Gilded Age witnessed a kind of publicly sanctioned taming of industrial capitalism.[6] At its extreme, as in Russia and Mexico, the transformation occurred amid revolutionary upheaval and gave birth to new regimes, but even when generally contained within older constitutional frameworks, the direction of change was the same. Industrial working classes—swollen by the transformations of previous decades and in some cases accompanied by an aroused peasantry—entered the political process (whether formally invited and recognized or not) in a big way. Alongside them, significant sections of the middle classes also challenged entrenched power on both economic and moral grounds. Among this latter group, a small but crucial new sector of intellectuals emerged to give voice and often leadership to the rising popular demands on the state. Whether as liberals, progressives, social democrats, or social revolutionaries, a highly educated elite everywhere played an outsized role in the political institution-building of the young twentieth century.

The engagement of educated elites in statecraft, however, also affected the substance and direction of that enterprise. "Policy intellectuals," as political scientist Ira Katznelson has argued, characteristically advanced an agenda "between pre-modern conservatism and Spencerian laissez-faire, on the one side, and the wholesale rejection of liberal markets and citizenship [or revolutionary socialism], on the other."[7] Such a via media swept up the so-called American Progressives in its tow as well.[8] Notwithstanding an overlap of understandings as applied particularly to the ills of the capitalist marketplace, however, the policy intellectuals organized themselves differently—and with different effects or outcomes—in different countries. Thus, one can argue, ideology alone did not mark the difference between U.S. intellectuals and their international counterparts. In what respects, then, *did* reform ideas here emerge from a distinctive institutional base and with what related problems of social influence?

Looked at through a comparative lens, U.S. intellectuals present a curious paradox of accomplishment and failure. On the one hand, their impact has forever since claimed a twenty-year stretch of time as their own: the Progressive Era. And within that era, the historian can point to an almost endless series of initiatives that bear their imprint: from labor to welfare reform, women's rights and suffrage, prohibition, civil rights and anti-lynching, anti-monopoly, conservation, clean government. Moreover, their characteristic habitats are also forever fixed in the collective memory of the era: churches, settlement houses, universities, third parties, government commissions, newspapers, small magazines, women's groups, Greenwich Village. On the other hand, their presence as reformers seems fleeting and comparatively ineffectual. Not only did they make no revolution (which, to be sure, only a fraction of them sought), they brought no sustained new political party or coherent legislative program to the fore. Not lacking in ideas, they ultimately looked in vain for a vehicle to which to effectively harness their energies for social transformation.

By way of comparison, I begin with a quick gloss on two influential movements abroad—the German Verein für Socialpolitik and the British Fabian Society—each of which was clearly associated with new currents of "social politics" borne of the late nineteenth century. However internally varied, social-political thought shared an antipathy to an older set of policy assumptions—commonly identified as laissez-faire, neoclassical economics, or "Manchester liberalism"—in addressing yawning chasms of social inequality, urban misery, as well as rising disorder with targeted governmental intervention. Most famously perhaps, the new Prussian state of the 1870s directly meshed its higher education system, and particularly the findings of its research scholars, with state policy designed to soften social conflict, enhance public welfare, and strengthen the social foundations of empire. The Verein für Sozialpolitik, established as early as 1872 as an association of younger German economists, not only served as an intellectual rallying center for "historical" (or context-specific) versus "liberal" (or universal and market-centered) norms of economic thought but also actively collaborated with state officials in the formation of labor, agricultural, and social insurance policy. Indeed, it was to the classes and lectures of early Verein leaders Gustav von Schmoller, Adolph Wagner, Lujo Brentano, and their collaborators to which future American reformers and "new economists" like Florence Kelley, Richard T. Ely, Henry C. Adams, Simon Patten, and Edmund James would flock as students for inspiration.[9]

Conceptually, the Verein-centered economists offered young American Progressives-in-training two important beachheads from which to attack classical economic liberalism. First, they viewed market relations as a product of historical development, not unchanging natural law. Second, they challenged the very concept of the "freely acting self," substituting an assumption of social interconnectedness for the liberal model of acquisitive individualism.[10] The Americans, following their German teachers, turned to the state as a source of market correction and distributive justice. As urban reformer Frederic Howe internalized the message, "[Germany] takes it as a matter of course that many things must be done by the state in order to protect its life and develop industry."[11] While generally abstaining from direct political roles themselves, Verein members cultivated contacts with both administrators and politicians. Albeit lampooned from both the political right and left as mere "socialists of the chair," they possessed an influence uncommon to their social station, claiming a leading role in the development of Germany's pioneering social insurance programs.[12]

To be sure, the German model of engaged scholarship was not an uncomplicated one. Rooted in a privileged professoriate altogether dependent on the monarchic state for support, the Verein largely ignored issues of democracy and generally opposed the socialist workers movement. As "state-run training schools for the higher civil servants," the university incubator for the Verein was only as free as the state itself allowed.[13] The vaunted ideal of *Lehrfreiheit*, a privileged dispensation offered to a valued elite, thus "distinguished sharply between freedom *within* and freedom *outside* the university."[14] Identifying their own interests with Germany's national revival, for example, it was easy for Verein members like Schmoller to become ardent advocates of Alfred Tirpitz's turn-of-the-century naval buildup.[15] More ominously still, the reformers' "patriotism" veered toward anti-Semitism, as in Wagner's association of Jews with "Mammonism" or his student Werner Sombart's resort to a race-based eugenics theory.[16]

Generally speaking, the academic intellectuals bobbed and weaved in a political setting controlled by others. Thus, whereas Bismarck's anti-socialist laws of 1878 had initially dissuaded the Verein from open public agitation, Emperor Wilhelm II's more tolerant "new course" after 1890 at once widened the Verein's ranks but also left it internally divided, particularly around the intellectuals' reaction to the rise of social democracy. Paradoxically, increasing pluralism in the larger prewar political culture proved, according to historians Dietrich Reuschemeyer and Ronan Van Rossem, "the beginning of the end of the political project of the Verein," remanding it to "mere academic discussion" before it dissolved in 1936, only to return in similarly muted form in the immediate post-World War II era.[17]

If the Germans established a state-based, professional, and university-centered arena for social-political thought, the British offered a decidedly more autonomous, civil society-based sector for intellectual agitation. Of course, this had much to do with England's much-vaunted "liberal state"

and a resulting freedom of expression protected by both a widening electoral franchise and common law legal system. Just as influential, however,
were other factors particular to Britain, including a cozy governing elite
that had rubbed shoulders in private schools; a tradition of "amateurism"
in civil service resting on classical, liberal arts education; and, correspond-
ingly, a variety of self-initiated centers of political inquiry and activism.[18]
No doubt, the beehive of such intellectual-centered policy thinking was the
Fabian Society, established in 1884 as a political spinoff from the more
spiritually oriented and Tolstoy-influenced Fellowship of New Life.
Directed by Sidney Webb and his freethinker wife Beatrice Potter-Webb,
the Fabians were mainly independent men and women of letters who drew
on a litany of free-thinking literary and political *prominenti*, including
George Bernard Shaw, H. G. Wells, Annie Besant, Graham Wallas, Sydney
Olivier, Oliver Lodge, Ramsey MacDonald, and Leonard and Virginia
Woolf. Less bounded institutionally, the policy authority wielded by the
Fabians initially depended less on university degrees than on personal con-
nections and journalistic documentation of select social problems, as pre-
sented through its Fabian Tracts, such as "Education Muddle and the Way
Out," "Houses for the People," and "Life in the Laundry."[19]

Only in 1895, as the product rather than the incubator of Fabian agitation, was the London School of Economics chartered to investigate (in
Sidney Webb's words) "the problems of municipal and national administration from a collectivist standpoint."[20] The social-democratic thinking
that quickly dominated the originally eclectic Fabian group was, unlike
their German Verein counterparts, tied to specific political strategies—
initially seeking infiltration of the Liberal Party (including entry into the
London County Council to push municipalization programs), then, following an alliance with the Labour Representation Committee in 1899, ever
closer connection to the emergent Labour Party until effective merger when
Webb himself joined the party's executive committee in 1916. By 1922, ten
Fabians had been elected to Parliament in a party that elected fellow-Fabian
Ramsey MacDonald as its leader.[21]

Like the Verein, the Fabians held considerable appeal for middle-class
American men and women of conscience. Whereas the British society found
it necessary to make a formal break between its initial religious impulse and
subsequent determinedly scientific and political direction, the Fabians' American cousins more comfortably blended social politics with the Social Gospel.[22] Thus, among American visitors who followed up "afternoon tea and

conversation" with the Webbs into formal Fabian affiliation were WCTU founder Frances Willard, Rev. W. D. P. Bliss (son of American missionaries and active Christian socialists), and Andover Seminary student Robert A. Woods, a pioneer of American social settlements.[23]

For their part, Fabian leaders, though often scornful of American "backwardness," maintained regular conversation and travel links with a variety of American Progressive counterparts, including Jane Addams, Florence Kelley, and (as we shall see) Richard T. Ely.[24] Though presenting no shortage of the raw material for an American facsimile of the British Society, the American Fabian League, as chartered by Bliss in 1894 (and recruiting such luminaries as Edward Bellamy, Henry Demarest Lloyd and William Dean Howells) never really gathered steam in its six years of existence. An early astute commentary on its failure cites the scattered interests of its members and impatience for results as sources of decline. Perhaps more importantly, they lacked the organizational discipline provided by the Webbs: "nearly all were given to broad moral generalizations, few to factfinding."[25] The fact that, following the decline of populism and the Knights of Labor, they also lacked a mass political movement eager for their expertise no doubt also diffused the energies of would-be American Fabians.

Thus, even as both strictly academic and more activist intellectual formations abroad beckoned to young American progressives, home circumstances dictated that they fashion an instrument suitable to their particular circumstances. Of all the initiatives of American progressive policy intellectuals, the one that took on the most sustained, tangible form developed at the University of Wisconsin from 1890 to World War I, roughly coincident with the academic presence of labor economist Richard T. Ely on the one hand and the statewide political influence of Robert La Follette on the other. The "Wisconsin Idea," first coined by state legislative librarian Charles McCarthy in 1912 but retrospectively attributed to the reign of four Republican governors (most notably La Follette, 1901–1906, and Francis McGovern, 1911–1915), describes a policy mindset that at once helped lift the state of Wisconsin from the doldrums of the depression of the 1890s and proved a blueprint for a national social policy agenda. As a process, the Wisconsin Idea applied social science research, as conducted by university-trained scholars, to the general problems of statecraft and social welfare.

Substantively, the ideas of Wisconsin Progressives trumpeted a mixed public-private economy combining the resources of farm and factory with science, engineering, and human welfare expertise rooted in a state university system centered in Madison. The policy initiatives were legion. After years of retrenchment, Wisconsinites turned to "tax fairness" as a way of redistributing the burden for vital government services, inaugurating an inheritance tax on the rich and raising rates for railroads, insurance companies, and utilities. The wage-earners of the state—recognized as victims of "predatory wealth" and suffering under "unequal conditions of contract"—were rewarded with pioneering statutes in worker's compensation, health and safety regulations and extension schools for adult education.[26]

As a model of intellectual policy influence, the Wisconsin Idea proved something of a cross between the German Verein and the British Fabians. Like the Verein, generative new ideas emerged from within protected university walls and relied on disciplinary expertise to enhance their authority. Like the Fabians, however (and unlike their German counterparts), the Wisconsin reformers openly, if cautiously, displayed their political allegiances and relied on a social network that extended far beyond academic circles.[27]

While certainly distinctive, Madison appears not so much singular as one of several American higher education institutions at the turn of the century attempting to integrate a service ethic within its teaching and research agenda. The German model was relevant here, but so too was the Protestant Social Gospel. To be sure, "service" as a means of connecting the university to civic stewardship and as a source of cultural renewal proved an expansive idea among educators and one hardly limited to self-identified progressives. The University of Chicago's politically autocratic William Rainey Harper, for example, trumpeted service (including the nation's first extension program), albeit partly to offset the Rockefeller-funded institution's reputation as the "university of Standard Oil."[28] And even Columbia University's conservative president Nicholas Murray Butler declared in his 1902 inaugural address that the "university is not for scholarship alone. In these modern days the university is not apart from the activities of the world, but in them and of them. . . . The university is for both scholarship and service. . . . Every legitimate demand for guidance, for leadership, for expert knowledge, for trained skill, for personal service, it is the bounden duty of the university to meet."[29]

By that time, however, a few other institutions had already put the ideal into practice. In an important sense, "practical" or policy-oriented expertise depended on a prior ideal of specialized knowledge that itself had only taken recent root in the United States. Though an earlier model of broader "liberal arts" education remained a staple of the American four-year under-graduate curriculum, a German-influenced ideal of more specialized, research-oriented training was manifest in the proliferation of "graduate universities" (i.e., those with Ph.D. programs, now simply called universi-ties) beginning with Johns Hopkins in 1876.[30] Wisconsin, as it happened, experienced the bounty of a graduate university grafted onto an institution already directed toward strongly reformist social ends.

Although ultimately piloted by professional researchers, the kernel of the twentieth-century Wisconsin Idea had been planted as early as the 1870s by president John A. Bascom. A seminarian-cum-philosopher who migrated to Madison from Williams College in 1874, Bascom, though pre-siding over a campus of only a few hundred young men and women, never-theless made an enduring impression. Balancing a Congregationalist faith with deep learning (a compromise that would not permit a full embrace of evolutionism), Bascom challenged students to engage the world around them. An ardent prohibitionist, Bascom also gravitated toward increasingly radical positions on political-economic issues, as influenced in part by the works of Richard T. Ely.[31] By 1887, as enunciated in *A Christian State*, Bascom had tied the university's reputation to "the degree in which it understands the conditions of the prosperity and peace of the people"; for him, moreover, such understandings now included labor's right to strike and endorsement of Knights of Labor cooperatives as well as women's suf-frage. It was no wonder that many latter-day Wisconsin Progressives, including Robert La Follette and future university presidents Charles Van Hise and Edward Birge felt that they had learned their principles from the "classroom of John Bascom."[32]

If Bascom set a moral-political tone for the campus, the effective infra-structure for practical research was laid by others. As chief of the state geological survey, Thomas Chamberlin, who succeeded Bascom following the latter's personal dispute with the trustees, was equally committed to the service ideal. As he declared in 1890, "Scholarship for the sake of the scholar simply is refined selfishness. Scholarship for the sake of the state and the people is refined patriotism."[33] Moreover, committed to a strong research agenda, Chamberlin leaned heavily on the Germanic model pioneered by Daniel Coit Gilman at Johns Hopkins to build a new university faculty. Indeed, within four short years of taking office, he had recruited four schol-ars from Gilman's institution, including the newly minted historian Freder-ick Jackson Turner in 1890 and, most notably for our purposes, Richard T.

Ely, to take over the new School of Economics, Political Science and History in 1892.[34]

If not the most brilliant economist of a talented, German-trained generation, Richard T. Ely, as historian Daniel Rodgers properly judges him, was surely the boldest.[35] There is no doubt that by the time he arrived in Madison as the highest paid faculty member on campus, he carried about him something of an aura of transformative social science thinking and policy prescriptions. The son of well-read but struggling Presbyterian farmers from western New York, Ely first established his reputation at Johns Hopkins after imbibing the social gospel at Columbia University and pursuing a graduate degree at Heidelberg under economist Karl Knies. It was in Germany that Ely became immersed in the new thinking of his day—and especially keen on toppling the laissez-faire inclination of the then-dominant Manchester school of political economy—a stance institutionalized in the creation of the American Economics Association (AEA) in 1885. If Ely's political antennae shifted a bit over the years, his antipathy for the "excessive individualism" of classical political economy proved a mainstay. Indeed, in the 1883 preface to his first book, *French and German Socialism in Modern Times*, he even invoked Marx's own ridicule of liberal orthodoxy to the effect that "they wanted, to say all in a word, unbounded liberty, and have produced the meanest servitude."[36]

The lofty German idea of the state's role in diffusing social conflicts offered Ely not only a powerful economic tool but an arena where his previously instilled Christian sociology could also happily take root.[37] Already, he had gone far beyond mere scholarly descriptions of the world around him. For years, Ely was a mainstay on the Chautauqua lecture circuit, and his published messages of Christian sociology (particularly *The Social Aspects of Christianity and Other Essays*, 1889, and *The Social Law of Service*, 1896) proved virtually canonical for Protestant social reformers.[38] Even as Ely's new social science message attracted many younger recruits with a background as Sunday school teachers as well as Union and Republican Party stalwarts, it was also no accident that many of his early students themselves became ministerial leaders of the social gospel movement as well as social workers and charity leaders.[39]

By the 1880s, however, Ely, applying a characteristically idealized empiricism, had come to identify the labor movement as "the strongest force outside the Christian Church making for the practical recognition for human brotherhood."[40] For a time, moreover, he believed he had discovered its ultimate humanitarian expression in the example of the Noble and Holy Order of the Knights of Labor. One of several political economists to look to cooperative idealism as a promising alternative to class conflict, he pinned his hopes on the Knights to find a "midway" position that "begins within the framework of present industrial society, but proposes to transform it gradually and peacefully, but completely, by abolishing a distinct capitalist class of employers."[41] Amazed, albeit in a patronizing way, at the biracial nature of the order's southern district assemblies ("thus they bring an elevated influence to bear upon the more ignorant blacks"), Ely nearly envisioned the Order as a practical working out of a Hegelian unity of opposites in binding up the nation's deepest social class divisions: "Strange, is it not? that the despised trades-union and labor organizations should have been chosen to perform this high duty of conciliation! But hath not God ever called the lowly to the most exalted missions, and hath he not ever called the foolish to confound the wise?"[42]

Notwithstanding his commitments, Ely tried to protect his flank from criticism and to maintain his role as a professional, scientific, not to mention elite observer of developments among the "lowly," in short to balance the roles of respected expert and prophetic truth-teller. From the beginning (and for good reason as it turned out) he was determined to protect himself from political censure, declaring in his first book that his own "impartial presentation" ultimately renders a most valuable "service to the friends of law and order." In 1886, amid his virtual identification of the Knights of Labor as the very embodiment of Christian idealism, he nevertheless covered himself with a vague and opportunistic cloak of "dissent from some of its principles . . . and from its course in some localities."[43] And again in 1894, Ely's *Strengths and Weaknesses of Socialism* was self-consciously couched "in a conservative spirit," with its author carefully situated between the "anarchists of the poor" on one extreme and reactionary "mammon worshipers" on the other.[44]

There were clearly moments when Ely sensed that his political opinions had become too exposed. He took snappish offense, for example, at his student Edward R. Bemis, who, thinking he was following in his teacher's footsteps, apparently offended conservative charity circles in Buffalo. Apologizing for his indiscretions, Bemis begged forgiveness: "When, in my letter to you I said I might yet become as "radical" as you, I meant that I should yet write and speak as do you, in fearless condemnation of what I don't agree with especially along moral lines."[45]

All told, Ely was already walking a fine line when he arrived in Madison in 1892. A philosophical economist who had strayed far from accepted intellectual as well as political conventions, he set himself up to try to serve at least two irreconcilable constituencies—university (and larger academic-professional) gentility and a popular clamor for labor rights, welfare, and more general attack on social privilege. It proved an impossible balancing act. Between the tumult of the 1886 Haymarket affair and the Pullman boycott of 1894, two of Ely's most prominent acolytes, Henry Carter Adams at Cornell and Edward Bemis at Chicago (soon to be followed by E. A. Ross at Stanford), had already been dismissed from their academic positions.[46] University of Chicago president William Rainey Harper likely represented the dominant wisdom of the period when he warned faculty against the dissemination of "untested" ideas or "unsettled" opinions as the "truth," propagating "partisan" views, using "sensational methods" to influence students or the public, speaking "authoritatively" on subjects outside his specialty, or failing to exercise "common sense.'"[47]

Indeed, even Johns Hopkins University, which had spawned so much original investigation of social and economic issues, hedged on the question of free expression: in June 1894 the trustees agreed to "regard the discussion of current political, economic, financial and social questions before the students of this University as of such importance that the lessons should be given only by the ablest and wisest persons whose services the University can command."[48] When, in 1894, against his normal cautionary pattern, Ely asserted his pro-labor sympathies during a local printers' strike simultaneous to the larger Pullman conflict, he paid the price of a formal (and for him humiliating) investigation by the Board of Regents. Their investigation was precipitated by a letter to *The Nation* (reprinted in the *New York Evening Post*) from Oliver E. Wells, the Democratic state superintendent of education, charging Ely with "encouraging" strikes and "practicing" boycotts, while generally undermining the principles of law and property in his writings and teachings. Fortunately for Ely, Wells was already disdained as a bombastic troublemaker by many in positions of state authority, and his insinuations were vigorously refuted by a blue-ribbon string of witnesses.[49]

Although Ely was ultimately fully vindicated (and Wells, in turn, censured by the Regents), there is little doubt that the incident—exacerbated by his concurrent removal from the Chautauqua circuit and continuing loss of influence within the AEA—wounded Ely and noticeably robbed him of his public confidence and writerly exuberance.[50] First, in the face of Wells's accusations, Ely quickly reinvented himself (with coaching from university president Charles Kendall Adams) as a conservative scientist with no interest in public agitation or direct contacts with the workers' movement.[51] Moreover, in the aftermath of his trial, he virtually promised Adams he would take a breather from public advocacy.[52]

Amid the public assault on America's radical young political economists, Ely, like most of the others, retreated.[53] For the next thirty years, his own writings, which gradually turned to a focus on law and property and land economics, were clearly more directed to an academic than a popular audience, and were generally free from explicit criticism of the dominant economic order that characterized his earlier work.[54] There is no sign of a public rebuttal, for example, when the New York Times in 1897 referred to municipalization and other "fads that the half-baked have picked up from Prof. ELY and other socialistic writers."[55] In effect, he had abandoned a bully pulpit for relative academic quietude. There is little doubt, moreover, that by 1918 and his open support for World War I—which included leadership in the Loyalty Legion as well as the campaign to unseat antiwar senator La Follette—and his participation in the postwar Red Scare, followed in the 1920s by his turnabout on public-owned utilities, controversial receipt of research funding from private interests, and ultimate embrace of the presidential candidacy of Herbert Hoover, that Ely had taken a decidedly more conservative turn.[56] His principal biographer goes so far as to suggest that the "well-informed prophet-preacher" was replaced by a "more inarticulate, cautious, and fearful academician."[57]

Yet—excepting his wartime disillusionment—a too-quick, post-trial pigeonholing of Ely misses his most signal contribution to progressive politics. Rather than a full-scale retreat after the Pullman strike, what we may be tempted to call Ely's post-advocacy years seem in retrospect to have engendered a creative realignment of intellectual firepower and political will, an accommodation of radical ideas to political reality and practical results. Whatever the appearance on the outside, Ely turned his continuing reputation, influence, and political network to the creation of an infrastructure for real-world policy influence. In short, it was not the cloistered image of the ivory tower that grabbed Ely's imagination in the aftermath of the public attack but the dogged pursuit of public influence on policy and public thinking on new grounds. This unheralded moment—the key to the transition from advocacy to what historian Mary Furner calls "commissioned" or "authorized" expertise—I suggest, points to the first real embodiment of the Wisconsin Idea.[58]

Ely's twenty post-trial years at Wisconsin witnessed the application of his full intellectual powers and administrative authority in the cause of progressive social policy. First of all, this was the same period when Ely effectively saved and resuscitated the careers of three other politically persecuted social scientists, and former Ely students—Bemis, Commons, and sociologist Edward A. Ross; the latter two he personally recruited and helped financially establish in Madison.[59] Second, these were the years when, sustained by this Madison beachhead, progressive intellectuals mounted their most effective attack on what remained of the doctrines of an independently self-executing (or laissez-faire) market economy.

Intellectually, Ely had in no way backed down from the AEA's original 1884 missionary call for a "progressive theory of legislation." In significant ways, he challenged the rudiments of anti-statist, individual property-based freedom doctrines, or what we have previously labeled the American Ideology. In contradistinction to Herbert Spencer's juxtaposition of "individual freedom" and "state-coercion," for example, Ely, in an address to the Madison Literary Society in 1897, starkly labeled "regulation by the power of the state" a basic "condition of freedom."[60] To counter the 1890s depression, Ely openly prescribed public work projects, a federal employment bureau, public loans to individuals, a state program of medical services, as well as public ownership of natural monopolies.[61]

His writing, at least at a substantive level, betrayed even less sign of discontinuity. Encapsulating his strong-regulatory message in an esoteric text, *Property and Contract in Their Relations to the Distribution of Wealth* (1914)—a thesis subsequently honed by both Commons and Columbia University legal scholar Robert Hale—Ely documented how property and contract relations had long been framed by government-based legal boundaries: as such the putatively sacred wall separating public from private spheres of activity was largely imaginary. In this gathering of his classroom lectures across the previous fifteen years, Ely again openly drew on his German studies, emphasizing the "internationalism of our thought and life, showing the inadequacy of the idea that law is local and that we do not need to study foreign systems of law." And, as if to define the niche he had helped secure at Madison, Ely exalted, "The German universities have for two centuries or more held a position in German life like that which American universities,

and especially the University of Wisconsin, have begun to occupy in the life
of the American nation. They have been largely engaged in preparing men
for civic life, for positions as civil servants, as trained and specialized *Beamten*,
to use the German term which is well defined as *Offiziere* in the army." In
addition to degree programs, for example, Ely pointed to "working fellow-
ships" (for graduate students) in connection with the State insurance, tax,
and railroad commissions, "the appointees working half-time in the University and half-time in the service of the commissions, the design being to train
men for the service of the State."[62]

What kind of educational ideal was Ely aiming for in Wisconsin's School
of Economics, Political Science, and History? In his 1938 memoir, *Ground
Under Our Feet*, he summarized the Ely-Commons approach as the "look
and see" method: "We encouraged the kind of knowledge which would lead
to action, for knowledge without action is dangerous. . . . This is a world full
of work to be done and knowledge has its practical purpose." The "down-
and-out" or "undercover" investigations in which Ely took great interest once
they first appeared in Germany in the 1890s mixed a scientific, even labora-
tory-like approach with underlying sympathy toward their subjects.[63] Moreover, it was apparently a scholarly mission that Ely imagined for women as
well as men. Ely took great pride when his daughter Anna and her friend
Alice Van Hise (daughter of university president Charles Van Hise)—
apparently both matriculating as graduate students in economics at Madison—took jobs in a canning factory in upstate New York:

> They knew what it meant to work all night when the peas were
> coming in to be canned. They learned by first-hand observations
> about the harsh realities which lay behind the theories they studied.
> And this is what we wanted our students to have—an understanding
> of economics, based not alone on book knowledge, but on first-
> hand experience. We wanted them to "look and see" for them-
> selves.[64]

Characteristically, it was Ely who in 1905 assumed the inaugural presidency of the American Association for Labor Legislation, the American
wing of an international clearinghouse for progressive measures "stocked
with German-trained social economists."[65] It was a tribute to a modest-
sized university's disproportionate influence that the national headquarters
of an international network should initially be sited in Madison; indeed,

even Ely worried that "so many Wisconsin men "filled up its inaugural conference proceedings."⁶⁶ Soon, Ely had helped secure the selection of Commons as executive secretary and Commons's student John Andrews as first permanent paid staffer, while relocating the association's office to New York City. Nor did Ely simply ride on past reputation. Rather, he continued a vigorous correspondence on social issues with a virtual who's who of American progressives, socialists, labor leaders, and international social democrats, including Jane Addams, Florence Kelley, Samuel Gompers, Robert Hunter, Graham Taylor, A. M. Simons, Frederic Howe, Sidney Webb, and Graham Wallas.⁶⁷

Though generally outside the limelight of public recognition (as well as the glare of public scrutiny and potential censure), Ely's work habits and progressive program-building continued unabated. A few examples suffice by way of illustration. First, the recruitment of Commons alone was no mean feat. The university itself (under Van Hise) could commit to cover only one-third the $30,000 price it would require to establish Commons's teaching position and research funds necessary for what would become the monumental *Documentary History of American Industrial Society* (10 vols., 1910–12). It was Ely who reached out to a circle of influential progressive contacts to seal the appointment. Learning from fellow economist John B. Clark in April 1903 that Commons had fallen into a "rather depressed state" (a finding Commons himself vociferously contested), Ely prevailed on nonacademic fellow reformers Jane Addams, Frederic Howe, and Robert Hunter to tap their philanthropist friends—including International Harvester heir Stanley McCormick and Teachers College benefactor V. Everitt Macy—for the needed complementary funds.⁶⁸ When word reached him of the appointment, Edward A. Ross, then in Lincoln, Nebraska, exulted, "It is poetic justice that he who has always thought of truth and principle should get some of the academic loaves and fishes after all. With Commons well placed in a University and Bemis [too] I should feel like saying "Lord, let now thy servant depart in peace!"⁶⁹

Meanwhile, Ely, if now in a quieter way, resumed efforts on behalf of labor reform. In his private correspondence, for example, we find populist-cum-socialist Henry D. Lloyd first begging off a request from Ely in December 1902 to testify at the anthracite strike commission hearings: "The truth is," said Lloyd as he tried to excuse himself, "in recent years I have given comparatively little attention to the labor movement. My work has been directed along other lines." Yet, within a month, the evidently persuasive

Ely was thanking Lloyd for "your argument before the Commission."[70] Moreover, Ely was still pressing Lloyd on labor-related matters, this time to surreptitiously secure a copy of the "personal service contract" of the International Harvester Company, which typically released a company like Harvester (ironically, the very source of the wealth Cyrus McCormick's son Stanley would soon devote to the Commons professorship) from liability in case of workplace accident. "What I am working at," explained Ely, "is to show that free contract cannot give us industrial liberty; that contract must be regulated and the employees protected."[71]

As evident in the log-rolling for the Commons appointment, Ely had knit strong ties to a larger progressive community, and particularly to a network of female professionals centered at the social settlements. His relations with Jane Addams's Hull House were a case in point. From the mid-1890s on, Ely served as a kind of intellectual/literary executor for Hull House publications, including the path-breaking *Hull-House Maps and Papers*.[72] At one typically candid moment, Addams apologized to Ely for her co-worker Florence Kelley's undiplomatic rebuff of a suggestion regarding map layouts; in another moment, however, Kelley herself begged Ely not for compliments but for "criticism . . . such as the German inspectors get" after factory inspection reports.[73] Not surprisingly, Addams and Ely also readily exchanged professional favors.[74] It is likely from his prior social gospel work that Ely had learned to appreciate women as serious professional peers, even as reform-minded women were drawn to his call for "practical Christianity." The early AEA, for example, thus enjoyed an uncommonly high female membership of nearly 10 percent, albeit with continuing instances of sex segregation in its social affairs.[75] Feminist Helen Sumner, who became Ely's secretary, contributed to the history of American labor edited by Commons and Ely, as well as to an important volume for the Bureau of Labor Statistics *Report on the Condition of Woman and Child Wage-Earners in the United States* (1910).[76] And Emma O. Lundberg and Katharine Lenroot, who would play leading roles in the reform-minded Children's Bureau from the teens through the 1930s, both matriculated into what historian Robyn Muncy calls the "female dominion in American reform" under the tutelage of Ely and Commons at Madison.[77]

Even if Ely, by the turn of the century, considered himself "something of a back number" in relation to the budding contemporary socialist movement, he nevertheless maintained a lively correspondence with the more activist community. Perhaps his closest uninterrupted conversation with the activist types was with his former undergraduate student Algie M. Simons, who gravitated from the Socialist Labor Party to the left-wing of the Socialist Party (as editor of *International Socialist Review* and *Appeal to Reason*) before breaking with the movement in World War I. As a young charity worker newly imbibing a more revolutionary message, Simons had first approached Professor Ely "as I knew you always wished to keep in touch with life and I always feel that it is to our Universities we must look for guidance of the power that is being generated to effect the coming social revolution."[78]

Perhaps drawing a permanent lesson from his time of public duress, Ely generally stayed out of the partisan limelight. Except for a brief period in 1903 where he joined Commons and university president Van Hise for regular "Saturday lunch clubs" with Governor La Follette, Ely was self-confessedly never a "close personal advisor" to La Follette. Still, he supported him beginning with the nomination to the governorship in 1900, and, indeed, within a year was already lobbying the new governor for the appointment of an academic friend to a state agency. Ely was surely one of those responsible for the appointment by 1911 of an estimated 46 faculty members to one state commission appointment or another.[79] As late as 1912, Senator La Follette, in turn, looked to Ely for guidance on how to keep the "Wall Street program" from infecting scholarly treatments of money and banking questions.[80] Moreover, as a sturdy as well as influential advocate for the university, Ely helped to prop up the Wisconsin Idea even after it had lost some of its pubic luster. His quiet cultivation of former governor McGovern, for example—including a focus on such incidentals as support for an "Irish evening" and Irish-related artwork on campus—helped to get McGovern to publicly disavow the 1915 Allen Survey that called for a controversial tightening of university managerial structure.[81] Charles McCarthy thus simplified, but perhaps not by much, when, in explaining Wisconsin's progressive movement, he pointed to a singular conjuncture: a state with a large German population, a reform-minded university administration, and the fortuitous arrival of "a new teacher" in the form of Richard Ely in 1892.[82]

Among Ely's quieter but perhaps most influential legacies was his contribution to the formalization of academic freedom. Begun as an initiative of the AEA and other social science associations, the American Association of University Professors in January 1915 appointed a committee of fifteen to examine the problem of academic freedom. Alongside philosopher

Arthur O. Lovejoy of Johns Hopkins, Roscoe Pound of Harvard Law, and committee chair Columbia University economist E. R. A. Seligman sat Ely. Aside from the needs for free inquiry in research and integrity and independence in instruction, the resulting Report of the Committee on Academic Freedom and Tenure tied academic freedom to a new and peculiarly American justification: "to develop experts for various branches of the public service." In words that likely originated with Ely's advocacy, if not his own pen, the declaration, which emerged as an enduring, almost sacred doctrine of the academic vocation, further explained:

> In almost every one of our higher institutions of learning the professors of the economic, social, and political sciences have been drafted to an increasing extent into more or less unofficial participation in the public service. It is obvious that here again the scholar must be absolutely free not only to pursue his investigations but to declare the results of his researches, no matter where they may lead him or to what extent they may come into conflict with accepted opinion. To be of use to the legislator or the administrator, he must enjoy their complete confidence in the disinterestedness of his conclusions.[83]

Of all Ely's moves in Madison, it is likely the Commons appointment in 1904 that proved most socially transformative. "I was born again," Commons later recalled, "when I entered Wisconsin, after five years of incubation."[84] Dismissed from Syracuse (technically his chair was terminated) in 1899, Commons's own incubatory period, just as Ely's relative quietus posttrial, had proved formative. Indeed, Commons's temporary exile from academe (what he later called "my Five Big Years"[85]) drew him into contacts and engagement with labor, business, and other associations that would prove crucial to the triad of state-civil society-university faculty ties that would long burnish the very word "Wisconsin" in the nation's political vocabulary.

Investigatory experience with the U.S. Industrial Commission of 1902 and the U.S. Bureau of Labor, followed by full-time staff work for the National Civic Federation (where, among others, Commons developed an enduring friendship with AFL president Samuel Gompers) endowed Commons with both field experience and expertise on themes of taxation, labor, immigration, trusts, and prices possessed by no other contemporary social scientist.[86] Though he had, like Ely, somewhat moderated his earlier radical political prescriptions by the time he reached Madison, Commons, more than his mentor, still brought a penchant for ambitious, labor-friendly, statist intervention to bear on industrial relations problems.[87]

Once Commons arrived, the university likely most measured up to the service role to which its presidents since John Bascom had regularly subscribed. Commons and an extensive team of graduate students (many who had first helped with the labor history project) quickly fanned out on a wide variety of both state and national level policy-oriented projects, including the Pittsburgh Survey, drafting of the state's civil service and utility regulatory codes, laws for worker's compensation, unemployment compensation as well as the workplace safety enforcement as established by the state industrial commission (on which Commons served).[88] With access to state-based policy-making facilitated and welcomed by "progressive Republican" state administrations beginning with La Follette in 1900, Commons's conduit from campus to statehouse was particularly facilitated by state legislative reference librarian Charles McCarthy, who had first been attracted to the University of Wisconsin by Ely's reputation and gone on to do a Ph.D. in history under Frederick Jackson Turner. With close ties to the surrounding academics, McCarthy ran his reference service as if it were a state-focused policy institute. At the national level, meanwhile, Commons and McCarthy would also closely collaborate on the Commission on Industrial Relations, chartered by President William Howard Taft in 1912.[89] For years after Ely and Commons's heyday, the graduate students they trained would not only maintain a determined "historical-institutionalist" cohort within the Economics department at Madison and a few other academic centers, they would also continue to draft public policy, perhaps most prominently on display in the work of Commons's students, Edwin Witte and William M. Leiserson, on New Deal social security legislation.[90]

The state's Industrial Commission, chaired by attorney and La Follette confidant C. H. Crownhart, with Commons as a designated commissioner, offers a particularly telling example of both the ambition and creativity of progressive state-making. In Commons's mind, the commission—a democratically representative form of governmental administration—was nothing less than a "fourth branch of government," combining (if not superseding) the work of the other three. Soon after its creation, for example, the Industrial Commission actively intervened on public health grounds to set standards of operation for bakeries across the state. The

first "bakery school" in America—with initial branches in Milwaukee and
Kenosha and extended through the state's continuation, or adult education,
schools—engaged in a "scientific study" to "produce the best bread in the
most economic manner." Within two years a system of licensure begun
among bakeries also included candy and ice cream makers. In other initiatives, the commission's "committee of arbitration" also quickly reached in
to mediate industrial disputes. In one instance, commission deputy Leiserson was deputized by the commission to settle a shoeworker strike in Milwaukee. Leiserson gained the employer's initial (albeit temporary) assent to
a collective bargaining agreement so long as it was kept "out of the newspapers." In this and other disputes, the commission's priority was to get the
parties to "commit to the principle of collective bargaining" and thus the
"recognition of unions."[91]

Even as he had clearly set the wheels in motion, there seems no doubt
that Ely's direct impact on Madison's progressive policy apparatus notably
dimmed across the first two decades of the twentieth century. Contemporary correspondence and later memoirs of student activists thus offer an
invidious comparison of the university's two leading economics mentors.
The tight circle of students around Commons—including, among others,
David Saposs, Witte, Leiserson, Helen Sumner, Elizabeth Brandeis Raushenbush, Ira B. Cross, E. B. Mittelman, Andrews, and Sumner Slichter—
generally cultivated a kind of Young Turk identity that separated them from
their institutional patriarch. By 1907, for example, a young David Saposs,
who had grown up under the influence of Victor Berger's socialist movement in Milwaukee and even worked in a union-organized brewery before
going to college, regularly joined Witte and Leiserson at meetings of the
university's Socialist Club. By that time, Witte, who was raised in a conservative farm family, had become an ardent "La Follettite"—more of a "populist" sympathetic to limited government ownership of railroads and
utilities than to the full-scale socialist agenda that Saposs at the time
endorsed.[92] Proudly considering themselves "disciples of John R.," whom
they considered at least "sympathetic" to socialist reform measures if not
openly class-conscious, they dismissed Ely, recalled Saposs in 1964, as
something of an "old fogey." Saposs even remembered two clubs of graduate economics students: "one was called the Richard T. Ely Club which
we scorned and ridiculed, [then] there was the economics club where we
comrades met."[93] As the radical young immigrant Selig Perlman reported of

a 1910 seminar on Marx overseen by both Ely and Commons, "I lead the attack on the Ely forces."[94]

Given their close personal attachment to Commons, it is likely that the younger political economists imbibed as well something of their advisor's resentment of Ely's condescending solicitude toward a colleague who was only eight years his junior. In March 1904, for example, Ely took the liberty of addressing Commons frankly "about one or two things concerning your future," as "we must try to be helpful to each other in every way." First, Ely, in a kind of gruff acknowledgment of mutual affection, urged Commons to regard his new Wisconsin appointment "as permanent and to make all your plans accordingly. This will be a wise thing to do even should anything arise to bring about a change later." Then, Ely hinted that "a little criticism" about his younger colleague had come his way. Two anonymous friends in addition to Ely himself were worried that Commons has "tried to do too much." "This is a mistake," counseled Ely, "that I myself have made." Likely reflecting Ely's own hard lessons in broader public advocacy, he urged Commons to "concentrate your strength upon economic theory and economic problems, giving up all interest in other directions. Let absolutely alone proportional representation [about which Commons had written considerably since 1896] and other political problems." As if such intellectual directions were not enough, Ely also beseeched Commons to avoid "contributions to second-class periodicals like the [social gospel monthly] *Arena* . . . I would also, generally speaking, avoid the popular magazines and write for the economic quarterlies."[95] While stopping short of his students' revolutionary élan, Commons nevertheless engaged in a sustained and direct way with the state's progressive political wave. His own economic thinking displayed a pragmatic adaptation to the immediate environment. Originally drawing heavily from both Ely and Sidney Webb (the third lesson in a political economy class he offered at both Oberlin and Indiana University in the early 1890s was entitled "Socialism—the Ideal Plan for Social Reform"), Commons soon sought out a more hard-boiled political middle ground. Reporting in 1895 on a two-day visit to Iowa's "Amana Society of Communists" (the communal colony of German Pietists established at mid-century), Commons acknowledged the "idyllic life these quaint people live." On the positive side, Amana boasted "no paupers, no criminals, no sweaters, no over-worked, no able-bodied idlers, no illiterates, no millionaires, no spendthrifts, no heiresses." On the other hand, society in Amana was not only generally tedious ("too humdrum, too slow, too ancient"), but much of the hard work, he discovered, was performed by outside hired laborers.

Rather than full-scale socialism, which he viewed as Amana writ large, Commons thus endorsed a doctrine he called "progressive individualism," a La Follette-like recipe for a mixed economy with selective government intervention (including, for example, public control if not ownership of railroads) as an alternative to the "lethargy of socialism."[96] Soon Commons sounded as enthusiastic as any of his students about La Follette Progressivism. "It might almost be said," he intoned in a 1910 article, "that The Present of Wisconsin is The Future of America." Indeed, as Commons elaborated, if Wisconsin had "achieved a more perfect control of her own government than any other State in the Union . . . [it was] not because the people are more democratic than the people of other States, but because they have had a leader."[97] This was a message through which both faculty and students could (at least for an extended season) enter into practical state-making.

Personal jealousies and tensions among faculty, a continuing staple of academic life, were hardly the only conflicts the young Wisconsin cohort encountered during their student days. Generally feeling removed both socially and politically from their more gentrified peers, the young comrades also tried to make war—albeit ultimately unsuccessfully—on the Greek system that dominated student government organizations as well as campus social life in Madison. Saposs and other likeminded "Barbarians" reportedly opted for Friday night debating society events over the fraternity- and sorority-sponsored parties: "social life" recalled Saposs, "insofar as dances, insofar as taking out girls . . . was something to be scorned."[98] In addition, the attraction of several Jewish recruits (including Saposs, Leiserson, Mittelman, and Perlman) to Madison's radical economic corridors similarly challenged the conventions of a generally WASPish community. Even those who otherwise revered John R. suspected him (and perhaps even more so his wife Nell D.) of various anti-Semitic cultural prejudices, including character judgments that may have cost both Mittelman and Perlman deserved honors or positions.[99]

Still, there was no doubt but that the intense life—at once academic, political, and social—of the Wisconsin students created tight cohort bonds and long-lasting friendships. For example, while the young industrial relations scholar Sumner Slichter was engaged in investigatory work in Washington in 1915, he reported back to his friend William Leiserson that

"Washington is a very pleasant place to work and there are a great many Wisconsin men here who make it more so." Even when Leiserson gained a teaching position at prestigious Stanford University, he looked back longingly to the more socially grounded mission in Madison. As he wrote Ira Cross: "I am eager to get out of Stanford for several reasons. First, the place is hard up for money. We have enough of the filthy lucre but a 'pin-headed' business manager and board of trustees see fit to spend it on lawns, beautiful buildings, flower gardens, automobile roads, memorial churches and the like with the result that the academic side of the University suffers badly."[100]

Notwithstanding their internal frustrations and divisions, the pre-World War I Wisconsin institutionalists managed a remarkable feat of public influence both within the state and beyond. One contemporary account estimated that more than 90 percent of Wisconsin state legislative acts from 1901 to 1921 were composed in McCarthy's "bill factory" or legislative reference library office. The host of measures that McCarthy christened the "Wisconsin Idea" included direct primaries for all state offices, establishment of state railroad and civil service commissions, creation of an extension division of the university, and, in a tide of legislation in 1911 alone, passage of worker's compensation, an industrial commission pioneering in health and safety regulation, child and female labor regulations, continuation schools for workers on the European model, and creation of a state board of public affairs with a planning capacity for a further reform agenda.[101]

Remarkably, the arbiters of the "Wisconsin Idea" also happily cooperated, at least until World War I, with the advocates of what Victor Berger called the "Milwaukee Idea"—what Marvin Wachman later elaborated as an "interlocking directorate" between the city's Social Democratic Party and the state's trade unions. Commons himself (who rejected any wholesale socialist program) accepted Berger's invitation to integrate various municipal socialist ideas into an administrative whole in 1910. As he later commented about his meetings with Socialist Party officials and aldermen: "I appeared at these caucuses, with blueprints and charts, to report progress and answer criticisms. Nearly all of those present were mechanic and trade-unionists. Never before, even in England, had I met such a capable and rational body of men in charge of a city government." Likewise, McCarthy personally drafted the worker's compensation bill first introduced in the legislature by the socialist representative, Danish cigar maker Frederick Brockhausen.[102]

Assessing social reformers almost inevitably invokes glass half-full speculations. Did they author genuine advances or mere palliatives that retarded more thorough breakthroughs? In the case of the Wisconsin Progressives and the "Wisconsin School" labor economists in particular, judgments are likely to hang on assessments not only of the political possibilities of *their* time but also of the mood of the contemporary questioner. Not too long ago, for example, it was easy to assail the edifice of a limited social welfare state combined with bureaucratic collective bargaining institutions—both of which bore the mark of Ely's and Commons's students—as symbols of conservative social control. As a young New Left historian Maurice Isserman summarized the wisdom of his day in 1976, "Commons' social vision was motivated by the desire to preserve the capitalist system of private ownership of the means of production by granting organized labor its rights as a competing and cooperating interest group within the system."[103] After an extended era of business dominance capped by an onslaught of deregulatory fervor, however, the social compromise eked out by an earlier generation of intellectuals and activists may now not look so meager.

Like their political cousins, the German Verein and the British Fabians, the Wisconsin economists pushed beyond middle-class careerism as well as the intellectual fashions of their day to try to re-shape society toward more egalitarian ends. Indeed, invocation of the state and public authority to balance private interests and plan for a common future—the core assumptions of the first generation of progressives—seems almost as far-fetched a vision today as it must have struck many contemporaries at the time. In such circumstances, historians are likely to be more charitable toward intellectual reformers who in the face of considerable hostility, opposition, and even recrimination in their day, still managed to push the ball forward.

At the same time, the structural limitations on the Wisconsin experiment are undeniable. In functional terms, the Wisconsin-style progressives look most like an American version of their earlier German counterparts: albeit operating with more personal and political independence than the Verlein, they too relied on sympathy, if not outright patronage, from the surrounding state apparatus. Dependent on an encouraging, university-state administrative connection, the collective research agenda (let alone the "bill factory") established in Madison thus also proved susceptible to changing political winds. The post-La Follette deflation of the university-state alliance (as even the faculty repudiated the senator for his antiwar stance in 1917) blocked the pathways to policy influence by intellectual reformers. In turn, Wisconsin state politics continued to swerve from left to right in a pattern that has continued to the present day.[104]

Aside from the immediate political climate, moreover, the reward structure for academic social scientists was also steadily moving away from the Ely-Commons model of institutional engagement with labor or other social movements toward a more self-insulated professional and discipline-based culture. Even as the "action" for engaged left-wing intellectuals in Britain moved from the Fabian Society into the Labour Party and, more tragically in Weimar Germany, to create institutions like the radical Deutsche Hochschule für Politik in Berlin and the openly Marxist International Institute of Social Research at Frankfurt, American academics by the 1920s had no equivalent vehicle through which to make their mark on society, especially at the national level.[105] In this sense, we can identify early twentieth-century roots for a problem not generally commented on until the end of the century—the peculiar public space available in the United States to "academicized" or "tenured" radicals. Criticized from both the Left (for being too timid and career-oriented) and the Right (for subversive advocacy or thought immune to popular influence), reform-minded academics early claimed a place, however contested, in the American political order.

In the case of the academic-based labor economists, their fortunes—as well as social-political perspective—would shift over time. Beginning in the 1920s, a managerial ideology, with a strong imprint of social psychology, made its way into a field that had initially focused on the political resolution of workplace conflicts. Most prominently associated with the Hawthorne experiments of Harvard Business School sociologist Elton Mayo, "human relations" would jockey with "collective bargaining" as well as "workers' education" approaches for dominance in the industrial relations field over the next few decades. By 1945, with organized labor's growing political influence combined with a general fear of strikes, the program was bolstered by establishment of the University of California's Institute of Industrial Relations, headed by labor economist and future university president Clark Kerr (who, appropriately enough, had received his Berkeley Ph.D. under the direction of Commons's student Paul S. Taylor) and Cornell University's New York State School of Industrial and Labor Relations.[106]

Together, figures like Kerr and Harvard economists Sumner Slichter and John Dunlop shifted the field's professional focus, according to a recent commentary, "from progressive advocacy to establishment expertise through mediation, arbitration, and analysis of collective bargaining in unionized industries and via contributions to post-war liberal consensus thinking." Then, beginning in the 1970s, with the decline of unions and business indifference to collective bargaining, the influence of the entire IR project was "sharply curtailed."[107]

When we think of great democratic advances, we are ordinarily ready to cheer on disciplined mass movements for change, leaders who bravely take up the cudgels for the people, and legislators who push for the rights and welfare of working people or are willing to stand up to defy those who would sweep them away. Yet, as the Wisconsin Idea suggests, a vigorous, scientific search for truth may well precede the formulation of progressive legislation, and "legislation" itself may prove no more important than effective "administration" once it is in place. Moreover, to arrive with satisfaction at all three of these objectives, some degree of collaboration among social investigators and reform-minded politicians, together with a popular mandate, is also crucial. That was what Richard T. Ely, John R. Commons and their students—in combination with the "La Follettite" wing of the Republican Party—once attempted to mold in Wisconsin. And that too, to quote the most popular chant heard in Madison's 2011 streets, is "what democracy looks like."

Chapter 4

Labor's Search for Legitimacy

Since nations have grown to the wisdom of avoiding
disputes by conciliation, and even of settling them by
arbitration, why should capital and labor in their
dependence upon each other persist in cutting each other's
throats as a settlement of differences?
—U.S. Strike Commission, 1894

The legend of Eugene Debs's prison conversion focuses on the Pullman
strike leader's six-month confinement in a Woodstock, Illinois, cell in
1895 on a contempt of court conviction. According to the story subsequently promoted by Debs himself, he emerged from jail ready to pro-
claim his commitment to socialism as the sole alternative to the collusive
power of rapacious employers and the capitalist state.[1] Less well known
(indeed unacknowledged in any of the Debs biographies or Pullman
chronicles) is a prior "conversion" of the labor leader following his initial
indictment and refusal to post bail on the contempt charge, resulting in
a week-long stay in a rat-infested Cook County jail cell in July 1894. By
that point, Debs had already watched the struggle of a quarter million
workers in twenty-seven states utterly come apart under a joint offensive
by the employers' General Managers' Association and the federal government. As a final insult, his appeal to Samuel Gompers and the AFL to
raise the social ante by way of a general strike had been categorically
rejected. Exhausted, he saw the strike officially called off and the Pullman
works reopened during his own two weeks of bed rest at his Terre Haute
home. Now, in mid-August, even as he was preparing his defense against
charges of both contempt and conspiracy (the former of which would

land him in the Woodstock jail even as the latter was unceremoniously dropped by the government), he was called before the U.S. Strike Commission, a government body convened by President Cleveland to seek post-Pullman remedies for industrial unrest.[2]

At that moment, still apparently confident of his ultimate legal exoneration and still striving to stave off the destruction of his American Railway Union, Debs played the role less of marginalized political radical than a savvy policy insider. The issue over which Debs, Commissioner Carroll R. Wright, the nation's most distinguished labor statistician and first U.S. commissioner of labor, and Illinois circuit judge Nicholas Worthington most intensely sparred was one largely lost to posterity: compulsory arbitration. In an esoteric exchange over whether and how competing unions could hypothetically be held liable for their actions by a court-ordered board of arbitration, Debs allowed that the major stumbling block for him was "how an average body of men would proceed to file a bond" as part of securing the union's legal status before such a body. Yet, if they could resolve such technical matters, Commissioner Worthington implored the labor leader, "would [it not] show that the representatives of the Government were endeavoring to do something to relieve the trouble [the workers] complain of with the corporations?" Debs belatedly agreed, "Yes: I think it would have that effect, that an effort at least was being made to provide remedies by law for the grievances of which they complain."[3]

The very obscurity of the terms under discussion offers testimony to the subsequent defeat and burial of these ideas on the American mainstage.[4] That there is no institutional court of resort for aggrieved parties (workers or employers) in workplace disputes, and that the state has no compelling interest in ensuring fair outcomes in labor-management disputes, is today taken for granted. The fact that such issues were once discussed at all, however, and especially by such key protagonists in a pivotal political drama, suggests the need to look again at key policy choices facing Americans during the Long Gilded Age. It was, in short, not just in campus-based "idea factories" that alternative conceptions of the law—and labor's place within it—were thrashed out. Political actors, engaging state action across oceans, also had their say.

All the world's industrial powers experienced a period of mass distress and unrest that broke out even before the extended depression of the 1890s. The result, across a wide variety of political regimes, was a near-universal proliferation of state-centered measures aimed variously at securing the public welfare and maintaining social control. In the course of their own confrontation with the most severe of capitalism's crises to that time, American policy-makers—public officials, social investigators, independent labor reformers, as well as union and business leaders—would locate themselves as never before in a larger, international spectrum of economic experience. This wider tableau of understanding is repeatedly apparent in congressional and other public debates and even more in a series of expert-led investigations of labor relations commissioned by Congress from the mid-1880s through World War I. And, while reaching out anecdotally to examples on the European Continent, turn-of-the-century American commentators tended, logically enough, to concentrate on English-speaking countries with a similar legal-political inheritance: the UK, New Zealand, Australia, and (to a lesser degree) Canada.

In assaying the models embodied by their closest politico-cultural counterparts, American reformers were effectively beckoned by two, competing strategic roads. One, which for simplicity's sake I will call the "British road," looked to clear away state and especially court-sanctioned interference to allow organized workers to wrestle with employers on a more even playing field. In the UK (as in all her former colonies), modern industrial relations had first to overcome primitive master-and-servant and criminal conspiracy doctrines rooted in the common law that contradicted democratic norms. To this end, beginning with the 1906 Trade Disputes Act, British unions notably inoculated themselves from injunctions and other civil penalties in a regime of what is commonly dubbed "collective laissez-faire"—permitting economic conflict between organized employers and workers—that largely lasted until the Thatcherite reforms of the 1980s. The alternative path, which after both the Australian and New Zealand examples, we will label the "Australasian road," headed in the opposite direction toward a statist regulation of labor-management relations and workplace standards most famously represented by the institution of compulsory arbitration. These arrangements also enjoyed an extended shelf life: though New Zealand bent toward a more market-driven system amid the pressures of "globalization" beginning in the mid-1980s, Australia has maintained a modified version of its arbitration system to this day.[5]

Many Gilded Age Americans seeking labor reforms were pulled in both directions but alas, their country arrived at neither destination. Just why, as we shall see, was a mixture of political structure, distinctive ideology, business intransigence, and perhaps no small measure of strategic blind spots among pro-labor advocates themselves.

Worker anger, mass mobilization, and recurrent state repression in an era of global economic depression set the stage for modern-day labor relations across the English-speaking world. In Britain union fortunes had followed the trade cycle, with a major upswing punctuated by the "dockers' tanner" strike of 1889—a bitter conflict settled by the intervention of Catholic Cardinal Henry Edward Manning—followed by economic downturn and an employers' counter-attack. The latter challenge to union picketing (legally protected from civil prosecution since the mid-1870s) led to the notorious Taff Vale judgment of 1901, which held the leading railway union liable for crippling monetary damages.

What seemed a gathering conspiracy against labor by established political and legal authority—an impression stirred by the half-measures recommended by the post-Vale Royal Commission on Trade Disputes—quickly strengthened the hand of incipient independent labor political forces. A cross-class reform impetus together with an ensuing electoral landslide effected by a Liberal/Labour pact in 1906 parliamentary elections at once "created the Labour Party" (in the words of British political theorist G. D. H. Cole) and ushered in important new legislative measures. In addition to workmen's compensation, undoubtedly most significant among the latter was the Trade Disputes Act of 1906 that secured pre-Taff Vale protections for peaceful picketing and union immunity from claims for damages that effectively insulated the industrial work stoppage from civil prosecution.[6]

Interestingly, one usually pro-trade union voice on the Royal Commission who had consistently dissented from the more popular push for "full immunity" from state intervention was Fabian socialist leader Sidney Webb. Alongside a few moderate railway and coal-mining union officials, Webb took the position that in the long run, the working class had more to lose than to win from no-holds-barred collective bargaining. Better, this opinion suggested, to use the recognition accorded the unions (even as a suable party) to make legally enforceable agreements and push as well for compulsory arbitration of irresoluble disputes.[7] Effectively, Webb and friends were endorsing the "Australasian solution."

By the 1890s the two countries the British called the Antipodes were jointly relying on state intervention to craft a new social order. Essentially, in a period of extended economic crisis, New Zealand and Australia cut a deal between workers and domestic manufacturers to maintain prices and wages for both parties by a combination of labor arbitration, tariff protection, and immigration restriction (hence the enduring concept of "White Australia")—while relying on commodity exports (especially coal, mutton, and wheat) to build the larger social surplus. The combination of worker-friendly dispute resolution and wage-setting instruments led political scientist Francis Castles to the apt description of the countries as "wage-earners' welfare states."[8]

The ideological and political origins of the antipodean arbitration systems are worth teasing out. In New Zealand, a disastrous drop in farm prices brought the Liberal Party along with a group of Independent Labour representatives to power in 1890 in a "Lib-Lab" coalition to enact what Americans a few years later would have called a "progressive" political agenda. Among the most dramatic innovations, beginning in 1891, Minister of Labour William Pember Reeves shepherded through parliament an elaborate set of Factory Acts ("the fullest labor code in the world") and then, in 1894, the world's first compulsory arbitration legislation (Industrial Conciliation and Arbitration Act).[9] Reeves, whose combination of radicalism and worldliness soon led him out of the country as New Zealand's representative to the UK and subsequently director of the London School of Economics, was doubly influenced by the distress of the unemployed and his own readings of Edward Bellamy, Henry George, and the British Fabians. Following closely on a measure proposed four years previously to the South Australian parliament by workingman's advocate Charles Cameron Kingston, the New Zealand system centered on an arbitration court with three members: one selected by employer associations, one selected by the unions, and an appointed supreme court judge. Together, the panel would take on and legally resolve disputes submitted either by the disputing parties or by an affected third party. Certain features of the system clearly bolstered the country's labor unions and generally satisfied the working-class citizenry. In particular, the very process of registration, required to take part in the system, enfranchised organized employees as legitimate partners in the larger process of social bargaining. Arbitration in Australasia thus emerged more from a "need for trade union recognition" than vice versa.[10]

Not surprisingly, given its more complicated economy, Australia followed a rockier but ultimately equally decisive move toward a state-mandated system of industrial dispute settlement. In August 1890, wage cuts in a slipping economy provoked all four of Australia's major employee groups—seamen, wharfies (dockworkers), coal miners, and pastoralists (sheep shearers)—to strike action. Within two months, a general strike of 50,000 workers provoked the government to invoke the Riot Act and dispatch special constables to break the strike.[11] Three years later, with unemployment now reaching depression proportions, the ports futilely erupted again. In the face of industrial defeat, however, organized workers had begun turning to a new weapon: the ballot box. By 1892, New South Wales had given birth to the upstart Australian Labor Party (intentionally adopting the American spelling of "labor" in admiration of the Yanks' Homestead-era militancy): from 1898 to 1910, the ALP steadily gained in influence until it had captured the provincial government with 49 percent of the vote.[12]

As in New Zealand, rising class tensions across several of the Australian colonies (which would unite in a federal commonwealth in 1901) produced a move to the political center among a professional elite of lawyers, manufacturers, and labor-oriented politicians. Charles Kingston thus proved to be just one of several lawyer-legislators among the Commonwealth's "Founding Fathers" who effectively functioned as what the British called "new liberal" thinkers (and the Americans would dub "progressives"), embracing the state as a source of both social order and public welfare. Following on the recommendations of the New South Wales Royal Commission on Strikes (established in the immediate aftermath of the 1890 maritime debacle), Australian public policy as led by Kingston, Alfred Deakin, and Henry Bournes Higgins moved irrevocably toward an interventionist, compulsory arbitration model, crowned by the Commonwealth's Conciliation and Arbitration Act of 1904. The commissioners themselves had variously located the seeds of such a reform in more restricted settings in a range of countries, including the U.S. and the UK, but they proved particularly intrigued by the French "Conseils des Prud'hommes," which had long invoked a tribunal of worker and employer representatives around local judges to resolve conflicts affecting existing contracts.[13] After 1904 a national arbitration court, though continually buffeted by political forces from all directions, held tremendous authority over labor and welfare standards. Likely most influential of all its decisions was Justice Higgins's precedent-setting Harvester Judgment of 1907 that established a family-based (or male breadwinner) criterion for the minimum industrial wage.[14]

Overall, antepodian developments did not so much replace labor-management conflicts as *politicize* them—ensuring continuous fierce debate not only between the labor movement and its antagonists but also within the labor movement over the nature of its collaboration with governmental authority.[15] Nevertheless, however otherwise contested by contemporaries or subsequent historians, the arbitration systems did seem to confer one unalloyed, long-term result on posterity: they guaranteed the trade union a legitimate place in the national civic order.[16]

As far back as the 1870s and continuing through the 1880s, the American labor movement imagined a positive role for government in buttressing workers' power and adjudicating major industrial disputes. Even as the commonly invoked term "arbitration" floated ambiguously as a signifier—here meaning "conciliation," there meaning "collective bargaining," and only occasionally specifying what later industrial economists would define as "compulsory arbitration"—there was no denying support for an active, interventionist state within the popular ideology of what historians have called "labor republicanism."

Indeed, as witnessed by the special Senate Committee on the Relations Between Labor and Capital commissioned in 1883, the concept generally reverberated in most favorable terms among otherwise quarreling labor leaders as well as among several of the inquiring legislators. It was perhaps not surprising that Robert Layton, general secretary of the broadly reform-minded Knights of Labor (KOL) would imagine where "a certain number of employees should meet an equal number of employers; they to select an umpire, whose decision should be final. Then let the men make their demands, and let the employers produce their books, and if it appears that they cannot afford to comply with the men's demands, that decision [of the umpire] will made, and must be final."[17]

As John J. O'Neill, Democratic representative and former Workingmen's Party candidate from St. Louis, emphasized in a semi-official volume of Knights of Labor thought in 1887, "Workmen, as a rule, have always favored arbitration, and the submission of their differences to an impartial tribunal." With extended references to examples in both Britain (with special attention to the worker-employer committees operating under A. J. Mundella's Nottingham Hosiery Board in the 1860s) and the Continent, O'Neill hailed arbitration as "far superior to any other method of settling differences."[18] Indeed, John McClelland, secretary of the KOL General Executive Board, placed such invocation of governmental authority alongside a broader call for nationalization of the telegraph industry and general public control over monopolies.[19]

Positive reference to some sort of compulsory arbitration, moreover, was hardly limited to the politically inclined spirits of the Knights of Labor. As early as 1873, for example, the German socialist party document that had first impressed young cigar maker Sam Gompers with "the fundamental possibilities of the trade union" had pointed to "industrial arbitration courts and the simplification of judicial procedures" as key goals of the international workers' movement.[20] A decade later, W. H. Foster, a printer by trade who served as the first general secretary of the craft union federation that would shortly become the American Federation of Labor, did not sound much different from his Knights of Labor counterparts before the Senate Committee. When asked for a remedy to disputes over hours and wages, Foster pointed to a system of arbitration: "Instead of having it as now, when the one often refused to even acknowledge or discuss the question with the other, if they were required to submit the question to arbitration, or to meet on the same level before an impartial tribunal, there is no doubt but what the result would be more in our favor than it is now, when very often public opinion cannot hear our case."[21] Another Foster, this one Boston printers' leader Frank Foster (no relation), spelled out further the terms that, in principle, seemed reasonable to many in the organized skilled trades. Arbitration, he insisted, must be matched by full legal legitimation, and even encouragement, of organization among the workers themselves. "Experience among individuals and among classes," he suggested, "is the same in this respect as among peoples." "It is only the strong nations that arbitrate with each other. Very rarely a powerful nation arbitrates with a feeble one."[22]

Foster's analogy of workplace arbitration to the arena of international dispute resolution was probably instinctual given the political backdrop of the times. Not that Foster and his contemporaries would necessarily remember much about specific prior uses of this negotiating tool. Since the American Revolution (most notably the John Jay Treaty of 1794) and the War of 1812 (Treaty of Ghent), the U.S. had regularly resorted to arbitral forms to settle differences with Great Britain short of continuing war. Moreover, if Americans had sometimes dealt from weakness, late nineteenth-century associations with the process likely centered on the post-Civil War Treaty of Washington, where the British swallowed humble pie in acceding to American claims stemming from the *Alabama* (and other Confederate destroyers built in British shipyards), the boundary of North Atlantic fisheries, and the northwest San Juan Islands. The coming years would only witness more such "strong nation" resort to arbitration by the Americans—most famously, by pressing the judicial measure on the British in the case of Venezuelan land disputes in the late 1890s and again, before the Hague Court in 1904.[23] By the turn of the century, not only was arbitration regularly in the air as a preferred pathway to international peace, but some voices—perhaps most notably the Women's Christian Temperance Union (WCTU)—loudly made the connection, advocating for its use on both the international and domestic fronts.[24]

Foster's "strong nations" argument, however, would also serve as the very branch that other craft unionists would use to climb down from their original expressions of interest in arbitration. At the time of the Senate hearings in 1883, future AFL leaders like Gompers and carpenters' leader P. J. McGuire were already parsing their reservations about a doctrine that had generally united the cross-class labor reform community of the early Gilded Age. "I am in favor of arbitration when that can be accomplished," Gompers complained, "but [it] is only possible when the workingmen have, by the power of organization, demonstrated to the employers that they are the employers' equal."[25] McGuire, citing recent post-strike agreements among both telegraphers and railroad engineers with their bosses, put the point more graphically: "Arbitration never will come until the employer recognizes that the workman is his equal, and that never can be established until the workman, by a class struggle, through a strike, proves that fact to the satisfaction of the employer." Thus, for leaders of the most skilled workers, the creation of strong unions with a capacity for militant collective action superseded any commitment to the machinery of dispute resolution. As McGuire declared, "No strike is a loss or a failure to the workers, even if the point sought is not gained for the time being. If naught else, they at least teach the capitalists that they are expensive luxuries to be indulged in."[26]

Given later disparagement by the Gompers-led AFL of most state-sanctioned interventionism including arbitration, workers' compensation, and hours legislation as somehow "un-American," the initial circumspection of the movement regarding means and ends is noteworthy.[27] While reaching out simultaneously in multiple directions for a source of institutional stability and material support, the labor leadership took necessary note of what seemed the limits of both employer cooperation and American statecraft. As carpenters' leader McGuire, who had traveled to Great Britain and Germany two years before his testimony to the Senate Labor and Capital Committee, reported, "While the workers [there] do not perhaps have as much money, they are better off from a social standpoint and an economic standpoint and a sanitary standpoint and, upon the whole . . . enjoy life better than our workers do." Citing the Saturday half-holiday and shorter working hours prevailing among British workers, McGuire suggested "they come nearer to that which humanity generally desires, a contented existence." The United States, on the other hand, seemed caught up in its own digestive system. "This is a country," lamented McGuire, "that is intent chiefly on making money, getting wealth somehow, and our people care little for social comforts or public enjoyment if they are to be had at the expense of the money-making propensities."[28]

In such circumstances, the nearly autonomous national and local unions within the larger labor federation took a decidedly pragmatic, case-specific approach to arbitration systems. In Chicago, for example, the building trades hammered out a series of favorable settlements under the imprimatur of sympathetic federal judge Murray F. Tuley. In 1891, again, the city's carpenters secured a two-year agreement including the eight-hour day and compulsory arbitration through the duration of the Chicago World's Fair in 1893. Workplace-centered militancy as much any cooperative spirit secured such beachheads; by 1899 the employers' Building Contractors' Council successfully locked out unionized workers, setting off years of further labor-management turmoil.[29]

Industrial unrest centered on the railroads—at once catalyzed by the Great Southwest Strike conducted by the Knights of Labor on the Gould line in 1886, and then reignited two years later by a joint walkout of railway brotherhoods against the Chicago, Burlington, & Quincy Railroad—first pushed serious talk of arbitration to the fore of national legislative consciousness. The principal proposal, originally offered in early spring 1886 by Representative O'Neill and ultimately shepherded into law by Texas Democratic Representative William H. Crain as the Arbitration Act of 1888, envisioned only voluntary arbitration in future railroad disputes.[30] Yet a strong undertow existed for more radical measures, including compulsory arbitration. West Virginia Democratic Representative Eustace Gibson, a Virginia-born former Confederate officer and presumably no partisan of federal power in the abstract, nevertheless demanded more than the Crain Bill offered. On the one hand, Gibson related, "skilled labor" had furtively combined in "an unarmed army for protection; "and on the other hand we have organized capital, with its paid attorneys in every Legislative Assembly that meets in this land—whether it be National or whether it be State—passing through the legislative halls and leaving their slime on every act of legislation that is passed."

The remedy, as attested to by growing evidence both at home and abroad, was obvious. Citing the Constitution's interstate commerce clause, which seemingly invited regulation of railroad traffic and rates, Gibson asked, "So why not wages and hours?" Gibson followed with a series of further rhetorical questions: "Why do we want national legislation on this subject? Is it true that questions of supply and demand will not regulate themselves? Is it true that labor is weak and unable to compete against the power of money? Is it true that the money-power has acquired a hold upon the legislation of this country which it requires the masses of people by their votes at the ballot-box to break? If it be true then we must step in and legislate."[31]

Sharing Gibson's assumptions, Kansas Republican John A. Anderson went one step farther. Relying on both the interstate commerce and the general welfare clause (and thus the power to compel any corporation with a public charter to perform its duty), Anderson sought a permanent investigatory commission over railroad disputes, whose "voluntary" recommendations, if rejected by the parties, would be examined by the courts and transformed into a "compulsory" settlement. In a characteristically partisan explanation, Anderson insisted that principles on this pivotal matter divided on party lines: "The Democratic doctrine is that of supreme State rights . . . under the strictest construction of the Constitution. . . . The Republican doctrine is that of a Government strong enough and wise enough to protect its people, no matter what may be the form of attack, nor where."[32]

Though Anderson surely exaggerated mainstream Republican commitment to a compulsory arbitration bill, his assessment of the anti-statist presumptions among most Democrats—and especially those most closely identified with the craft unions—was not inaccurate. A portent of battle lines to come was signaled by the position on the Crain Bill of Martin Foran (D-Oh.), president of the Coopers International Union. Foran opposed the conciliation bill not because it was too weak but because it was too strong. Once Congress started meddling in industrial relations, even by mere investigatory process, he worried, where would it end? "May not some future Congress," he conjectured, "pass laws making it a felony . . . for employees to interfere with the commerce of such roads or the transmission of the mails by striking?" As a potential "entering wedge" to crush organized labor, such would-be government assistance must be opposed. Not by legislation, Foran insisted, but only "through organization that labor will work out its freedom . . . and exact from capital . . . its just reward."[33]

Foran's coolness, moreover, was just the tip of an iceberg of opposition by the soon-to-be dominant AFL toward the entire concept of arbitration. From early on, Samuel Gompers himself led the AFL defiance of the reformers' interventionist efforts. Already by the time of the Homestead Strike in 1892, when a friendly Ohio legislator had asked for his bill-drafting help, Gompers and his tight leadership circle had sharpened a questioning skepticism into unalterable opposition to compulsory arbitration.[34] Already dodging hostile judicial verdicts, the idea of putting any more power in the hands of the federal government had by then proved anathema to the AFL high command. As P. J. McGuire chided an arbitration advocate at the federation's national convention in December 1892, arbitration "smacked of the Elizabethan age. If the Government makes arbitration, why should it not also regulate wages and the hours of labor? The powers that now direct the militia against strikers would then use the Board of Compulsory Arbitration."[35]

By the time of the 1894 Pullman Strike Commission, Gompers introduced a new argument. The economic "compromises" that would likely emerge from arbitration, he suggested, would surely favor less the just than the clever claimant: "the employing class are usually more alert—necessarily so; if they have not the brains themselves they buy them; continually on the alert, continually thinking, more watchful of events. . . . I don't think the workers would get much the best of it."[36] Reiterated as the official AFL position in 1900, opposition to any and all compulsory arbitration became a principle from which it never subsequently deviated.[37] Gompers that year went so far in an address to the National Civic Federation conference to equate any settlement imposed on labor by arbitration with a "demoralized, degraded, and debased manhood." It was no less than "a negation of liberty and a return to serfdom."[38]

In the end, therefore, the Crain Bill of 1886 galvanized no major working-class constituency. Even as the AFL was drawing an increasingly hard line against the incursion of state authority on union autonomy, the more politically oriented Knights of Labor pointedly remained on the sidelines. Unlike proposals for land or currency reform, the legislated eight-hour day, or government ownership of the railroads, telephone, and telegraph—which all received enthusiastic endorsement in the course of the Knights' national assembly in June 1886—the arbitration issue did not command the delegates' attention, one way or the other.[39]

Over the next two decades, industrial conflicts would continue to spur demands for federal reform of American industrial relations. Indeed, public discussions triggered by the Pullman boycott of 1894 and again by the anthracite strike of 1902 regularly re-engaged the arbitration theme. A decade later, the Commission on Industrial Relations (1912–1915), convened after the deadly bombing of the *Los Angeles Times* building during an ironworkers' strike, once again probed for systemic policy alternatives. In the end, however, state intervention in American industrial relations arrived less from domestic disturbances (as in Australasia) than from foreign ones, as in the emergency of the Great War.

During the prewar years, the argument for public intervention in industrial conflicts, either through arbitration or other state-based measures, regularly mixed moral with political-economic justifications. On the moral-philosophical front, an appeal to class conciliation echoed alike in the social justice principles of Pope Leo XIII's encyclical *Rerum Novarum* (1891), in the teachings of nonresistant Leo Tolstoy, and, relatedly in the social settlement practice at Jane Addams's Hull House. The Russian author—who had drawn heavily on his own readings of American writers Ralph Waldo Emerson, Henry David Thoreau, and abolitionist William Lloyd Garrison in his prescriptions of nonviolent resistance—proved in turn a catalyst for others seeking a resolution of social conflict. Inspired by Tolstoy—and moved to visit him at his country estate in 1896—Addams nevertheless questioned both his ascetic individualism and his unremitting disdain for government. As fellow Tolstoy acolyte Aylmer Maude would note, the very inattention to the poor had "driven her, and Hull House generally, into politics."[40] For Christian pacifists—whether individuals like Maude or organizations like the WCTU—recourse to compulsory arbitration was thus but one of the ways the state could live up to its moral responsibility to the surrounding community.[41]

On the domestic political front, likely the most powerful voice for arbitration in industrial affairs was the Civic Federation of Chicago (CFC), a body that gave way to the National Civic Federation in 1900. Linking capitalists like Chicago banker and future secretary of the treasury Lyman Gage and flour king Charles A. Pillsbury, politicians led by Mark Hanna, labor leaders including Gompers and Mitchell, and clergymen like Washington

Gladden and Father John A. Ryan with reformer/social scientists Carroll D. Wright, Jane Addams, Ralph Easley, Henry Carter Adams, Henry Demorest Lloyd, and Edward Bemis, the Civic Federation presented a social bloc of considerable potential significance. Tellingly, in accord with both a national and transnational intellectual mood, the Federation's gaze fell early and heavily on the subject of compulsory arbitration. Only months after the collapse of the Pullman strike, Gage convened a conference in Chicago to build support for national legislation on the subject. The spirit in the room was reflected in business editor James D. Weeks's attack on the principles of traditional political economy as a "gospel of grab . . . not in accordance with our civilization."[42]

Citing the commerce clause of the Constitution, Representative James A. Tawney, Republican of Minnesota and a former machinist, offered perhaps the most developed rationale for compulsory adjustment of "such controversies as impede or obstruct . . . our commerce between the states." Tawney neatly contrasted the treatment of the nation's two main "instrumentalities" of commerce, water and rail. In the case of the former, as he accurately cited maritime law stretching back a century, "the medicine in the chest, the license to the engineer, the commission to the captain are all governed by federal statute; even the machinery on the vessel, including the boilers, cannot be used until thoroughly inspected, tested and its safety certified to by a duly authorized government inspector." What was more, he counseled his listeners, Congress had also brought the instrumentality of rail within its regulatory gaze with the Interstate Commerce Act of 1887. Now, urged Tawney, it was time to go farther. "The right of the employees of railroad companies to go out on strike is not denied, but the necessity for the exercise of the right should be removed by giving to either party to the controversy an adequate, peaceable remedy."[43]

Generally in line with the logic of the Civic Federation, the 1894 U.S. Strike Commission tried again to raise the banner of compulsory arbitration.[44] Given the unequal power relations in which they found themselves, writer-activist Demorest Lloyd testified to the commission, industrial workers had no chance to cope on their own against obdurate employers: "The attitude of the employer amounts simply to this: Reason shall not arbitrate between us, because there is a Judge sitting on your case who always decides in my favour, if he has time enough—Judge Hunger."[45]

Led by their chairman, Carroll Wright, the commissioners attempted to move the American system towards an accommodation with foreign

examples of state engagement. As an issue affecting "quasi-public corporations," asserted their final report, railroad regulation—including questions
of compulsory arbitration as well as government ownership—"is one of
expediency and not of [inherent] power." Applauding a move away from
class strife and toward the institutionalization of the "rights of labor"
within "conservative" trade unions, the commission noted that "capital
abroad prefers to deal with these unions rather than with individuals or
mobs, and from their joint efforts in good faith at conciliation and arbitration much good and many peaceful days have resulted."[46] Building on what
it claimed was now a common agreement among both workers and
employers internationally in favor of peaceful collective bargaining, the
commission sought self-consciously to advance "harmonious relations of
equal standing and responsibility before the law."[47]

Leaving aside larger questions of industrial governance, the commission's report urged strong intervention in future railroad disputes by a permanent strike commission empowered, like the ICC with respect to freight
rates, to resolve disputes by decisions enforceable through the courts. In
any particular "controversy," both the affected union and employer would
have a right to select a representative as a temporary member of the commission, but each side would be subject to governmental discipline:
employers could not discharge workers for union membership, unions
could not "intimidate" nonstriking workers in the course of the dispute.[48]

The commissioners were clearly eager to identify their recommendations as a basic rebalancing of the national scales of social justice. While
acknowledging that the "growth in corporate power and wealth has been
the marvel of the past fifty years," they expressed the hope that the next
half-century would witness "the advancement of labor to a position of like
power and responsibility." The key to their proposal—like the plans developed in New Zealand and Australia—was institutionalization of the labor
movement through a combination of incorporation of trade unions, collective bargaining, and compulsory arbitration. As the commission concluded,
"Since nations have grown to the wisdom of avoiding disputes by conciliation, and even of settling them by arbitration, why should capital and labor
in their dependence upon each other persist in cutting each other's throats
as a settlement of differences?"[49] The point was to set limits to collective
protest while legitimating and normalizing the presence of trade unions
within the industrial order.

Encountering repeated skepticism from most of their trade union witnesses (who for almost a decade now had rejected the arbitration option)
the commissioners bent over backward to recruit at least a few working-
class representatives—and Eugene Debs in particular—to support their
proposal. But Debs's qualified and provisional conversion to compulsory
arbitration demanded no giant leap from the ARU leader. As we saw in
Chapter 2, he had skillfully deployed Minnesota's arbitration statute to win
recognition from the Great Northern Railroad in 1893. Even amid the hos-
tilities of the Pullman strike and boycott, Debs had twice offered to submit
the issues to arbitration, albeit in vain, as a way to entice the AFL into fuller
support for his cause.[50]

The unequivocal recommendation of the Pullman commission may
have been the nation's best, if not its last, chance for a fundamental shift in
industrial social policy. Despite the commission's own considerable intellectual heft, however, neither President Cleveland and his party nor prevailing elements of the organized business or labor community made the
recommendations their own. The closest turn-of-the-century reformers got
to a serious role for government action in industrial disputes was the Erdman Act of 1898, which, mandating only mediation and voluntary arbitration on the railways, was not concretely applied until 1906. The Anthracite
Coal Commission, established by President Roosevelt following his settlement of a strike during the harrowing winter of 1902, pushed for a
strengthening of Erdman—including a penalty for whichever party initiated
a strike or lockout without first resorting to the machinery of arbitration—
but this appeal, too, was lost on Congress. The sole legacy of Pullman-era
energies was a series of federal railroad acts limited to the running trades
and aimed at averting any further catastrophic work stoppage by way of
conciliation, investigation, or at most voluntary arbitration.[51]

Despite the continuing odds against a regulated industrial relations system, public discussion of the subject was kept alive by the new generation
of institutional economists who had gained a foothold in the universities in
the 1890s (see Chapter 3). These intellectual reformers first seized a
national platform amid the deliberations of the United States Industrial
Commission (USIC), a four-year investigation (1898–1902) of American
economic institutions instigated by President McKinley. With a tripartite
structure of business, labor, as well as congressional representatives, the
nineteen-member USIC fairly took the measure of its times. Though both

USIC secretary E. Dana Durand, a Stanford economist, and staff investigator John R. Commons initially assembled comprehensive and generally
positive reports on arbitration procedures abroad, the commissioners, after
hearing sustained opposition from both business and labor representatives,
quickly dropped arbitration and other strong-state interventions from their
policy playbook. In line with both corporate and the AFL's own insistence
on "voluntarism," even Commissioner of Labor Carroll Wright retreated
from his prior, post-Pullman advocacy. As an alternative, Commons
pushed in vain for "labor councils" (common to France, Belgium, and
Austria) as a state-centered system of mediation, but, according to historian
Clarence E. Wunderlin, Jr, he was never authorized to submit draft recommendations to Congress. In the end, Durand, following his mentor and
USIC senior economist Jeremiah Jenks, trimmed away all mention of cor-
poratist alternatives in a largely voluntarist set of final recommendations
encouraging only collective bargaining, child labor laws, and eight-hour
workdays.[52]

Without a labor or political champion (Mark Hanna died in early
1904), arbitration largely fell out of the national progressive toolkit in precisely the years of most fertile reform agitation on most other subjects. In
its place, for the most part, continued an ongoing war between hardline
"open-shop" employers on one side and "closed shop" trade unionists on
the other. In the long run, the stalemate surely worked to the distinct disad-
vantage of the labor forces. Not only would the unionists search in vain for
the elixir that would put the U.S. on the British road of collective laisssez-
faire, but the open versus closed shop debate lent employers an important
ideological edge as champions of "voluntary" individual rights against
"compulsory" union membership.

As one of the idea's foremost advocates, Jane Addams also sensed when
the air was leaving the arbitration bag. In Pullman's aftermath, Illinois had
established a State Board of Conciliation and Arbitration, but to Addams's
regret its voluntary apparatus went largely unused. In 1896, for example,
Chicago clothing manufacturers determined to break the cutters' union,
precipitating a strike. In the pages of the *Hull-House Bulletin*, Addams
chided the owners for their disavowal of the "fundamental principle of
representation, upon which our entire government is founded," as well as
for a basic "lack of discipline." Still appealing for arbitration, she counseled
the parties, "Trained and responsible people do not try to settle their diffi-
culties by fighting."[53] The following decade sapped her hopes. "There is no

doubt," she wrote after the city's bitter teamster strike in 1905, "but that ideas and words which at one time fill a community with enthusiasm may, after a few years, cease to be a moving force, apparently from no other reason than that they are spent and no longer fit into the temper of the hour. Such a fate has evidently befallen the word 'arbitration,' at least in Chicago, as it is applied to industrial struggles."[54] Without legislative advance on the issue, what was left on the edges of the industrial scene were a select series of local experiments in employer/union cooperation (sometimes including voluntary arbitration machinery) as well as the continuing reports of a phalanx of social scientists and reform thinkers still looking at various international alternatives.

The most prominent of such experiments occurred in garment manufacturing. Following upheavals and militant strikes among semi-skilled, largely immigrant and female labor force, two new industry-wide unions— the International Ladies' Garment Workers' Union and the Amalgamated Clothing Workers—gained a foothold, respectively, in the women's and men's clothing industry on the basis of mediated settlements that institutionalized arbitration in the settlement of industrial disputes. It was no accident that such agreements were reached within a relatively homogeneous surrounding of large, Jewish-owned firms at once susceptible to community pressures and capable of imposing a floor of work-based standards under all competitors.

In New York City, progressive Boston attorney (and future Supreme Court justice) Louis Brandeis negotiated the industry's first "Protocol of Peace" following the cloakmakers' Great Revolt in July 1910. As a tripartite agreement between labor, management, and the public, the protocols— quickly established across the needle trades—promised both industrial peace (secured through a no-strike, no-lockout pledge from the parties and binding arbitration for future grievances) and labor rights, the latter vouchsafed by a union-management committee on working conditions and a "preferential" union shop.[55]

A similar logic prevailed in Chicago. Following a walkout of 40,000 workers at Hart, Schaffner, & Marx settled by arbitration in 1911, Sidney Hillman and fellow strike leader (and future spouse) Bessie Abramowitz led a rebellion against the corrupt leadership of the United Garment Workers and chartered the ACW in 1914 with a combined commitment to industrial unionism, scientific efficiency, and cooperative adjudication of disputes. That same year, a model ACW settlement was signed with the garment giant Sonneborn in Baltimore; there, German Jewish attorney and reformer Judge Jacob Moses arbitrated an agreement that included pensions, safety measures, and a new medical unit as well as union recognition. In return the union would discipline its members, forsaking wildcat strikes in favor of arbitration to establish "joint control" of the industry.[56]

The logic of "industrial democracy," to cite a favorite phrase of Brandeis, developed in the special circumstances of the big-city garment districts as in no other places. Both a flexible labor leadership—for example, willing to accept a "preferential shop" over the unions' preferred "closed shop"— and "moderate" owners (like Lincoln A. Filene, Meyer Bloomfield, and bankers Jacob Schiff and Louis Marshall) worried about low-wage competitors could come to terms around the long-term health of the industry as well as worker welfare. Unlike most other industrial conflicts, the big-city garment strikes attracted numerous middle-class supporters, determined to find a pathway to long-term labor peace. Moreover, the very fact that the "manliness" of the workers was not at stake in an industry dominated by women semiskilled operatives may have heightened cooperation among the parties. As discovered elsewhere, arbitration appealed particularly to a labor force not confident of its own combative strength. Here, then, according to Brandeis's vision, was an arena where the raw inequalities of industrial capitalism could be softened by countervailing power in the hands of workers as well as management.[57] Organized garment workers could thus look back with pride on several years of stable employment and rising wages. Even in this selective sphere, however, as post-World War I conflicts flared up over union bureaucratization and lack of democracy as well as between labor and management, "protocolism" proved no magic elixir of social harmony.[58] In the United States, room for even a trial run for arbitration was thus most narrowly confined.

Even before his arbitration experience, however, Brandeis had recognized the need for a dramatic breakthrough from the legal constraints defining American labor relations. Preparing to teach a course on business law just as the Homestead Strike of 1892 erupted, Brandeis later explained how the conflict had first upset his conventionally sanguine assumptions about the capacity of the legal system to offer equal protections to all: "I saw at once that the common law, built up under simpler conditions of living, gave an inadequate basis for the adjustment of the complex relations of the modern factory system. I threw away my notes and approached my theme from new angles."[59]

How to trump the common law and its bias toward the employer's property rights became a central strategic preoccupation not only of legal reformers like Brandeis but a host of progressive scholars not to mention the stewards of the labor movement itself.[60] Their concern was not misplaced. After 1880, employers customarily sought injunctive relief and subsequent suits for damages in the case of strikes or boycotts; indeed, from 1880 to 1931, 1800 injunctions would be issued in U.S. courts against strikes alone.[61] The dominant legal voice echoed in two opinions from the bench only a few months before the Pullman conflict of 1894. In the first, Circuit Court Judge William Howard Taft, disallowing strikes and boycotts to enforce the closed shop, ruled that the constitutional provision of the conservative Brotherhood of Engineers requiring members to act in solidarity with brothers on strike "make[s] the whole brotherhood a criminal conspiracy against the laws of their country." In the second, a Wisconsin federal court similarly compared striking railroad workers to surgeons suspending work in the middle of an operation: "It is idle to talk of a peaceable strike. None has ever occurred."[62]

A crucial division nevertheless erupted among those who would uphold trade union rights. Brandeis and university-based policy intellectuals like John R. Commons (whom we followed in Chapter 3) generally leaned toward a variety of "statist" interventions. Tripartite investigatory commissions, conciliation and arbitration panels, obligatory incorporation of unions, as well as minimum wage and maximum hours legislation were generally all part of a mix of interventions into the private marketplace, consistently pushed by Progressive labor reformers and regularly recommended in high-level forums convened after major industrial conflicts and meant to set an agenda for national ameliorative action.

The mainline AFL (i.e., excepting the garment unions and railroad brotherhoods) tended to rebuff all such initiatives in favor of a determined pursuit of what we have identified as the path of collective laissez-faire. Again and again, pro-labor legal strategists looked for a single legislative remedy that would legitimize the unions' normal behavior—i.e. accepting a role for disciplined, collective action in industrial conflicts including the inoculation of labor strikes from civil prosecution for damages. Alas, they never found the cure. The closest they got by World War I were Sections 6 and 20 of the Clayton Antitrust Act of 1914, exempting unions from antitrust provisions of the Sherman Act (that had been used against the Pullman strikers) and famously declaring that "the labor of a human being is not a commodity or article of commerce."[63]

By themselves, however, such doctrinal changes in statutory law—what Gompers at the time christened as labor's "Magna Carta"—could never shut the door to the coercion available to employers (and sympathetic justices) via case law. In part, American courts (with the power of judicial review), unlike their British counterparts, owed no constitutional deference to legislative mandate. In this particular arena, for example, whereas British legislation as early as 1875 had "statutorily specified strike offenses," American laws, notes historian David Brody, through the Clayton Act and beyond, "never overrode the authority of the courts to decide what "intimidation [of non-strikers] meant." With its intentionally vague and open-ended definitions of what in the end constituted lawful acts, Clayton opened a hole that justices could ride a carriage through.[64] Generally impressed with American progressive thinking on social welfare issues while touring the U.S. in 1914, the great Australian jurist H.B. Higgins expressed a mixture of admiration and sympathy for the political position of his hosts (who included Brandeis, Felix Frankfurter, and National Consumers' League leader Josephine Goldmark). "It is to America," he wrote Frankfurter, "that we must look for the humanizing of our civilization . . . and yet you are horribly shackled by your constitution."[65]

Divisions in the pro-labor ranks were perhaps most crucially on display when, in the full flush of Progressive reform fever in 1912, President William Howard Taft appointed a federal Commission on Industrial Relations (CIR) to recommend solutions to "a state of industrial war." Three years of exhaustive investigations overseen by a tripartite panel of business, labor, and public representatives—all sympathetic in principle to a role for organized labor in the body politic—in the end produced a policy stalemate between the allies of the commission's chair, radical attorney and AFL confidant Frank Walsh, and those of its most distinguished public member, Professor Commons, as aided by Wisconsin legislative librarian Charles McCarthy.[66]

Pointedly, both sides adopted what they recognized as the British road of untrammeled collective bargaining by endorsing a U.S. replica of the 1906 British Trade Disputes Act. But Commons's proposals went further, including calls for minimum wage regulation and other worker safety and welfare measures combined with a proposal for the institutionalization of Wisconsin-style industrial commissions. If self-consciously less "compulsory" than New Zealand arbitration's system, the commission model nevertheless anticipated a permanent investigatory role for government in labor-management disputes. The idea was abhorrent to the Walsh-led trade union bloc.[67] With more sharply anti-capitalist language, Walsh and the labor commissioners called for stringent inheritance taxes, nationalization of utilities, and no restrictions on the right to strike, but warned against German-style "bureaucratic paternalism" and "ponderous legal machinery" that would subject business and workers equally to "the whim or caprice of an army of officials, deputies, and Governmental employees."[68]

In the end, when the "legal machinery" of the state arrived only two years after release of the CIR Report, it was packaged in irony. With U.S. entry into World War I, two old labor-management foes and equally fierce advocates of the industrial "free contract"—William Howard Taft and Frank Walsh—became co-chairs of the War Labor Conference Board, which quickly morphed into the more administrative National War Labor Board (NWLB). The NWLB presided over a joint no strike-no lockout pledge by leading employers as well as the AFL. In addition to a guarantee of the right to organize (without coercive methods), the wartime federal government would also impose an eight-hour workday as the industrial norm. Finally, and most dramatically, the NWLB inserted itself as a powerful broker of industrial disputes; its offers to arbitrate were voluntary but—freighted with the authority of the "national interest'—once accepted by the parties, its judgments were enforceable under law. Despite the efforts of Walsh to extend the life of the wartime board, the edifice of government-backed industrial relations quickly came asunder in the face of employer opposition. Within months of the armistice, the war labor agencies had collapsed."[69] In retrospect, it was obvious that "wartime fervor" more than "progressive ideals" had accounted for the experiment in expanded government that included the NWLB.[70]

Still, we might ask, could an arbitration system of some sort (outside of wartime) have proved both constitutionally and politically acceptable in the U.S.? Brief experimentation in two states—Colorado and Kansas—throws some light on the question. In the wake of the Ludlow Massacre at John D. Rockefeller, Jr.'s Colorado Fuel and Iron Company and the subsequent recommendations of the CIR, Colorado in 1915 became the first American jurisdiction to authorize the compulsory investigation of labor disputes. Extending the logic of the Canadian Industrial Disputes Investigation Act of 1907 (whose chief legislative advocate, former Canadian labor minister and future prime minister MacKenzie King served as Rockefeller's official consultant in Colorado post-Ludlow) and citing the recommendations of the CIR's John Commons, the Colorado Industrial Commission established a 30-day cooling-off period in disputes for all industries "affected with a public interest," during which time the CIC would use the journalistic mode of exposé as well as its subpoena power of investigation to arrange a settlement.[71]

With similar intentions following a devastating coal strike in the fall 1919 (part of the larger strike surge of that year), the state of Kansas created the Court of Industrial Relations, an ambitious system of dispute resolution, initially boosted politically by two powerful friends, Governor Henry J. Allen and progressive journalist William Allen White. It set up a three-judge panel charged with adjudicating disputes respecting wages, hours, and working conditions in any business "clothed with a public interest"— specifically those involving food, clothing, mining, transportation, and public utilities. In framing the state's plan, the Governor reportedly studied the arbitration systems of New Zealand, Australia, and Canada, but chose to bypass the former's tripartite mechanisms in favor of a unitary judicial authority with appeal available only to the state supreme court. Significantly, though rhetorically recognizing the right to unionize, the Kansas tribunal (unlike the arbitration systems of Australasia) did not encourage or integrate unions or employer associations into its procedures. Disposing of some 166 cases during five years of activity before it was formally disbanded by the legislature in 1925, the Court challenged the legal and political norms prevailing in the rest of the nation. Controversial and politically besieged from its inception, the abrupt termination of the Kansas experiment calls attention to the sources of its limitations.[72]

Constitutionally, the U.S. Supreme Court delivered a key blow to the state initiatives in two related judgments, *Chas. Wolff Packing Co. v. Court of Industrial Relations* (1923, 1925). In opinions delivered by Chief Justice Taft (appointed to the bench in 1921) and Willis Van Devanter, the Court, relying on its oft-expressed connection of property rights and the 14th Amendment, denied the Kansas Industrial Court the power to set wages (1923) or hours (1925) for a Topeka-based meatpacking firm. As to when and under what circumstances the state or its agents *could* restrict a company's labor relations, Taft's opinion put the burden on the state to show "the indispensable nature of the service and the exorbitant charges and arbitrary control to which the public might be subjected without regulation." Unlike the potential "commercial paralysis" of a nationwide railroad strike, which the Court in 1917 had deemed justification enough to uphold a legislated eight-hour day for the running trades (*Wilson v. New*, 243 U.S.

332), disputes in more "common callings" were another matter; otherwise, feared Taft, "there must be a revolution in the relation of government to general business."[73] Since both Kansas and Colorado had already found themselves ill-fitted, by their limited jurisdiction, to handle national disputes in coal or the railroads, the Wolff decision, as historian Todd R. Laugen concludes, effectively "undermined the principle upon which the state arbitration movement rested."[74]

Apart from the legal questions, however, both the Colorado and Kansas experiments proved political failures, particularly attracting the ire of organized labor. In Colorado, invocation of the state's "ranger law," facilitating the mobilization of national guard units for strikebreaking duty in a 1920 coal strike, nullified the commission's prior, sympathetic intervention on behalf of union typographers, bakery workers, and the building trades.[75] From the beginning, the Kansas industrial court set itself against the power of the United Mine Workers, the state's largest union, led by the cantankerous Alexander Howat, who made even the notoriously independent UMW president John L. Lewis seem tame and conciliatory by comparison.

Even as the measure establishing the court was being debated in the state legislature, Howat secured Frank Walsh to attack the bill as "vicious[ly] antilabor" and a form of "state socialism."[76] With Walsh's apparent encouragement, Howat not only ignored subpoenas to address the court but authorized a series of wildcat strikes which ultimately landed him in jail for contempt of court. What was worse, in terms of the larger climate of the state's industrial relations, Gov. Allen invoked the punitive sanctions of new anti-vagrancy laws to force Howat's remaining followers back to work. As if inability to resolve the state's own industrial conflicts were not problem enough, Allen and the industrial court also quickly found themselves sucked into the nationwide railroad shopcraft strike of 1922. Rather than an honest broker, the state's Industrial Relations Act was turned into an aggressively coercive agent, outlawing picketing and arresting two hundred union leaders, even as the federal government helped stamp out the strike with its own prosecutions. In the end, William Allen White's public support for the strikers earned the editor an arrest (for displaying a union placard that purportedly contravened the Act's antipicketing provisions)—as well as a Pulitzer Prize for an editorial upholding free speech.[77]

Although in principle reformers might have picked up the policy baton to fashion a revised industrial relations plan following the Kansas debacle, in reality the die had likely been cast by 1920. What was wanting was less a policy option than political will. The fact was that at the end of the war, there were ideas on the table that might well have passed muster even with the conservative Supreme Court. Most obviously, lawmakers at the state or federal level might have advanced adjudication of disputes that might truly disrupt public commerce—as in a railroad, transportation, or possibly mining strikes and lockouts. Beyond such a limited arena of application, moreover, also lay other options. In particular, models drawn both from the experience of the National War Labor Board and post-war forums like the National Industrial Conferences in 1919 envisioned something of a step-ladder of encouragement of worker and employer representation and collective bargaining, followed, if necessary by government mediation, fact-finding, and, in the final moment, ad hoc compulsory arbitration. The tripartite collaboration envisioned by the conferences—held in the U.S. and Canada as well as in Great Britain in 1919—built off the proposal for joint labor-management industrial councils originally proposed by British Cabinet minister J. H. Whitley in 1917.[78] Contrasting the "council" idea to that of the "compulsory authority" assumed by the Kansas Court, the left-progressive *New Republic* thus endorsed the former, "which would work primarily in the hands of local people familiar with the industry, thus securing two essential features of a sound plan—maximum devolution in consideration of cases and consideration by a group which is an integral part of the industry."[79]

Still, such ideas proved non-starters. Tellingly, although the post-war industrial conference recommendations suffered a fitful political response in all three countries, only in the U.S. did simultaneous opposition from business, labor, and Capitol Hill alike amount to what union-friendly economist Jett Lauck called "a catastrophe both to the public and to industry."[80]

The common rejection of arbitration by the normally politically contrarian Taft and Walsh stands in for the larger story here. As indirect representatives of the nation's business and labor interests, these two figures had cooperated in wartime to fashion the nearest thing the U.S. ever got (at least with the exception of World War II) to the institutionalization of labor unionism within a politically circumscribed industrial order. Yet each returned, at least rhetorically, to pre-war ideological perspectives that precluded governmental oversight or a recognized role for consumer interests within the collective bargaining process.[81] In particular, Walsh's juxtaposition of confrontation and consent with his business antagonists summons the spirit of the absurd. At one point—just before the NWLB officially expired (and with the hope that a new body might more effectively take its place)—Walsh's lieutenant Basil Manly urged President Wilson to ignore the inveterately anti-union members of the current NWLB in favor of men like J. P. Morgan, Henry Ford, and John D. Rockefeller, Jr., men who felt a "genuine responsibility for the maintenance of the nation's stability."[82] The latter, of course, were precisely the lords of the capitalist empire (albeit sometimes with conciliatory language toward labor) against whom Walsh had fought for years. If he had not found common ground with them before, he surely would (and did) not while the corporate class smelled blood at the sputtering end of the national steel strike of 1919. Unable to buck the courts and equally unable to generate any alternative state-centered authority, the American labor movement limped into the 1920s as a weak counterpart to corporate control of the economy and the workplace. Determined to defend its own organizational autonomy and strategic room to maneuver from governmental interference, the AFL struggled in vain to construct a British road on American industrial soil.

Moreover, a recent reconsideration of the character of British industrial relations suggests that the Americans may have been looking in the wrong place. It proves too simple, it now appears, to attribute British Labour's extended twentieth-century "success" to workplace strength alone. Indeed, the sudden collapse of British trade union power under the assault of Thatcherite reforms in the 1980s, argues historian Chris Howell, should challenge assumptions that its power had ever fully been based on "voluntarism," "state abstentionism," or "collective laissez-faire." Rather, state actors themselves had carefully laid a framework (initially heralded by the 1894 Royal Commission on Labour and subsequent 1906 Trade Disputes Act) to promote collective bargaining among the parties, *but always within a politically regulated terrain*. Legal support for trade union rights and room to maneuver proved crucial to the stability of the British labor movement, but the government also regularly intervened in major disputes (usually citing the 1896 Conciliation Act) that threatened the civil order. Over time, Howell concludes, an underestimation of the unions' underlying "dependence on the state" permitted the growth of the "myth of bootstrap voluntarism," a self-delusion for which they would pay dearly in modern times.[83]

To the extent that the British road had always been paved by politics and sympathetic governmental oversight of their industrial relations system, the Americans had been doubly blindsided. First, they had hunted a

fox (to stick with British mores) that they could never catch. They simply
could not keep the courts from meddling with strikes. It was as if there
were a rule in the U.S. that hounds could not run in packs. Secondly, they
had misapprehended the degree to which, even in the idealized England of
outwardly no-holds-barred labor-management conflicts, there were, in fact,
rules to the game. Raise the costs too high, in short, and the government
would step in. Even more than their British counterparts, American labor
strategists—albeit determinedly "practical" men——paid a price for their
principled but ultimately impractical aversion to a more thorough-going
political strategy.[84]

Neither was the Australasian Road on easy offer. At several moments
Americans did seriously debate the option of a state-sanctioned system of
dispute resolution. But except as a solution-under-duress—devastating
strikes (1880s, mid-1890s), wartime (1918–19), and the special cases of
the railroads (1915) and the ethnically homogeneous garment trades—
arbitration was pointedly rejected by both business and organized labor
in America. In mainstream American circles, the idea of institutionalized,
preventive public intervention in labor-management relations thus
remained as exotic and undomesticated a creature as the Australian dingo.
Organized labor, in general, rejected a system that in exchange for certain
tactical limitations (particularly on the closed shop and sympathy strikes)
promised the possibility of a cross-class legitimacy for worker representation through unions as well as a mediated settlement of work-based disputes. To be sure, it was a prospect that beckoned unevenly to unions at
either end of a curve of independent market leverage: strong unions, as in
the building trades, thus eschewed "protections" that might have buttressed
workers in the service industries. Overall, however, the historical record
suggests that organized labor fared better—in both workplace density and
general public presence—in countries where it was incorporated in state-
based collective-bargaining or arbitration systems than in the U.S. where it
was left to struggle on its own.[85] That the current era of global marketplace
competition has weakened or upended national arbitration systems in Australasia further suggests the degree to which such systems likely aided workers more than they did employers.

If a stronger state-based system of dispute resolution—an option
repeatedly raised on the U.S. public agenda from 1880 to 1920—would
have simultaneously served the cause of worker welfare while still being
eminently compatible with a capitalist-centered industrial economy, why

did it not get established? I would point to four culprits. First, the effective recognition of trade unionism as a natural part of the industrial system, as required in any arbitration system, remained anathema to the most dynamic of American business lobbies in this era. Although, as we have seen, major industrialists like Carnegie and Rockefeller and financiers like Morgan gave at least momentary consideration to such alternatives, particularly through the entreaties of the National Civic Federation, Main Street employers looked in a decidedly different direction. Both the National Association of Manufacturers (at least post-1903) and the U.S. Chamber of Commerce (established in 1912) took a hard line against enforced collective bargaining and any state-led coordination of the economy. In crusading for the "open shop," autonomy-minded employers thus counter-posed the very principle of "personal liberty" to union discipline.[86] With no space for ideological reconciliation, the only "give" available would be through the courts or brute industrial warfare.

Politically, we have identified no shortage of articulate advocacy for an interventionist state, seemingly stronger among Republican than Democratic legislators. Yet, no single event or individual could catalyze these disparate elements into a positive reaction. The one political power broker, with sympathetic ties to labor as well as to a national bloc of manufacturers with an interest in tariff protection, was probably Mark Hanna, and he passed from the scene too early to see any such event through. Otherwise, even when they invoked arbitration (as did President Roosevelt after the anthracite strike) and Wilson during World War I on a de facto basis, the nation's political leadership never embraced the concept in any convincing way.

Nor could the state effectively intrude on labor-management relations without the consent, let alone active support, of at least a sizeable part of the labor movement. Third-party intervention, to be sure, never fully replicates what an organized body of workers wants for itself; nevertheless, both the isolated examples in the U.S. and the record in Australasia indicate that much can be gained by public leverage in the larger bargaining process. Since the 1890s, however, the forces within U.S. organized labor cleaved to a collective version of "personal liberty" or group autonomy in rejecting the dilution of industrial authority implicit in arbitration awards. Part hard-headed pragmatism, part macho braggadocio, the AFL (and subsequent AFL-CIO) attitude simply failed to reckon with how fragmentary, how limited was its own reach over the American workforce. To be sure, combined political and industrial mobilization in the New Deal Era did produce an extended interlude (roughly 1935–1975) of trade union buoyancy and restrained state repression, an era of so-called "industrial pluralism" that superficially resembled the heyday of the British collective laissez-faire. Neither the legal nor political grounds for this evanescent upsurge, however, were well-secured; as U.S. hegemony in the postwar world faded, so too did business tolerance of robust collective bargaining. For most of their history, therefore, American workers never found secure or official acceptance for their unions or a countervailing voice to corporate power at the workplace.[87]

Finally, as a cross-class model, a nationally sanctioned arbitration system required a core of professional-class advocates or public intellectuals to turn the idea into a public priority high enough to command attention from the political and industrial actors themselves. In Australasia the effective ramrod came from labor-sympathetic lawyers, writers, and journalists in alliance with select trade union and business figures. That same social formation existed in the U.S. in the amorphous circles of reform we call the Progressives. Powerful Progressive voices like Richard T. Ely, Jane Addams, Henry Demorest Lloyd, Louis Brandeis, and John R. Commons tried but failed to find an institutional alternative to class conflict and class subjugation in the form of state mechanisms of investigation, conciliation, and ultimate arbitration of workplace disputes. For all their energy and good will, American Progressives only rarely found a vehicle to translate the message of their speeches, writings, and commissions into determinative public policy.

Was the outcome "overdetermined" or did the actors suffer a failure of "will"? Scholars generally prefer the first explanation, but a single historical case argues the latter. Like the rest of an international bevy of reformers, the young Mohandas Gandhi was drawn to the nonresistance doctrines of conflict resolution beginning with his first exposure to London in 1888. In the company of Gujarati writer Narayan Hemchandran, he visited Cardinal Manning one year after the dockworkers' strike. Over the next few years, he also read deeply in Tolstoy and established his own "Tolstoy Farm" in South Africa to work out his philosophy of active nonresistance or *satyagraha*.[88] Soon after Gandhi returned to India, he became involved with the campaign of the textile workers in Ahmedabad in 1918, near his ashram on the Sabermati River. Quickly attaching himself to the demands of the skilled workers, who were demanding a raise retroactive to their service during a recent plague, Gandhi also closely consulted with the wealthy local Sarabhai family, which encompassed both a recalcitrant local mill owner and his sister, the latter an equally forceful advocate for the workers.[89] The three-week campaign ultimately led to Gandhi's first hunger strike. Just as notably, it ended with a successful resort to arbitration, a form of redress that decades later would become institutionally incorporated into the post-colonial state.

Of course, there was no simple path from initial commitment to arbitration (or the mutual recognition of social antagonists) to successful outcome in a particular conflict, let alone long-term public policy.[90] To become institutionalized, it likely needed both a context and a catalyst. The idea thus utterly failed to get off the ground in a country without either dingoes or a mahatma.

Chapter 5

Coming of Age in Internationalist Times

I awoke in a new world, with new viewpoints, new
aspirations and a dazzling view of the new and wonderful
work to do. All the universe pulsated with new life that
swept away the last vestige of the mists of creed and dogma
and the old ideas and beliefs.

—Kate Richards O'Hare, 1902

American socialists at the turn of the twentieth century certainly thought
they had more important matters in mind than focusing on personal identity. As Pauline Newman, who as an eight-year-old began working at the
Triangle Shirtwaist Company in 1901, later recalled of her entry into the
union and socialist movements, "All we knew was the bitter fact that after
working 70 or 80 hours in a seven-day week, we did not earn enough to
keep body and soul together."[1] Yet Joseph Schlossberg, who was also working in New York City sweatshops by the time he was thirteen, well recognized that his move from experience to political activism had been
mediated by a period of instruction and ultimately the acquisition of a
new group identity. As the future garment union leader remembered, "The
spokesmen, the interpreters of our grievances . . . brought with them from
the land of persecution high idealism and youthful enthusiasm. They were
Socialists."[2] Those drawn to the socialist movement like Newman and
Schlossberg anticipated nothing less than revolution, and all of them believed that they were remaking the world around them in significant ways.

In retrospect, we can also see that the young radicals who populated the
ranks of socialist, anarchist, and/or syndicalist groups like the Socialist
Party of America and the Industrial Workers of the World had been born

into a special time. They encountered an intellectual, political, and even spiritual world of heretofore unsurpassed international and cosmopolitan influences. The economic dislocations of worldwide capitalist development put people as well as ideas in motion as never before. However fraught with internal division and contradiction, the socialist message placed the idea of worker power at the top of its agenda. It also emboldened its followers with a heady internationalism, an assumption that workers the world over were cooperating in a common endeavor to replace production for profit with a social system more geared to human needs.[3]

As such, for a period of years (roughly coincident with what sociologist Daniel Bell called the "golden age of American socialism," 1902 to 1912) American-born as well as immigrant activists drew confidently from a global index of political and social thought, much like their industrialist counterparts.[4] It was a period when the perennial Socialist presidential candidacy of Eugene V. Debs crested with 6 percent of the national vote, three hundred socialist newspapers (including thirteen dailies) circulated across the country, and over a thousand socialist candidates took office, including 56 mayors. No doubt, Bell declared, "the voice of socialism was being heard in the land."[5]

Just how did individuals meld such world-transformative ideals with their own personal imperatives and ambitions and indeed with their own changing experience? Education both formal and informal, travel and migration, work and professional life, faith and philosophy, and romance—all pointed for many in a common direction. The political radicalism of the era entailed an intellectual expansiveness and a generational coming-of-age all at once: hence, we might call the mixture socialist identity politics.[6]

One of the most enduring comments about American socialists is Bell's judgment, meant as a requiem, that they were "*in* but not *of* the world." Bell, in turn, was invoking Max Weber's categorical distinction between a loyalty to "conscience" (or dedication to principle) and adherence to "responsibility" (or necessary compromises) entailed in a life of serious political engagement. Bell, himself a former socialist partisan, concluded that the American movement "could never resolve but only straddle the basic issue of either accepting capitalist society, and seeking to transform it from within . . . , or becoming the sworn enemy of that society."[7] To be sure, Bell's logic was quickly subjected to serious challenge. At least until World War I, there was little sign that American socialists were any more fixated on abstract principle over pragmatic politics than their European comrades.[8]

In a sense outside Bell's intended meaning, the alleged dreaminess of the socialists may yet be recovered as a useful category of historical analysis. For American socialists were not only adopting a vision, or as some would have it a creed, different from that which they had inherited and from that of most of their peers. It was more that they were *self-consciously* identifying with new and even foreign doctrines: indeed the very internationalist dimension of the socialist culture was for many one of its most compelling features. Even those who sought to mask such foreign and cosmopolitan connections went to self-conscious lengths to do so. In short, socialism at both the political and intellectual level was a multicultural and cosmopolitan enterprise and one that enveloped its adherents in a heady if ultimately frustrated search for transcendence from the here and now.

Rather than being removed from the world, American socialists, it might be fairer to say, lived in *several worlds*, a condition that regularly connected them to ideas, people, and movements beyond U.S. borders. In this respect, they shared a characteristic with cosmopolitan businessmen like Andrew Carnegie, whom we visited in Chapter 2. Also in this respect the early socialists may have served as harbingers of a latter day citizenry—today's era of globalization and transnational culture—even if today's radicals have yet to fashion anything like the common political umbrella of their progenitors.

The process had begun before the turn of the century. Like other budding social scientists of the era, twenty-four-year-old graduate student Florence Kelley had pursued a German path to history and social theory, in her case at the University of Zurich in the mid-1880s. There, she would recall, "among students from many lands, was the philosophy of Socialism, its assurance flooding the minds of youth and the wage-earners with hope that, within the inevitable development of modern industry, was the coming solution."[9] Across three decades leading up to World War I, young people attracted to the ideas and politics of Europe had formed a class of fellow travelers of a literal variety. For those of at least middling means, moreover, the educational influence of travel—facilitated as it was by an era of cheap and (generally) safe steam travel—only added to an overall sense of adventure, and even lurking danger, encountered in stepping outside one's normal orbit. As Upton Sinclair reported to *The Masses* literary editor Floyd Dell following a "charming" visit to Holland and Belgium in

1912, "I missed the *Titanic* by two days thank Heaven and I was so anxious beforehand to see how it would be on a new boat like that."[10]

The confidence of the early twentieth-century socialists was, of course, partly inherent in their ideological worldview. Whatever their internal differences, they were certain that history was moving in their direction. In keeping with the teleology (if not the strategy and tactics) of Karl Marx and Friedrich Engels's *Communist Manifesto* of 1848, the denizens of the Second International—founded by a gathering of twenty national delegations in 1889 in Paris—to which the newly formed Socialist Party of America (SPA) attached itself in 1901, were equally sure that they were part of a social evolutionary trend.[11]As influential but free-floating party intellectual Algie (or A. M.) Simons wrote in 1911:

> Like the commercial and plantation interests that brought about separation from Great Britain and formulated the Constitution, like the chattel slave owners that controlled the government and molded it for two generations, like the capitalist class that rode into power amid the blood and fraud and terror of civil war and Reconstruction, the working class has become in its turn the embodiment of the spirit of social progress, and is fighting for victory with a certainty of success before it.[12]

The SPA regularly attempted to square its positions with those of its European partners, especially the German Social Democratic Party, whose official or "orthodox" strategy was principally guided by Wilhelm Liebknecht, Karl Kautsky, and August Bebel. The orthodox position (defended in the United States by New York City leader Morris Hillquit, Pennsylvania labor chieftain James H. Maurer, and at least initially party standard-bearer Debs) posited a *political* path to socialist transformation, based on winning over both the labor movement and the voting public to a program of radical institutional change, at which point the socialist majority would assume control of both the political and, via nationalization, economic levers of power. In the meantime (i.e., prior to electoral majority), the advance of reform demands was to serve mainly as an *educational* tool, not a transitional path to power. This latter point was dutifully taken up by the American party: indeed, national party officials broke up incipient attempts (even expelling offending locals) that tried to cooperate with populists or create broader "labor party" formations.[13]

Beyond the tenets of party orthodoxy, American comrades in the steadily if still relatively slow-growing socialist political movement in the United
States took solace from truly dramatic gains overseas at the turn of the
century. From its regular "Socialism Abroad" column, *International Socialist Review* editor Simons thus exulted after collecting reports from Austria,
England, Italy, Denmark, and Japan (among other centers) in 1901, "Like
some famous monarchs, we socialists can proudly point to the fact that the
sun never sets in our realm."[14] And just as attuned (and generally deferen-
tial) to European advances was the headline in Victor Berger's center-right
Milwaukee Leader in January 1912, "Red Wave Sweeps All of Germany."[15]

The German-stamped "scientific socialism" favored by the Second
International was not the only well-developed body of thought that drew
recruits to the movement. For one, as other historians have well noted,
late nineteenth-century American writers like Lawrence Gronlund and
Edward Bellamy had previously assimilated socialist theories of economic
development into popular utopian political narratives.[16] In addition, as
events in Chicago in 1886 (and later in Berkman's assassination attempt
on Frick at Homestead in 1892) demonstrated, an anarchist tradition (associated in Europe and Russia with Mikhail Bakunin and Peter
Kropotkin) had successfully married itself, partly by way of the direct
immigration of Johann Most, to a native Garrisonian and John Brown–
derived tradition of political terrorism and moral action.[17] Even more
influential, in terms of electoral appeal, was likely the crossover from
populism to socialism.[18] Ethnic nationalisms, beginning with Irish radicalism and extending through their Yiddish and Finnish counterparts,
also regularly criss-crossed socialist political culture. The appeal of an
increasingly class-inflected and politically sharp-tongued Christian socialism must also be given its due in the contemporary swirl of political and
cultural influence. In addition, from the fringes of a white-dominated,
discriminatory political culture (even on the Left), African American
socialists raised the image of the New Negro. Finally, an upheaval in gender relations, or perhaps more exactly an assertion by feminist women
(and a number of male allies) of a new socialist-feminist ideal of love and
marriage also propelled the movement forward.

Rather than stacked up like separate college course credits, these ideological influences unfolded, and often intersected, in the course of individual lives, a point which returns us to the question of political identity
formation. But there was another, heretofore unemphasized, aspect of the

early twentieth-century socialist movement. One of the most striking qualities about a survey of American socialist notables is the youth of most of the movers and shakers. In the list of 60 movement leaders or otherwise prominent figures assembled from the secondary literature and grouped in Table 1, according to their ages at the point of takeoff of the movement—the vast majority (upward of 70 percent) at the beginning of the period were no more than "young adults," or no more than thirty-two years of age. Indeed, Eugene V. Debs, at forty-five, was already something of an elder statesman when he first ran for president on a socialist unity ticket in 1900. (In these years, miners' angel and peripatetic agitator Mother Jones stood out as a singular exception in the movement as a sexagenarian.) As such, for many of its adherents, socialism and the surrounding welter of reform thought and practices beckoned as a kind of experiment to young lives in various transitions— from servile work situations to independent unionism, from farms and small towns to cities, from Europe to America, from university studies to the professions, from racial outcast to proletarian inclusion, as well as (for women) from dependent helpmate to assertive free spirit.

Now, let us look more closely at some of the key players, with both the age factor and transnational influences foremost in mind. A. M. Simons offers a good example of the effect of international connections on the making of a moderate socialist. Son of a struggling farm family in Sauk County, Wisconsin, Simons had studied with both Frederick Jackson Turner and Richard T. Ely at the state university in Madison and graduated at twenty-five in 1895 with honors in economics. After two years of settlement house connections in Cincinnati and Chicago (including a survey of the stockyards district on which Upton Sinclair, author of *The Jungle*, would keenly rely), Simons repudiated "charity" work in favor of revolutionary agitation as writer and editor within the Socialist Labor Party, an effort for which he was soon joined in marriage with his childhood friend, schoolteacher May Wood. Quickly embroiled (like so many other SLP members) in factional turmoil, the Simonses suffered a personal tragedy when their eighteen-month-old son swallowed a lethal dose of poison from a medicine cabinet. As balm to their bereavement, a group of old settlement house friends, including Jane Addams and William English Walling, raised funds to send the couple to Europe. A generally restorative trip also contained something of a political revelation in their encounter with the pragmatic, nonsectarian socialist movement in Belgium. Encompassing farm cooperatives, craft unions, and municipal reform programs—all anathema

Table 1. Socialist Activists Age Chart (age in 1900)

Movement elders

Irons, Martin	73	Wayland, J. A.	46
Jones, "Mother" Mary	63	Debs, E. V.	45
Morgan, Thomas J.	52	Meitzen, E. O.	45
De Leon, Daniel	48	Winchevsky, Morris	44
Hagerty, Rev. Thomas J.	48	Mills, Walter Thomas	44
Parsons, Lucy	47		

Middle-aged

Kelley, Florence	41	Rauschenbusch, Walter	39
Kerr, Charles H.	40	Scudder, Vida	39
Berger, Victor	40	Herron, George	38
Cahan, Abraham	40	Maurer, James H.	36

Younger adults

Du Bois, W. E. B.	32	Spargo, John	24
Hillquit, Morris.	31	Simons, May Wood	24
William ("Big Bill") Haywood	31	Saint John, Vincent	24
Simons, A. M.	31	London, Jack	24
Goldman, Emma	31	O'Hare, Kate Richards	23
Trautman, William	31	O'Hare, Frank	23
Hickey, Tom	31	Walling, Anna Strunsky	23
Thompson, Carl	30	Walling, William English	23
Berkman, Alexander	30	Sinclair, Upton	22
Walden, May	30	Sanger, Margaret	21
Ameringer, Oscar	30	Stokes, Rose Pastor	21
London, Meyer	29	Reitman, Ben	21
Hall, Covington	29	Foster, William Z.	19
Stokes, J. G. Phelps	28	Meitzen, E. R.	19
Lunn, George R.	27	Korngold, Ralph	18
Conger, Josephine	25	Harrison, Hubert	17
Schlossberg, Joseph	25	Eastman, Max	17

Children

Thomas, Norman	16	Owen, Chandler	11
Dell, Floyd	13	Flynn, Elizabeth Gurley	10
Reed, John	13	Fraina, Louis	8
Haldeman-Julius, Marcet	13	Waldman, Louis	8
Haldeman-Julius, Emanuel	11	Newman, Pauline	7
Randolph, A. Philip	11		

to SLP purists—the Belgian success story made a permanent political mark on the American couple.

Soon, Simons was collaborating with SLP dissidents and the Social Democratic circle around Debs to form the new Socialist Party of America. As the first editor of the Charles Kerr-owned *International Socialist Review* in Chicago, he tried to explain and defend the major tenets of Second International thinking to a U.S. audience, while wryly acknowledging the challenge of applying "German metaphysics to English economic history with a French vocabulary."[19] Pursuing their educational outreach, Algie and May briefly formed the entire faculty at socialist Ruskin College in Glen Ellyn, Illinois, before Algie concentrated on his own publishing and writing efforts at the Chicago *Daily Socialist* (1904–1910). Even though he attended the IWW inaugural convention in 1905, Simons's extended engagement with electoral initiatives inexorably pushed him "rightward" within the SPA until in 1913 he joined the staff of Victor Berger's "revisionist" *Milwaukee Leader*, a position he would maintain until December 1916, when he resigned from the paper to attack his staunchly antiwar former colleagues, and much of the party hierarchy, for pro-German sympathies. At the same time, he began advocating for a more ideologically diffuse "labor" party on the lines of the British model, a position that had always been anathema to the "revisionist" as well as "orthodox" factions of the SPA.[20]

If Simons's career generally marked a course within the party on both international and domestic grounds from Left to Right, others identified more wholeheartedly with the appeal of the movement's Left Opposition centered on the IWW or "Wobblies." Among the former was William "Big Bill" Haywood. Joining his stepfather in the silver mines of Nevada as early as age fifteen, Haywood was soon drawn to the workplace militancy of the Western Federation of Miners (WFM) and a political ideology that quickly gravitated from populism to revolutionary socialism.[21] In 1905 Haywood and WFM president Charles Moyer—surrounded by a motley crew of older radicals including Lucy Parsons, Mother Jones, Daniel De Leon, and Debs—chartered the IWW in Chicago as a direct repudiation of both the AFL and go-slow municipal socialism. Rather, declaring themselves the Continental Congress of the Working Class, the meeting openly committed itself to "class struggle, having in view no compromise and no surrender" with the object of "emancipation of the working class from the slave bondage of capitalism."[22]

Naturally enough, Haywood and his supporters preferred to play on the movement's indigenous roots—in part by way of contrast with the

European or otherwise more formal bearing of other socialist and trade union leaders. "Syndicalism," he said, "is just the simple, beautiful gospel of us folks that work for a living" (or, in alternate wording "socialism with its working clothes on"). Similarly, Thomas J. Hagerty, a suspended Roman Catholic priest perhaps most responsible for the wording of the Wobbly preamble, insisted that it be written "in the plain, everyday language of the man in overalls."[23] Underscoring the significance and controversy over the appropriate representation of the working class, the opening of the Socialist Party's 1912 convention in Indianapolis was delayed over the question of whether the welcoming host himself had permission to address the meeting in overalls. Although an initial poll of delegates sustained the suggestion, the speaker, bowing to the wishes of the party's National Executive Committee, ultimately appeared in "plain, ordinary bourgeois pants."[24] The Socialist Party, the gesture seemed to say, preferred cosmopolitan to home-spun standards of thought.

Despite its native bluster, the IWW, like its factional counterparts, owed much to transatlantic influence. With roots in discussions of a general strike dating to the Socialist First International in the 1860s and most powerfully represented by the French Confédération Génerale du Travail (CGT) at the turn of the century, syndicalism was a widespread international movement by the time of the IWW takeoff. Brewery workers' leader and IWW secretary-treasurer William Trautmann, the New Zealand-born son of German parents, thus actively corresponded with CGT editor Émile Pouget about setting up an organization on "French" principles.[25] Going even farther in the French direction, young syndicalist (and future Communist Party leader) William Z. Foster argued in vain with IWW leader Haywood at the CGT headquarters in Paris that American labor radicals should reenter AFL unions and "bore from within."[26] Similarly, one of the most acute minds among American would-be Bolsheviks, Louis Fraina, once a devotee of De Leon, deepened his thinking via connection to the Dutch militant Anton Pannekoek.[27] Emphasizing the absolute autonomy and capacity of workers qua workers to transform their societies at the place of production, syndicalists were barred from the Second International by a "pledge of faith in political action"—though not in the United States, where, at least until Haywood's expulsion from the NEC in 1912, an ambivalent rhetorical passage about joint political and industrial action in the Wobbly preamble kept them just within the zone of ideological acceptability.[28]

Many who would harken to post-1900 syndicalism had cut their political teeth in an earlier decade of immigrant radicalism, symbolized by Chicago's Haymarket tragedy of 1886. There the "Chicago Idea" of confronting capital and its police agents through the organized body of trade unionists had rallied an influential sector of German anarchists (who veered away from the individualism of better-known anarchist Johann Most's "propaganda of the deed") as well as native-born rebels like 1877 strike leader Albert Parsons.[29] The prosecution and martyrdom of the Haymarket defendants that scared off many of the labor movement's respectable supporters only emboldened its more marginal elements, like Haywood's hard-rock miners or Mother Jones herself, to embrace an international spirit of resistance.

Sixteen-year-old Emma Goldman, for example, a rebellious Russian-Jewish child who had only been in the United States for four months when, in Rochester, New York, she learned of the Haymarket events, determined to act on anarchist ideals nourished since her earlier reading of Nikolai Chernyshevsky's 1863 novel *What Is to Be Done?*[30] Soon she was attending German Socialist Club meetings as well as following news of the Haymarket trials in the pages of Most's *Freiheit* while working in garment factories. Within three years, after twice marrying and divorcing the same man and continuing to quarrel bitterly with her parents, she found her way to New York City's anarchist circle. There, she would meet nineteen-year old Alexander Berkman, and together they would plot their own revenge against Henry Clay Frick for the destruction of the union at Pennsylvania's Homestead steel works.[31]

A youthful quest for commitment partly explains the couple's actions in these years. As Berkman would later describe his own search for masculine self-realization, "Could anything be nobler than to die for a grand, sublime Cause? Why, the very life of a true revolutionary has no other purpose, no significance whatever, save to sacrifice it on the altar of the beloved People. And what could be higher in life than to be a true revolutionist? It is to be a *man*, and complete MAN."[32] About her arrival in New York City at age twenty, Goldman would remember in opening her 1931 memoir: "All that had happened in my life until that time was now left behind me, cast off like a worn-out garment."[33]

There was no doubt about the Left Opposition's romantic appeal. The dramatic stance of the Wobblies, for example, quickly attracted seventeen-year-old Elizabeth Gurley Flynn. Dissatisfied with the merely social-democratic leanings of her parents and harking back to the insurgent tradition of grandparents involved in the Irish Rebellion of 1798, Flynn was on a soapbox at sixteen, and within a year, moved by speeches from Debs and De Leon, she had not only joined the Wobblies but married a Wobbly organizer and attended the movement's third convention in Chicago as a delegate.[34] Wobbly idealism was perhaps at its height during the Paterson, New Jersey, silk workers' strike of 1913, in which twenty-three-year old Flynn and twenty-six-year-old journalist John Reed organized outside support. Jailed for disturbing the peace, Reed questioned his fellow prisoners, as subsequently captured by historian Helen C. Camp:

> Reed asked a young Jewish worker, "What nationalities stick together on the picket line?" Holding up a clenched fist the man answered, "T'ree great nations—Italians, Hebrews an' Germans . . ." "But how about the Americans?" Jack pressed him. The men standing in a cluster around the burly young man from Oregon broke into slow smiles. "Mericans no lika fight!" a young Italian blurted out. "Not all like dat," another prisoner interrupted. "BeegBeel, he 'Merican . . . Miss Flynn, 'Merican. *Good!*"[35]

Within the Socialist Party itself, many young recruits swayed back and forth between the appeals of its Right and Left factions. Ralph Korngold, a writer of Dutch-Polish parentage who had emigrated to the United States in 1903 at twenty-one as a correspondent for the Amsterdam daily, *De Telegraaf* and had already established himself three years later as an SP organizer in Arizona, quickly began offering commentary in the English-language socialist press on the strengths and weaknesses of the American movement. Unlike in Europe (or in certain German- and Finnish-language locals that he observed in the United States), the American Party, for all its ideological huffing, argued Korngold, was doing little of tangible "benefit" for its members. Indeed, by this indicator, the IWW, he suggested, was making more of a difference for its members than the SP. By 1910, however, as associate editor under A. M. Simons at the *Chicago Daily Socialist*, Korngold stumped with Carl Sandburg for the election of Emil Seidel as first socialist mayor of Milwaukee. Even as Korngold was pulled from left to right (leaving the Party and ultimately taking up a business career after World War I), the notes of his second wife, Piri Korngold, indicate that he always kept a photo of the revered Debs on his bedroom wall.[36] Like Korngold, Simons and another former SLP firebrand, British immigrant John Spargo, also moved to the more moderate end of the Party as they grew older.

Outside formal Socialist International and Wobbly circles, at least three other ideological centers exerted significant influence on the socialist movement's young rank and file. First, no discussion of the period's socialist culture is complete without some accounting for the populist-to-socialist nexus.[37] As old Knight of Labor and Southwest Strike veteran Martin Irons declared in a schoolish metaphor only months before he died in 1900: "Populists are juniors; socialists are seniors."[38] Yet, particularly in the Southwest, where the Socialist Party ultimately scored its best electoral results outside several New York City assembly districts, the cultural as well as intellectual borrowing was unmistakable. Among the regular features of the socialist "encampments" on the Southern Plains, Bavarian-born Oklahoma organizer Oscar Ameringer would later remember the "Socialist songs, usually of Populist origin" but with familiar melodies like "Onward Christian Soldiers."[39]

Nationally, the ideological matriculation of which Irons spoke was most prominently associated with party standard-bearer Eugene V. Debs and the publishing estate around Julius A. Wayland. Both these Hoosier socialist elders had come of age in a period of fierce Midwest party competition among Republicans and Democrats. Solidly Republican by upbringing, Wayland, drawing on entrepreneurial talents that would long serve him well, at twenty-three was already running a Democratic county newspaper in Missouri. By 1882, he had reconnected to a Republican press outlet in the manufacturing town of Pueblo, Colorado, but just in time to get caught up in western mining and railroad wars. Backing the rising populist movement and making money at the same time (spreading publications as well as shrewd mineral investments), Wayland returned to the Midwest, following intense self-directed reading in 1893 with an eclectic left-wing populist stance that he dubbed the "One Hoss Philosophy." Projected through two prominent and nationally circulated newspapers—*Coming Nation* (1893–1895) and *Appeal to Reason* (established 1895, with three-quarters of a million readers by 1912)—Wayland's publications initially supported a cooperative colony in Ruskin, Tennessee, and ultimately served as the quasi-official propaganda and campaign apparatus for Debsian socialism.[40] All told, as historian Elliott Shore notes, "The *Appeal* and Debs were made for each other. They shared a utopian outlook and a sentimental vision for the coming of socialism. Their positions were sufficiently flexible to hide any disagreements for a long spell."[41]

Although determinedly trained on a public inherently skeptical of "socialist" messages and self-consciously folksy in style, Wayland's philosophy was hardly provincial or narrowly nationalistic in inspiration. Personally enamored of the works of British critic John Ruskin (whose own ten-year career as a newspaper editor served him as a model), Wayland relayed Ruskin's warnings of the "pillage of the laborer by the idle" in a three-column feature in the inaugural issue of the *Coming Nation*.[42] More generally, the socialist vernacular press in the nation's heartland—including the *Appeal* in Kansas, *National Rip-Saw* (St. Louis), and *The Rebel* (Hallettsville, Texas)—regularly coordinated with Charles Kerr in Chicago and Wilshire's publishing house to spread translations of European socialist classics.[43]

Among Wayland's most ardent "converts" were Kate Richards and Frank O'Hare, both twenty-four when they met in 1901 at Wayland's International School of Socialist Economy, located above a furniture store in Girard, Kansas. Both from Midwestern working-class backgrounds (indeed, Kate had already forsaken a teaching career to work as a machinist in her father's unionized shop, while Frank had first encountered socialist reading materials while working at a St. Louis hardware store), it reportedly took all of four days before romance and intention to marry blossomed between them. As Kate would later muse, "Do you remember that moonlight night when the snow creaked beneath your feet and all the world was radiant with its frost jewels on, do you remember that someone held your hand to keep it warm, how heartbeats smothered voices but without the spoken word you knew for the first time love's young dream?" Under the *Appeal's* canopy, socialism also swept Kate off her feet:, "I awoke in a new world, with new viewpoints . . . and a dazzling view of the new and wonderful work to do." Within months, the O'Hares were married at Wayland's Girard home by the school's director and popular socialist orator Walter Thomas Mills; the following half-dozen years would bless them with four children, including twins Eugene and Victor, after the socialist icon.[44]

Yet, even for the nation's best-known socialist, the pathway from inherited values to a Marxist-inspired class analysis of industrializing American society was hardly a smooth one. As his biographer Nick Salvatore sensitively details, Debs stepped gingerly and somewhat awkwardly into his new ideological and organizational shoes. At least through William Jennings Bryan's devastating presidential loss in 1896, for example, Debs's radicalism, although indirectly tapping socialist currents, remained more attached to "classless," "republican," and "populist" rhetorical moorings. Fending off Victor Berger's full embrace as late as 1897, Debs's still inchoate Social Democracy of America thus worried that an over-emphasis on class consciousness may "do mischief":

> [It] is a good servant but a bad master. Socialism is something more than a mere labor question. It is a demand for equalizing of burdens and an equalizing of benefits throughout the whole society. Class consciousness for the laboring man is safe where it is made a part of a high moral demand in the interests of society as a complete organism and not of one class only. . . . We must not make socialism obnoxious to the people.[45]

Where, then, to look for non-Marxist avenues to socialism? As Debs's own career well embodied, a labor-republican or left-wing populist critique might carry one a long way in the same direction. But Debs gestured toward an alternate, if often related, route when, in Newark, New Jersey, in 1897, he asked rhetorically, "What is Socialism?" and then answered "Merely Christianity in action. It recognizes the quality in men."[46] That Debs had himself long admired the atheistic rationalism of Gilded Age orator Robert Ingersoll suggests the complexity and ambivalence, not to mention opportunism, that accompanied his political quest.[47]

When it came to socialist mobilization, the role of religion truly worked itself out in mysterious ways. Conventionally—and this was taken almost as a truism in Europe—socialism beckoned as an antidote to specifically religious faith.[48] The picture, however, was decidedly more mixed in the United States. No doubt, a directly anti-religious sentiment could be found in the American movement as well. Naturalism and evolutionary science, in defiance of older revelatory faiths, cushioned the world view of many a budding socialist.[49] A fetching example is Floyd Dell, socialist editor and writer who grew up in a "vaguely Christian" working-class family in the river town of Quincy, Illinois. Looking back, Dell identified his initial act of independence in "an intellectual recognition of the falsity of the claims made in behalf of the Bible as a true record. There was in my school histories the story of the Spanish Inquisition and other churchly tyrannies. It required only the slightest use of the mind to perceive that all religions were superstitious and tyrannical." By sixteen, Dell and his best friend had decided that "atheism was not enough" and had taken the further step to declare themselves socialists. Still, the connection between political radicalism and religious apostasy continued to play itself out. At twenty-two, Floyd and Margery Currey, from an Episcopalian family, chose to further flout convention with a wedding officiated by a rabbi in a ceremony memorialized by Dell's poem "Epithalamium": "For licensing we did not shirk / To Give two dollars to the clerk; / We gave a preacher proper trouble / Marking our singleness double;— / Would lovers all did emulate / Our true regard for Church and State!"[50]

The secularizing trend is perhaps best documented in the Jewish diaspora, where the move from "synagogue to socialism" often repudiated religious identity but usually in a communal setting—or as the Arbeter Ring's publication described this fraternal order: "purely secular, thoroughly Jewish."[51] The father of future Socialist Representative Meyer London, for instance, was "educated to be a rabbi," but turned "radical" and started a Yiddish printing shop on his arrival in New York in 1888 and was already an "extreme" socialist when Meyer migrated there three years later.[52] Similarly, for writer and long-time socialist publisher Abraham Cahan (unlike his more ethically challenged fictional character David Levinsky), commitment to the socialist cause was concomitant with an embrace of a more self-consciously scientific outlook on life more generally.[53] Socialism, Cahan believed, could take the place of religion for a new immigrant: "You will become a new person. Life will become for you broader, richer, higher, and more beautiful."[54]

Among the most determined of militant secularists was Daniel De Leon, born in Curaçao of a Spanish Dutch Jewish family. Though his parents were apparently well established in the Sephardic Caribbean community, Daniel turned defiantly away from his roots and dismissed all religion as mere superstition. A determined naturalism defined De Leon's worldview. Adapting the Darwinian struggle to the historical canvas, he took refuge in anthropologist Lewis Henry Morgan's "stage theory" of social development and—wedding Darwin, Spencer, and Morgan to Marx—waited impatiently for society's next revolutionary turn.[55] Yet his flight from Judaism, in particular, was more pointed, especially after the death of his first (Jewish) wife in childbirth while delivering stillborn twins. Soon, established in New York City and teaching political science at Columbia University, De Leon concocted a story of aristocratic, Spanish-Catholic, and Venezuelan origins. Remarried to a Kansas schoolteacher he met on a speaking tour in 1891,

De Leon fathered five more children, including "Genseric," reportedly after the Vandal king who made the pope kiss his toes.[56]

As a mark of communal deviation, if not open defiance, a forthright secularism also appealed to two of the leading members of the always tiny African-American contingent of Golden Age socialists.[57] W. E. B. Du Bois, for example, who would offer fleeting support for the Socialist Party as he emerged as the dominant voice of the Niagara movement by 1907, had more unequivocally made his spiritual retreat years before.[58] Although he was raised in a happy Congregationalist fellowship in Great Barrington, Massachusetts, a reaction against the conventional moral and theological policing he encountered on setting off for undergraduate study at Fisk University in 1885 set Du Bois on an "intellectual journey," according to biographer David Levering Lewis, "that would end, after a very short time, in serene agnosticism."[59]

Like Dell's, Du Bois's philosophical rambling proceeded apace, punctuated in his case by a formative two years of graduate study on a Slater Fund scholarship at the University of Berlin, studying with the eminent historical economists (or "socialists of the chair" as discussed in Chapter 3), Gustav von Schmoller and Adolph Wagner.[60] Historian Axel R. Schäfer carefully pursues the influence of figures like Schmoller on Du Bois's evolving thought. Like his mentors, Du Bois "regarded knowledge as culturally dependent and sought a postliberal communal ideal based on shared will and conscience, not simply on pragmatic interest." Drawing from his historicist training, Du Bois's early writings including *The Philadelphia Negro* (1899), notes Schäfer, "presented black institutions, morals, and manners primarily as containing the germ of the ethical self realization . . . that would lead to the development of a broader moral vision."[61] Yet, while imbibing a kind of Hegelian moral ontology, Du Bois was also refashioning his own political perspectives on both Germany and the United States. Straying beyond university walls, Du Bois not only expressed admiration for German state reforms but attended SPD meetings during his Berlin sojourn. Something of that critical influence, suggests Lewis, entered the famous Niagara "Credo" of 1904, wherein Du Bois declared that the race problem "was but the sign of growing class privilege and caste distinction in America, and not, as some fondly imagine, the cause of it." In the same year, while still hesitating to call himself a "socialist," he privately acknowledged "many socialistic beliefs" and voted for Debs on the presidential ticket.[62] Briefly a member of New York Local Number 1 and later, in 1917, serving on the executive committee of the Intercollegiate Socialist Society, Du Bois enjoyed an on-again, off-again relation to the party across the prewar years.[63]

Less formally educated than Du Bois but more of a Socialist Party stalwart until turning to a "race-first" approach in 1916, Hubert Harrison shared with his better-known comrade an early grounding in religious skepticism. Born to a poor, immigrant English-speaking mother on a rural estate in the Danish West Indies, Harrison emigrated to New York City as a seventeen-year old orphan in 1900. A strongly motivated autodidact who pursued a high school degree through night classes, Harrison ultimately landed a post office job, and then lost it when he ran afoul of the vaunted "Tuskegee Machine." In the meantime a postal worker study circle and later a literary club offered a venue for wide readings that centered on the cause of free thought, as organized around the rationalist, anti-religious New York *Truth Seeker*. As if to complete his rebellion from the twin institutional centers—the church and the Republican Party—of the black community, Harrison turned to socialism in 1911 and soon became one of the party's few paid African American organizers. In addition to a ready embrace of "science" in its social diagnoses, the party attracted Harrison on the basis of its seeming flexibility when it came to organizing marginal constituencies: he hoped (largely in vain as it turned out) to reproduce in the black community a "special approach" evident in the party's National Woman's Committee and ethnic-based Foreign Language Federations.[64]

Frustrated by 1916 with the indifference and worse he experienced at the hands of white party leaders, Harrison turned to a new project of what he interchangeably called "race-first" or "racial consciousness" politics. Interestingly, this split from socialist universalism was no retreat to intellectual provincialism, as Harrison explicitly called on the examples of the Swadeshi movement in India and Sinn Fein in Ireland. The following year Harrison's *Voice* enunciated what would soon be recognized as the New Negro sensibility, combining an assertion of race pride at home and internationalism abroad. Harrison's Pan-Africanism, soon trumpeted by Du Bois himself as well as the young radicals A. Philip Randolph and Chandler Owen, suggested that the geopolitical as well as demographic boundaries of an immigrant-centered movement were expanding beyond their original Euro-American base.[65]

For all the energy that some socialists spent attacking theology and the organized church, others happily accommodated their radical political convictions in an ardent faith-based identity. Taking its lead from Second International policy, the SPA's formal position on religion was agnostic. New York's "antireligious" Jewish leader Morris Hillquit publicly proclaimed, "The socialist movement is primarily an economic and political movement. It is not concerned with institutions of marriage and religion."[66]

However officially sanctioned, separation of church (or synagogue) and state did not accurately describe the motivation or de facto practice of many socialist rank and file. Thus, to the secular laws of social development adopted by the party, many American socialists readily grafted their own spiritual quests. This extended even to Yiddish-speaking socialists openly dismissive of traditional Jewish observance. Ukrainian-born Louis Waldman thus arrived in New York City at seventeen in 1909 "up to his ears in Talmud." After stints in a chandelier factory and as a cutter's apprentice, Waldman completed an undergraduate degree in engineering at Cooper Union in 1916 and was drafted that same year as a state assembly candidate on the socialist ticket. The dominant pattern among Jewish immigrant socialists, suggests historian Gerald Sorin, was not of self-hating assimilationists but of a "prophetic minority, responding to biblical norms of social justice, interpreted in a modern context."[67]

A left religious tendency was even more formally institutionalized among young Christians. As Milwaukee party stalwart and former Congregationalist minister Carl D. Thompson explained to a heartland audience in 1903, "socialism" was decidedly *not* "anarch[istic], atheistic, or hostile to the family." Rather, the movement declared religion a "private" matter, even as "there are multitudes of Socialists, like the writer, who see in Socialism the only possible program for realizing the ideals of Jesus . . . [which have] no place in the brutal, monopolistic system of today."[68] Perhaps best known for its World War I-inspired pacifist cadre (including Presbyterian minister and future presidential standard bearer Norman Thomas), "Christian socialism" proved a powerful nesting place within the broader movement dating to the late nineteenth century.

It was a tendency that appealed at once through subtle moral and theological arguments to middle-class youth like Richard T. Ely and Jane Addams (see Chapter 4), and through a more vernacular "socialist Jesus" gospel particularly to the party's agrarian rank and file.[69] An announcement for a pamphlet by *Appeal to Reason*'s associate editor A. W. Ricker on "The

Political Economy of Jesus" perhaps suggests the general tenor of such initiatives:

> For more than a thousand years prior to the birth of Jesus, the workers had been organized into Trades Unions, some of which had attained to international strength. At that time the working classes were rebellious and ready for revolt on account of their conditions. Jesus and his followers were a part of the working-class movement, and their first missionary work was chiefly among its members. . . . He was crucified by the ruling class because of his economic teachings. The early Christians practiced communism for three hundred years or until [Constantine].[70]

At least something of the power of this formation was suggested in William English Walling's left-wing, intramural fulmination in 1909 against the "German machine, Russian machine, the AFL machine, and the Christian Socialist machine."[71]

As with so many of the political and intellectual influences at the century mark, Christian socialism enjoyed strong transnational roots. To begin with, the "higher criticism" from which it sprouted had spread from a German theological base, defining a more open-ended or "liberal" disposition toward biblical interpretation across most American Protestant seminaries and denominations since the 1870s. Indeed, the fundamentalist counter-response apparent by World War I attacked its dominant rivals precisely for succumbing to "German barbarism" and the "German destructive criticism which has found its way into the religious and moral thought of our people as the conception and propaganda of the Reds have found their way . . . into civil and industrial life."[72]

In German theological circles, the unassuming scholar Albrecht Ritschl (1822–1889) laid tracks of ultimately widespread influence. Seeking to preserve the moral authority of the church within a larger culture of scientific advance, Ritschl argued that religion was less about facts than values. Identifying the values of Jesus as the essence of Christianity and the "embodiment of humanity's highest ideal," Ritschl pointed to the acts of the "living movement"—the Christian community—as the only pathway to the "Kingdom of God."[73]

The most prominent American Ritschlian was Walter Rauschenbusch, also the leading intellectual light in the Christian socialist movement.

Rauschenbusch, who in 1897 at thirty-six had followed his German immigrant father to the Rochester Theological Seminary, transformed Ritschl's 'Kingdom of God' imagery into a political imperative. Soon, from the ranks of Ely, Washington Gladden, and Josiah Strong, he emerged as the left-wing leader of the Social Gospel movement.[74] Although never a Socialist Party member, his voluminous and popular writings—especially *Christianity and the Social Crisis* (1907)—offered a most trenchant justification for socialist activism. Beginning his study with the Hebrew Prophets ("the beating heart of the Old Testament"), Rauschenbusch presented them as champions of the "poorer classes": "If anyone holds that religion is essentially ritual and sacramental; or that it is purely personal; or that God is on the side of the rich; or that social interest is likely to lead preachers astray; he must prove his case with his eye on the Hebrew prophets, and the burden of proof is with him."[75]As Rauschenbusch would elaborate in later works, capitalist property relations stood directly in the way of the Kingdom of God. Profit derived from the exploitation of labor, he declared in *Christianizing the Social Order* (1912), represented "a tribute collected by power." Rather than piecemeal reforms, a structural social readjustment was required: "Political democracy without economic democracy is an uncashed promissory note, a pot without the roast, a form without substance."[76]

International contacts and experiences advanced the thinking and practice of many young Christian socialists. Vida Scudder, for example, took advantage of a term at Oxford University following her graduation from Smith College, where she absorbed one of John Ruskin's final lecture series and came away a lifelong activist. "It was at Oxford that I woke up to the realities of modern civilization," she later recalled, "and decided that I did not like them." Born to a Congregationalist missionary in India who drowned while she was an infant, Scudder followed her mother into the Episcopal Church and remained an Anglo-Catholic in her religious beliefs even as she plotted an ideological juncture of Marxism and Christianity during a teaching career at Wellesley College.[77]

"Millionaire socialist" J. G. Phelps Stokes, meanwhile, fashioned an even more eclectic intellectual-political blend. An Episcopalian by birth, Phelps met and fell in love with Polish Jewish immigrant Rose Pastor in the course of his work with New York City's University Settlement. In the same period, Phelps joined the Vedanta Society, an outgrowth of Hindu reformer Swami Vivekananda's visit to the 1893 Chicago World's Fair and soon after sketched an inclusive philosophy of "Omniism," encompassing "word,

effort, deed, and life . . . devoted to the advancement of the welfare not merely
of Self, nor of Others, but of that Whole which embodies All." Marrying Rose
in an Episcopal ceremony in 1905 at which his officiating brother agreed to
strike the word "obey" from the vows, Phelps insisted that both bride and
groom were "Christians" yet open to different faiths. Phelps himself would
long cultivate an interest in the world's religions, even as he turned his immediate attentions to the socialist movement, including leadership of the Intercollegiate Socialist Society, until he split with Rose over World War I and
communism, their marriage ending in divorce in 1925.[78]

Sometimes, as proved the case with the most popular Christian socialist
of his day, international connections amounted less to an influence than a
safety valve. The third in a troika of Hoosier socialist leaders (just behind
Debs and Wayland in influence), George Herron presented a fiery and charis-
matic presence that made him (at least briefly) the perfect religious comple-
ment for heartland *Appeal to Reason* devotees. Born to poor Dutch Reformed
parents and believing that he had "never been without the inner consciousness of God's compelling and restraining presence," Herron first encountered
and embraced the Social Gospel while leading Congregationalist churches in
Minnesota and Iowa in the early 1890s. At first a private supporter of the
Socialist Labor Party and then openly campaigning for the party of Berger
and Debs, Herron offered a formidable public presence. Demanding a reconstruction of society on the standards of Jesus, Herron also unhesitatingly
excoriated institutional Christianity. "If I were to stand before any representative religious gathering in the land and there preach actual obedience to the
Sermon on the Mount, declaring that we must actually do what Jesus said,"
Herron expounded in 1899, "I would henceforth be held in disrepute by the
official religion that holds Jesus' name." [By contrast], "if the head of some
great oil combination, though it had violated every law of God and man . . .
were to stand before any representative religious gathering with an endowment check in his hand, he would be greeted with an applause so vociferous
as to partake of the morally idiotic."[79]

But it was not his political activity that ultimately marginalized Herron
as a force to be reckoned with. Widowed lumber baroness Mrs. Carrie D.
Rand had helped Iowa (later renamed Grinnell) College recruit Herron to
a chair in "Applied Christianity" in 1893, and college president George A.
Gates had backed his star professor in chartering *The Kingdom* as a leading
voice of social Christianity and co-founding the utopian Commonwealth
Colony in Georgia, 1896–1900, an experiment that actually spawned the

"social gospel" name. In the same period, the unhappily married Herron began cohabiting with Mrs. Rand's daughter (also named Carrie), news of which did not sit well with the surrounding community. Shortly after Mrs. Herron secured a divorce in 1901, George was deposed from both his Congregationalist ministry and his academic position. Soon he and Carrie married and, along with the older Mrs. Rand, moved to live off the Rand endowment (which they also used to charter the socialist Rand School in New York City) at an estate in Fiesole, Italy—a location that later made Herron an important conduit for wartime diplomacy from President Woodrow Wilson.[80]

As evident in both the Stokes and the Herron-Rand matches, politico-religious identities in the Progressive Era might well correlate with shifting gender roles and sexual mores. Indeed, given the deep connection of renewed suffrage and feminist organization with the rising employment of women outside the home, some overlap between the evolving women's rights and socialist movements was surely to be expected. In a now classic treatment, historian Mari Jo Buhle neatly distinguished German American (or immigrant) from "grass-roots" (or native American) origins within the developing socialist feminist tradition. In its crudest version, Second International orthodoxy (drawing, in particular, on August Bebel's 1883 *Women and Socialism*) positioned women within a mechanistic march of progress, wherein expanding industrial employment would serve as a progressive wedge to "lead women out of the narrow sphere of strictly domestic life to a full participation in the public life of the people."[81]

Equally limited in their own way, early native-born activists, rooted in the WCTU and suffrage organizations, initially posited socialism as an extension of "social purity," defending the family (and traditional gender roles) against ruination by capitalistic industrialization.[82] Encapsulating such attitudes, Kate Richards O'Hare addressed women primarily as helpmates to the true proletarian of the family: "If he wants to talk Socialism to you," she counseled in a 1902 column of the *Coming Nation*, "when you want to talk about the new dress you need, just forget about the dress for a little while. Put your whole heart and interest in what he is telling you, do your best to understand it; tell him how much it means to you and the babies."[83]

Before long, however, a new generation of socialist women and some men on both sides of the Atlantic began pressing up against the dual barriers of economic determinism and Victorian morality. In Germany, for example, thirty-four-year-old Clara Zetkin, otherwise an adherent of SPD orthodoxy, began articulating a woman-centered socialist agenda through the pages of *Die Gleichheit* in 1891[84] And at the 1910 Congress of the Second International in Copenhagen, the Second Conference of Socialist Women (out of which emerged International Women's Day) adopted an ambitious agenda: municipal services and educational programs for women, universal suffrage, lengthy maternity leaves, homes for single pregnant women, at-home obstetric care, day care centers and kindergartens, school-based medical and dental services and lunches, and national health care as well as state pensions for widows.[85]

By that time, American socialist women (speaking out in a variety of publications championed by J. A. Wayland's niece, Josephine Conger) were also directly linking the social provisioning of the family to women's political and sexual freedom.[86] May Simons Wood, for example, an elected delegate to the Copenhagen Congress, openly called for socialized housekeeping.[87] On the same subject, Charles Kerr's wife, May Walden, who wrote regularly in the pages of Chicago's *Daily Socialist*, suggested that in the interim wives should start economizing—"to have more time and money to fight capitalism"—with regard to home purchases: "choose what is durable and becoming, rather than that which is stylish." Moreover, with regard to household furniture, the socialist homemaker should "discard carpets for rugs that may be easily shaken," and "never select upholstered furniture."[88]

By the second decade of the twentieth century, as historian Christine Stansell reminds us, the French term "feminism" conjured up for both women and men on the cultural left the ideal of the New Woman—"not just a claim to the vote or to making mothers' roles in society more honored but rather to economic independence, sexual freedom, and psychological exemption from the repressive obligations of wifehood, neighborhood, and daughterhood—a jettisoning of family duties for a heightened female individualism."[89] Feminist identity came in different shapes and sizes. To adoring crowds in Greenwich Village and other urban centers, Emma Goldman contrasted the beauty of "free love" to the "insurance pact" of conventional marriage.[90] Yet, with equal political passion, in Girard, Kansas, Marcet Haldeman, Jane Addams's niece, married young Jewish-socialist journalist Emanuel Julius: as part of the ceremony both changed their names to Haldeman-Julius.[91] Meanwhile, among other young couples, Rose Pastor Stokes referred to her husband as her "comrade-lover," and immigrant Jewish poet Anna Strunsky exchanged marriage vows with well-to-do activist William English Walling in a Paris ceremony attended by Karl Marx's grandson Jean Longuet. Disdaining a religious service, Strunsky explained, "Our love is as free as the soul. We hold each other and will hold each other forever, by no force in the world except the force of love."[92] In a similar spirit of social innovation, birth control crusader Margaret Sanger initially expounded her ideas in a column entitled "What Every Girl Should Know" in the socialist *New York Call*; fittingly, her wisdom on sex education and women's health was subsequently recirculated as a pamphlet produced by the Haldeman-Julius Publishing Company in Girard, Kansas.[93]

Although generally unheralded, Walden, who separated from Kerr in 1904 at thirty-four and struggled thereafter to support a daughter as a single mother, may have gone as far as anyone outside the celebrity bohemian Goldman in elaborating the ideals of socialist feminism. As early as 1907, for example, she insisted in print that in the future women must be free to choose to establish homes of their own without depending on men in any economic way. "Marriage as we know it," she predicted, "will be an unknown institution belonging to the age of women's slavery," an era when they lacked "the right to their own bodies."[94] In 1913, playing off Walt Whitman's anticipation of the "best women" in *Chants Democratic*, Walden projected an image (never published) of "what womanhood will be like under Socialism." Cataloguing the insults, big and little, that ordinary women suffered every day, she imagined a time, "when we shall no longer drudge over wash-boards; when we shall not HAVE to cook individual meals; when the broom and the dust-pan shall be relics in the museum at which our children shall wonder; when members of the same household will not snarl at each other over petty grievances, for the cause of those grievances will be done away with." Women's liberation, she counseled, would necessarily banish "the brutal father, Capitalism . . . to be known nevermore. And the Universe will rejoice when told that the Democracy is a Woman-Child."[95]

The twin distinctions of American socialism in effectively reaching out to youth and a larger world ended with the Great War. Soon linked in contemporary minds with the Bolshevik Revolution, the war signaled a well-known watershed for the fortunes of the political Left.[96] Even as party hierarchs (together with the IWW) withstood the defections (and even experienced a temporary boost from anti-war voters) from AFL trade unionists and prominent pro-war intellectuals (including Simons, Walling, Spargo, and Haldeman-Julius), the party—with its leaders jailed and its communications soon stifled—ultimately suffered severely from wartime repression. Already tarred with the brush of disloyalty if not treason, American socialists confronted a further, polarizing set of political choices with the establishment of the Communist International (Comintern) in 1919. Quickly, the so-called Old Guard of the Socialist Party, recoiling at the revolutionism of its foreign-language federations (who likely now composed a majority of party members) suspended the federations, even as the Left Wing itself split bitterly into two "communist" parties, each begging for official recognition from Moscow.[97] By the end of 1919, the Socialist Party itself claimed little more than 25,000 members, a quarter of its size at the beginning of the year.[98]

Ironically, the two searing international events scattered a movement (and a surrounding culture) largely built up on international and transnational influences. One has but to dip into the established, deep historiography of the period to note how a significant fraction of the prewar crowd (including Reed, Goldman, Haywood, Rose Stokes, Foster, Fraina, and Gurley Flynn) rushed, at least initially, into the arms of the Soviets, while an alternate stream (including Spargo, Max Eastman, Algie and May Wood Simons, and Lewis Corey [formerly Louis Fraina]) moved more or less quickly to abandon the Left altogether. Many socialist activists, to be sure, were caught in the middle, maintaining their convictions but looking for any port in a storm. A few, including Texan E. R. Meitzen, Louisiana-born Covington Hall, and the peripatetic Walter Thomas Mills ultimately found a home in new movements like the North Dakota Non-Partisan League.[99]

Others experienced a rockier journey. One of the more poignant paths was traced by Kate O'Hare, as artfully recounted by her biographer, Sally M. Miller. Imprisoned for fourteen months during the war in the Missouri State Penitentiary (where she briefly shared a cellblock with Emma Goldman), O'Hare emerged as a prison reformer and vociferous critic of the convict-lease system she had observed up close. Over the coming decade, however, the strains of maintaining a socialist newspaper (the *National Rip Saw*), a short-lived New Llano Cooperative Colony in Louisiana, and associated Commonwealth College in Arkansas led to the breakup of the long-running O'Hare political and domestic partnership. By the mid-1920s, Kate's traditionalist moral values were openly contested by the "ultra-modernists of the faculty and student body" at Commonwealth, and she soon left the school.[100] By 1931, she had remarried a businessman and moved to California. Politically, as she wrote to Eugene Debs's surviving brother Theodore, she now saw few signs of hope: "When I look around I can see no organization or movement that seems to offer a satisfactory field for my services. The organized labor movement seems to me slowly dying of dry rot, and the poor, pitiful . . . Socialist Party is to me a heart-breaking tragedy. So [in words that eerily recall Kate's original advice to young socialist wives] I cook my husband's meals and darn his socks and pamper him shamefully." Happily for Kate, 1930s social unrest and the New Deal opened a final chapter of fulfilling political engagement, helping to manage Upton Sinclair's EPIC campaign for governor in 1934 and later serving in the D.C. office of a Progressive Party Representative from Wisconsin.[101]

In addition to organizational upheavals, war-related embitterment hit hard against the culture of solidarity that had attracted younger recruits to the labor and socialist movements in the first place. For Americans who had looked to German, French, or British models of organization, the out-right enmity among former "comrades" easily bred disillusionment.[102] There was a practical side, as well, to the diminution of internationalism. From the U.S. side, severe barriers against immigration went up, and a new cluster of red tape complicated even temporary sojourns. As Joseph Schlossberg, looking back from 1935 on his own immigration in the 1880s remembered: "The freedom of movement was much less restricted then than now[;] passports and visas were almost unknown. "[103]

But age itself was also a factor. Beyond the changing political context, personal identities wrapped in youthful ideals almost inevitably encoun-tered a more complicated life course. Bell's "golden age of [American] socialism," at least for a substantial leadership cohort, was, as we have seen, very much a youth movement. Although the actors sought tangible goals and fought live battles with real and sometimes tragic consequences, they were also often experimenting with life, self-consciously extending their reach across geographic as well as intellectual, cultural, and even ethnoracial boundaries unknown to previous generations. As such, their world likely impresses us now at once with its exuberance and its naiveté.

The impression of an unstable "political life stage" is particularly acute when examining the activists' private lives. To take perhaps the most obvi-ous case, by 1910, forty-one-year old Emma Goldman and her thirty-one-year-old anarchist lover Ben Reitman found it hard to follow free love prin-ciples and maintain personal trust at the same time. Fiercely jealous, Emma confessed to Ben that "love is beginning to be a mockery to me," while, Ben, strangled with guilt, damned "civilization" "if it means a man must stop and think when he desires another man's wife."[104]

Other formerly freewheeling spirits similarly stumbled toward sobriety. As former *Masses* managing editor Floyd Dell (who drifted slowly from both socialism and feminism to the mental hygiene movement), later recalled, "The world of forward-looking ideas, once unified in my mind under the aegis of Socialism, was splitting up and scattering in different directions—and I had to keep in sympathy with the most diverse and irreconcilable conceptions of the Future, in order to feel that it was a Future in which human beings could live and enjoy life."[105]

As if to ward off disillusionment, some socialists had early on adopted a more clear-eyed distinction between public and private demonstrations of good faith. An exchange of correspondence between Charles Kerr and May Walden five years after their separation is instructive here. Having been approached by their fourteen-year old daughter Katharine for supplementary school supplies, Charles balked at exceeding the $20 a month child subsidy that was part of the divorce settlement; rather, he invited both mother and daughter to "keep all the money received" from selling copies of the *International Socialist Review* on which "my ability to supply money and Katharine's prospects for the future are largely dependent." May was not amused.

It is quite useless for you to become irritated over this and of supplying Katherine's necessities. Your obligation to her does not cease at twenty dollars a month nor when she is eighteen, just because it is so stated in the [decree]. I shall expect you to pay for the music lessons, her extra carfare, and her clothes and school supplies; the natural father of an only child could do no less.

At least as far as May Walden was concerned, the personal had provided an unwanted corrective to the political: in short, she could no longer take her ex-husband's project seriously: "my knowledge of the growth of the Socialist movement and of the *Review* leads me to the belief that its success does not at all depend upon what I can do to help the latter along, but . . . more upon your ability to hypnotize the people into thinking your company is a good thing."[106]

Disenchantment from youthful idealism surely knows no particular political domicile. The challenges and frustrations experienced by the mostly young socialists might thus have been subsequently passed off as but an early fork in the road of a swelling political alternative—a period of personal testing that ultimately redounded to the strength of the movement as a whole as it learned from mistakes and forged a more effective industrial, electoral, and cultural strategy. If only they had entered the war with a stronger, working-class base. If only they had earlier countenanced greater electoral cooperation with nonsocialist forces. If only. The problem for American socialism was that there was no second act. Like other youthful political upsurges that a 1960s-reared historian well recognizes, this one largely dispersed before it grew up. That left the individuals involved to fashion a myriad of pathways of their own. By and large that meant finding not only new instruments of social transformation but also new sources of group identity.

Epilogue

It is common practice among history editors (including mine) to subject their authors to an ultimate taste test: how does the story you are telling connect to the world we are living in today? We might call it the Then/Now Imperative. What follows is an impressionistic, selective response to that connective prod.

According to the current scholarly wisdom, the leap from the Gilded Age to the present is facilitated by a few well-spaced conceptual spotters. Depicted in the broadest strokes, after a halting Progressive Era start, American society finally broke free of the constraints of its Gilded Age prejudices, when, beginning in the 1930s, it created the New Deal welfare state framework—accomplished via mass mobilization and seminal regulatory reforms, and sustained by the long-term economic growth wave unleashed by World War II. Then, as first signaled by the OPEC oil embargo of the early 1970s and accelerated by the Reagan-Bush policies of deregulation, the effects of "globalization" or a competitive world economy gradually undercut New Deal era gains and plunged American workers and their families back into a Second Gilded Age, exacerbated since 2008 by the Great Recession.

In keeping with this progression, today's readers can relate to the original Gilded Age precisely because it highlights so many themes of our own era. As historian Steve Fraser pithily phrased it in early 2008, "Crony capitalism, inequality, extravagance, Social Darwinian self-justification, blame-the-victim callousness, free-market hypocrisy: thus it was, thus it is again!"[1] Yet, the very logical (if inevitably simplified) framing of the two-Gilded Ages model begs one big question: how did it come to pass? How could Americans, having long since jettisoned the laissez-faire doctrines of a William G. Sumner and the chaos of unplanned growth, allow themselves to fall back into some of the most notorious of the country's old vices?

One response might be that the New Deal—especially its Wagner Act endorsement of collective bargaining together with its multipronged expansion of a national welfare state—was an aberration, or what one recent commentary calls a "Long Exception." In short, absent the trauma of the Great Depression, such thinking goes, the default position of the American social-political order generally veers toward "Gilded Age" individualism, business dominance, and fragmentation of the dispossessed in a way that ordinarily makes it impossible to maintain a powerful labor movement and advance a program for democratic social welfare. The fact that as these words are written, massive resistance is still threatened in the name of "individual freedom" against even a national health program dependent on private insurance companies would seem to offer further support for the assumption of a deeply conservative political consciousness as the normative core of American Exceptionalism.[2]

Yet, I can think of three reasons to resist such thinking. First, as I have argued throughout these essays, "American" developments, rather than being imprisoned in a domestic set of givens, were regularly tied to the dynamics of a larger world order. Thus, even as we may speak (as in the Introduction) of a historical ebb and flow in the *intensity* of the transnational flow of people, goods, and ideas, we should never assume an isolated or entirely autonomous terrain of national action. A recent treatment of the New Deal by political scientist Ira Katznelson emphasizes the degree to which a period marked by depression and fascist or communist dictatorships was haunted by transnational "fear" of the possible collapse of all liberal democracies.[3] Likewise Daniel T. Rodgers, in assessing international policy options in the 1930s, writes of an "intellectual economy of catastrophe."[4] Finally, if we extend the concept of the Long New Deal to 1970, we must also attend to the constant contestation over the meaning of that model as it engaged with (often to the point of domination of) the rest of the world. International communism, of course, proved a prod to both reform as well as reaction in U.S. policies at home and abroad.[5] But the battle over core New Deal principles of unionism, welfarism and the role of the state also never ceased: indeed, in some ways, the terrain of combat merely widened. To take but one example, North Carolina textile magnate Luther Hodges was just one of a distinct cohort of anti-New Deal, postwar American businessmen who helped lure foreign investments homewards while also campaigning to stamp the Marshall Plan with free-market principles.[6]

Second, the New Deal itself, rather than "breaking free" of the pre- and post-New Deal worlds to which, at either end, it was tethered, contained many of the same assumptions and internal conflicts that accompanied the supposedly more typical stretches of American institutional life. Take industrial relations as a prime example. To be sure, the 1930s witnessed an important breakthrough in the protection, and even original encouragement, for labor unionism encompassed in the National Labor Relations (aka Wagner) Act. Yet, as Fraser himself perhaps best documented, most of the ideas and key players involved in New Deal era labor reform emerged from industrial and political battles (especially surrounding the garment trades) in the century's first two decades. The proto-Keynesian labor policies of the New Deal (simultaneously attempting to stabilize production, facilitate worker representation, and stimulate mass consumption) emerged from a coterie around Senator Wagner (and his economic advisor Leon Keyserling), Amalgamated Clothing Workers leader Sidney Hillman, legal strategist Felix Frankfurter, and Wisconsin-trained industrial relations experts like William Leiserson, Edwin Witte, and David Saposs—who had all frequently rubbed shoulders during Progressive Era conflicts. Indeed, the very philosophy behind Roosevelt's first coherent game plan for dealing with the crisis (as encapsulated in the National Industrial Recovery Act) was reportedly drawn from former University of Wisconsin president Charles Van Hise's 1912 thesis on the control of trusts.[7]

Moreover, for all the "triumph" of long-sought principles in the 1930s act, a mortal weakness was also left over from its Long Gilded Age inheritance. Appealing at best to the interstate commerce clause allowing Congress to set appropriate economic policy for the national interest, the Wagner Act was not rooted in deep constitutional principles (such as the Bill of Rights) that would demand respect for unions as a necessary pillar of American democracy. Except for the tripartite commissions (including labor, business, and public representatives) of the World War II National War Labor Board, the unions themselves had no guaranteed voice in the application of the nation's foremost law affecting their welfare.[8] As such, its administrative effectiveness began to come undone as early as the 1947 Taft-Hartley Act with its "right-to-work" and other disabling clauses.

Once Title VII of the Civil Rights Act of 1964 took effect, as Nelson Lichtenstein has argued, it was clear that the already decaying 1930s edifice would play permanent second fiddle to an alternative, better-constitutionally-sanctioned set of antidiscriminatory legislation.[9] Again, in its protection of individual over group (or aggrieved class) rights, even the post-Wagner Act industrial relations regime proved that the American Ideology of Chapter 1 was alive and well. In short, the failure to secure a beachhead for the collective interests of workers vis-à-vis their employers—as imagined or practiced in numerous systems of compulsory arbitration—carried long coattails. Without active government intervention *on the side of* collective agreements, a dog-eat-dog world of "industrial pluralism" (or what the British had called "collective laissez-faire") prevailed in twentieth- and twenty-first-century America, and the big dogs unsurprisingly dominated the contest.

Third, just as the Gilded Age, New Deal, and "Second" Gilded Age are knit together by their structural limitations, so are they connected by a common quest for social-political transformation. By way of illustration, let me zero in on two different sectors that each reflect a logic of structural persistence. First is the centrality of youth culture and the role of higher learning as a force for change in American politics. Since the turn of the twentieth century, at least, a youthful awakening has shaken up the political order on recurrent occasions. In Chapter 5 we witnessed the injection of a host of new, young energies into a socialist movement that simultaneously challenged both the economic and cultural conventions of mainstream America. In Chapter 3, moreover, we saw how an institution created for the training of the young—in this case the research university—also proved a powerful conduit for progressive ideas of social and political reform. This Long Gilded Age legacy has also regularly reproduced itself. For the 1930s, the "brain trust" idea is associated with talents from the nation's leading law schools (especially Columbia and Harvard), from which FDR recruited Raymond Moley, Rexford Tugwell, Adolf Berle, Felix Frankfurter, David Lilienthal, and Donald Richberg, among others.[10] In the same period, the University of North Carolina at Chapel Hill under the tutelage of Howard W. Odum and Frank Porter Graham applied a Wisconsin-style notion of "service" to the rural South, even as Howard University trained a new generation of African American social scientists.[11] Farther to the left, a combination of urban night schools and residential labor colleges and summer schools constituted what one historian has called "an infrastructure for the Popular Front social movement."[12]

By the 1960s, youth as both a demographic and political fact dominated popular conceptions of "change agents" in American life. The universities proved then not only a source of future policy prescriptions; they became themselves a key locus of national political contestation. Ironies, of course, abound in the twists of time. Clark Kerr, who as University of California president and "social liberal" turned a deaf ear to the era's free speech and

New Left radicals, was himself a Wisconsin-style, labor-oriented industrial economist, as trained by 1930s era radical Paul S. Taylor.[13] Most recently, youth reared its head as the primary constituent of both the "Wisconsin Moment" of mass protest versus conservative Republican attacks on public-sector unionism and the Occupy Wall Street movement formed in response to growing economic inequality.

There are other echoes, and perhaps even lessons, from the past within the contemporary workplace. The argument throughout these chapters has pointed to recurrent opportunities to better align labor strategies with the power of government and, where possible, discover points of overlap with sectors of the business community as well. For the moment, for example, a "statist" strategy perhaps holds most promise in the service sector. Union-ism and collective bargaining currently have little sway here, but a robust set of state or federal minimum wage laws—along lines first initiated in the Progressive era—mark a hopeful and productive path forward. As for labor-management collaboration, we may well wonder what sectors of capi-tal today might be willing to forge a new social compact with labor and the progressive state, not unlike the NCF in its more hopeful moments? Part of the answer, surprisingly, may come via globalization. European auto giants like Volkswagen, even when locating manufacturing plants in the low-wage American South, it appears, are more open-minded than native employers when it comes to unionization and collective bargaining.[14] Other parts of the private employment sector, like health care, may also prove more ame-nable to cooperative labor relations. New York health care union 1199SEIU, for example, has long partnered with the Greater New York Hospital Asso-ciation in lobbying state government for operating revenues. Indeed, SEIU President Andy Stern, who built the biggest private-sector union in the country before retiring in 2010, took the "partnership" to a new level; Stern's top-down, industry-wide, "template" agreements with hospitals and nursing home management recalled nothing so much as John Mitchell's entente with Mark Hanna and NCF manufacturers.[15]

Finally, and perhaps most strikingly, and drawing on imagination as well as desperation, new workforces continue to demand new ways of doing things. In the twentieth century, new immigrants and southern migrants compelled (as in the case of John Mitchell in the anthracite fields) or pushed aside (as in the case of the CIO revolt from the AFL) an established labor leadership to press their demands on recalcitrant employers and/or state officials. Of course, whether the "formula" that worked across a first half-century of mobilization can still bear fruit in the twenty-first century remains an open question. If the workers of the extended New Deal generation were in an important sense the children and grandchildren of the Long Gilded Age laboring classes, the same cannot be said for the connections between the postwar Boom Era and today's Second Gilded Age. Yet, if a powerful labor movement is to reemerge in the United States, it will no doubt draw on both the resources and grievances of a new immigrant generation, heavily Latino and pan-Asian. Already, the current rebellions in the U.S. laboring world—whether quickie strikes at MacDonald's, domestic workers' bill of rights, warehouse organizing campaigns, not to mention mobilizations for the legalization of the undocumented—regularly connect youth and immigrant community energies.[16]

Perhaps, then, we should move to regather rather than separate the strands of our national political and social movement history. In both time and place, we can make some productive new connections. Like the purported Long Exception of the New Deal, the time of the Great Exception—of the United States as a land with a history largely of its own making—has passed.

Notes

Introduction

Epigraph: E. J. Hobsbawm, *The Age of Empire, 1875–1914* (New York: Pantheon, 1987), 54.

1. President Bush catalyzed growing contemporary use of the phrase in his September 11, 1990, speech to a joint session of Congress on the Persian Gulf War and his hopes for post–Cold War great-power unity, a speech subsequently known as his "Toward a New World Order" speech. Address Before a Joint Session of the Congress on the Persian Gulf Crisis and the Federal Budget Deficit," http://en.wikisource.org/wiki/Toward_a_New_World_Order.

2. Carl N. Degler, *The Age of the Economic Revolution, 1876–1900* (Glenview, Ill.: Scot, Foresman, 1976), 2–3.

3. Carl N. Degler, *Out of Our Past: The Forces That Shaped Modern America* (New York: Harper & Row, 1970), 248–59.

4. Degler, *The Age of the Economic Revolution*, 74–75; Herbert G. Gutman, "Class Composition and the Development of the American Working Class, 1840–1890," in Ira Berlin, ed., *Power and Culture: Essays on the American Working Class* (New York: Pantheon, 1987), 385.

5. *The La Pietra Report: A Report to the Profession*, Organization of American Historians, September 2000, http://www.oah.org/about/reports/reports-statements/the-lapietra-report-a-report-to-the-profession/.

6. M. S. Anderson, *The Ascendancy of Europe, 1815–1914* (London: Pearson Education, 2003), 17, 146, 159; on wheat, and its centrality to world economic panics, see Scott Reynolds Nelson, *A Nation of Deadbeats: An Uncommon History of America's Financial Disasters* (New York: Knopf, 2012).

7. Thomas Bender, *A Nation Among Nations: America's Place in World History* (New York: Hill and Wang, 2006), 250–55.

8. Charles Emmerson, *1913: In Search of the World Before the Great War* (New York: Public Affairs, 2013), 455; see also Daniel J. Sargent, "The United States and Globalization in the 1970s," 49–64 in Niall Ferguson, Charles S. Maier, Erez Manela, and Daniel Sargent, eds., *The Shock of the Global: The 1970s in Perspective* (Cambridge, Mass.: Harvard University Press, 2010), 55 (figure 2:1); quotation Charles Emmerson, "Eve of Disaster: Why 2013 Looks Eerily like 1913," *Foreign Policy* (January 4, 2013).

9. For an outstanding exception, see David Montgomery, *The Fall of the House of Labor: The Workplace, the State, and American Labor Activism, 1865–1925* (Cambridge: Cambridge University Press, 1987), chap. 1.

10. Leon Fink, *Workingmen's Democracy: The Knights of Labor and American Politics* (Urbana: University of Illinois Press, 1983), 229.

11. Werner Sombart, *Why Is There No Socialism in the United States?* (White Plains, N.Y.: International Arts and Sciences Press, 1976 [1906]), 10. Among several serious updates on Sombart's classic work, see Seymour Martin Lipset and Gary Wolfe Marks, *It Didn't Happen Here: Why Socialism Failed in the United States* (New York: Norton, 2000).

12. The fullest development of counter-exceptionalist thinking was found in Eric Foner, "Why Is There No Socialism in the United States?" *History Workshop* 17 (Spring 1984), although I think a key seed had been sown as early as E. P. Thompson's "The Peculiarities of the English," *Socialist Register* 2 (1965).

13. Ira Berlin, "Herbert G. Gutman and the American Working Class," in Gutman, *Power and Culture: Essays on the American Working Class* (New York: Pantheon, 1987), 4–9; David S. Brown, *Beyond the Frontier: The Midwestern Voice in American Historical Writing* (Chicago: University of Chicago Press, 2009), 85.

14. James R. Green, *Grass-Roots Socialism: Radical Movements in the Southwest, 1895–1943* (Baton Rouge: Louisiana State University Press, 1978), xix.

15. See Michael Kazin, *The Populist Persuasion: An American History* (New York: Basic, 1995).

16. I have borrowed the phrase, albeit with a more circumscribed meaning, from James L. Peacock, *Grounded Globalism: How the U.S. South Embraces the World* (Athens: University of Georgia Press, 2007), see esp. 9–10.

17. See, e.g., Andrew Zimmerman, *Alabama in Africa: Booker T. Washington, the German Empire, and the Globalization of the New South* (Princeton, N.J.: Princeton University Press, 2010); Ian Tyrrell, *Woman's World/Woman's Empire: The Woman's Christian Temperance Union in International Perspective 1880–1930* (Chapel Hill: University of Carolina Press, 2010); Donna R. Gabaccia, *Foreign Relations: American Immigration in Global Perspective* (Princeton, N.J.: Princeton University Press, 2012); Julie Greene, *The Canal Builders: Making America's Empire at the Panama Canal* (New York: Penguin, 2009).

Chapter 1. The American Ideology

Epigraph: Abraham Lincoln, address at a Sanitary Fair, Baltimore, Maryland, April 18, 1864, http://teachingamericanhistory.org/library/document/address-at-a-sanitary -fair.

1. "Americans for the Arts: Arts and the Private Sector: Volunteerism," http:// www.artsusa.org/information_services/research/impact_areas/arts_private_sector/ 005.asp.

2. Richard Swedberg, *Tocqueville's Political Economy* (Princeton, N.J.: Princeton University Press, 2009), 262. See also Lucien Jaume, trans. Arthur Goldhammer, *Tocqueville: The Aristocratic Sources of Liberty* (Princeton, N.J.: Princeton University Press, 2013); and Seymour Drescher, *Dilemmas of Democracy: Tocqueville and Modernization* (Pittsburgh: University of Pittsburgh Press, 1968).

3. Pierre Rosanvallon, *The Demands of Liberty: Civil Society in France Since the Revolution* (Cambridge, Mass.: Harvard University Press, 2007), 1–9, 153, 168–85, quotation 180.

4. Alexis de Tocqueville, *Democracy in America*, vol. II, Book 2, Ch. 20 (New York: Vintage, 1945 [1835]), 168–71.

5. See Gerald Friedman, *State-Making and Labor Movements: France and the United States, 1876–1914* (Ithaca, N.Y.: Cornell University Press, 1998).

6. Robert J. Steinfeld, *The Invention of Free Labor: The Employment Relation in English and American Law and Culture, 1350–1870* (Chapel Hill: University of California Press, 1991), 171–72.

7. William J. Novak, *The People's Welfare: Law and Regulation in Nineteenth-Century America* (Chapel Hill: University of North Carolina Press, 1996), 235–48, quotations 244.

8. Christopher Tomlins, *Freedom Bound: Law, Labor, and Civil Identity in Colonizing English America, 1580–1865* (New York: Cambridge University Press, 2010), 231–95, quotation 16.

9. Herbert G. Gutman, "Labor in the Land of Lincoln: Coal Miners on the Prairie," in *Power and Culture: Essays on the American Working Class* (New York: Pantheon, 1987), 117–212; "Interview with Herbert Gutman," 332–33.

10. Thomas G. Andrews, *Killing for Coal: America's Deadliest Labor War* (Cambridge, Mass.: Harvard University Press, 2008), 48, 181–82, 193, 195–96.

11. Eric Foner, *The Story of American Freedom* (New York: Norton, 1998), 120–23; Leon Fink, "Labor, Liberty, and the Law: Trade Unionism and the Problem of the American Constitutional Order," *Journal of American History* 74 (December 1987): 904–25; For an excellent recent overview of the jurisprudential treatment of free labor, see David Brody, "Freedom and Solidarity in American Labor Law," in *Labor Embattled: History, Power, Rights* (Urbana: University of Illinois Press, 2005), 110–37.

12. Christopher L. Tomlins, "The Ties That Bind: Master and Servant in Massachusetts, 1800–1850," *Labor History* 30 (1989): 196.

13. Foner, *Story of American Freedom*. See also David Montgomery, *Citizen Worker: The Experience of Workers in the United States with Democracy and the Free Market During the Nineteenth Century* (Cambridge: Cambridge University Press, 1993); and William E. Forbath, *Law and the Shaping of the American Labor Movement* (Cambridge, Mass.: Harvard University Press, 1991).

14. Ray Stannard Baker, "The Right to Work: The Story of the Non-Striking Miners," *McClure's Magazine* (January 1903), 323–35, quotation 325; Elizabeth Tandy Shermer, *Sunbelt Capitalism: Phoenix and the Transformation of American Politics*

(Philadelphia: University of Pennsylvania Press, 2013), 93–115. As historian David Brody has argued, "In America, where individual liberty weighed so heavily, labor law more than in any other country discounted the claims of solidarity in favor of the nonunion workers and, more to the point, the antiunion employer," *Labor Embattled*, 140.

15. Montgomery, *Citizen Worker*, 30.

16. Foner, *Story of American Freedom*, 124; Gutman, "Labor in the Land of Lincoln." Cf. David Brion Davis's famous argument of how the broad anti-slavery argument might also provide ideological cover for the "free-labor" marketplace of industrial capitalism. *The Problem of Slavery in Western Culture* (Ithaca, N.Y.: Cornell University Press, 1969).

17. David Montgomery, *Beyond Equality: Labor and the Radical Republicans, 1862–1872* (Urbana: University of Illinois Press, 1981 [1967]), 251–60, quotations 251–52.

18. Foner, *Story of American Freedom*, 127 quoting Omaha platform of 1892.

19. George E. McNeill, ed., *The Labor Movement: The Problem of Today* (Boston: A.M. Bridgman, 1887), 459.

20. Preamble and declaration of principles of the Knights of Labor of America, Extract from *Journal of United Labor*, the official organ of the order of the Knights of Labor (Philadelphia, ca. 1885).

21. William E. Forbath, "The Ambiguities of Free Labor: Labor and the Law in the Gilded Age," *Wisconsin Law Review* (July/August 1985): 806–8.

22. Paul Michel Taillon, *Good Reliable White Men: Railroad Brotherhoods, 1877–1917* (Urbana: University of Illinois Press, 2009), 68, 75.

23. Ibid., 69.

24. David Montgomery, "Workers' Control of Machine Production in the Nineteenth Century, *Labor History* 17 (Fall 1976): 485–509.

25. Taillon, *Good Reliable White Men*, 69, 90.

26. Alice Kessler-Harris, *A Woman's Wage: Historical Meanings and Social Consequences* (Lexington: University Press of Kentucky, 1990), 33–56, quotation 37.

27. Roseanne Currarino, *The Labor Question in America: Economic Democracy in the Gilded Age* (Urbana: University of Illinois Press, 2011), 98.

28. Eric Arnesen, "'Like Banquo's Ghost, It Will Not Down': The Race Question and the American Railroad Brotherhoods, 1880–1920," *American Historical Review* 99 (December 1994): 1601–33.

29. William M. Reddy, *The Rise of Market Culture: The Textile Trade and French Society, 1750–1900* (Cambridge: Cambridge University Press, 1984), 3.

30. Ibid., 9, 11, 13–14, 335–36.

31. Andrew Gyory, *Closing the Gate: Race, Politics, and the Chinese Exclusion Act* (Chapel Hill: University of North Carolina Press, 1998), 20–21; Scott Reynolds Nelson, "After Slavery," in Emma Christopher, Cassandra Pybus, and Marcus Rediker, eds.,

Many Middle Passages: Forced Migration and the Making of the Modern World (Berkeley: University of California Press, 2007), 153–56.

32. Gyory, *Closing the Gate*, 3, 21, 67, 177, quotation 183, 245.

33. Daniel E. Bender, *Sweated Work, Weak Bodies: Anti-Sweatshop Campaigns and Languages of Work* (New Brunswick, N.J.: Rutgers University Press, 2004), 47, 42, 36–37.

34. Ibid., 75–100, quotations, 78–79, 82.

35. Gunther Peck, *Reinventing Free Labor: Padrones and Immigrant Workers in the North American West, 1880–1930* (New York: Cambridge University Press, 2000), 84–89.

36. Ibid., quotation 89, 230.

37. Vanessa H. May, *Unprotected Labor: Household Workers, Politics, and Middle-Class Reform in New York, 1870–1940* (Chapel Hill: University of North Carolina Press, 2011), 100, 103.

38. Glen A. Gildemeister, *Prison Labor and Convict Competition with Free Workers in Industrializing America, 1840–1890* (New York: Garland, 1987), 207.

39. Brian Greenberg, *Worker and Community: Response to Industrialization in a Nineteenth-Century American City, Albany, New York, 1850–1884* (Albany, N.Y.: SUNY Press, 1985), 143–60.

40. Alex Lichtenstein, *Twice the Work of Free Labor: The Political Economy of Convict Labor in the New South* (London: Verso, 1996).

41. Preamble to the Constitution of the Knights of Labor, 1878, http://www.historytools.org/sources/knights.html.

42. Joseph G. Rayback, *A History of American Labor* (New York: Macmillan, 1959), 163; Gildemeister, *Prison Labor and Convict Competition*, 225–48; "Convict Lease System," *New Georgia Encyclopedia*, January 10, 2014, http://www.georgiaencyclopedia.org/nge/Article.jsp?id = h-2635.

43. See esp. Alex Lichtenstein, *Twice the Work of Free Labor: The Political Economy of Convict Labor in the New South* (London: Verso, 1996), and Douglas A. Blackmon, *Slavery by Another Name: The Re-Enslavement of Black Americans from the Civil War to World War II* (New York: Doubleday, 2008).

44. Blackmon, *Slavery by Another Name*, 1–2.

45. T. V. Powderly, *Thirty Years of Labor* (Columbus, Ohio: Excelsior Publishing, 1890), 243–46. Clearly, for most male labor activists (including Knights of Labor), women's very presence in the industrial labor force represented one of the "distortions" of an ideal labor market, and republican community structure. Whether the threat posed by women workers would meet with open restriction (as practiced by most of the craft unions) or dilution (by narrowing their competitive advantage through higher wages) was, except for a tiny feminist minority, a strategic rather than ideological distinction. See Susan Levine, "Labor's True Woman: Domesticity and

Equal Rights in the Knights of Labor," *Journal of American History* 70 (September 1983): 323–39.

46. See, e.g., the description of the 1903–1904 Colorado coal miners' strike in Stephen Brier and Ferdinando Fasce, "Italian Militants and Migrants and the Language of Solidarity in the Early Twentieth-Century Western Coal Fields," *Labor: Studies in Working-Class History of the Americas* 8 (2) (2011): 89–121.

47. See, e.g., Leon Fink, "From Autonomy to Abundance: Changing Beliefs About the Free Labor System in Nineteenth Century America" in Stanley L. Engerman, ed., *Terms of Labor: Slavery, Freedom, and Free Labor* (Stanford, Calif.: Stanford University Press, 1999), 116–36.

48. Montgomery, *Citizen Worker*, 4–5.

49. Theresa A. Case, *The Great Southwest Railroad Strike and Free Labor* (College Station: Texas A&M University Press, 2010), 107–10, 114; Leon Fink, *Workingmen's Democracy: The Knights of Labor and American Politics* (Urbana: University of Illinois Press, 1983), 119–21.

50. Case, *Great Southwest Railroad Strike*, 91–96.

51. Ibid., 112, 117.

52. Ibid., 126.

53. Ibid., 185–220; Fink, *Workingmen's Democracy*, 121.

54. Fink, *Workingmen's Democracy*, 122–42; Case, *Great Southwest Railroad Strike*, 214–20.

55. Case, *Great Southwest Railroad Strike*, quotations 207, 182.

56. Strauss Magazine Theatre program, March 31, 1913, as reproduced in Alfred Lief, ed., *The Brandeis Guide to the Modern World* (Boston: Little, Brown, 1941), 134.

57. John P. Enyeart, *The Quest For "Just and Pure Law": Rocky Mountain Workers and American Social Democracy, 1870–1924* (Stanford, Calif.: Stanford University Press, 2009), 41.

58. David Brody, *In Labor's Cause: Main Themes on the History of the American Worker* (New York: Oxford University Press, 1993), 139–42, quotations 142, 245.

59. Richard A. Greenwald, "Labor, Liberals, and Sweatshops" in Daniel E. Bender and Greenwald, eds., *Sweatshop USA: The American Sweatshop in Historical and Global Perspective* (New York: Routledge, 2003), 79–83, Stolberg quotation, 82; Colin Gordon, *New Deals: Business, Labor, and Politics in America, 1920–1935* (Cambridge: Cambridge University Press, 1994), esp. 87–127.

60. Cong. Rec., House, 63rd Cong., 2nd sess., 1914, 51, pt. 14:14359.

61. Jerold S. Auerbach, "Progressives at Sea: The La Follette Act of 1915," *Labor History* 2 (Fall 1961): 353–54.

62. House, 63rd Cong., 2nd sess., 1914, 51, pt. 14:14356.

63. See Eric Hobsbawm, "Custom, Wages and Work-load in Nineteenth-Century Industry," in *Labouring Men: Studies in the History of Labour* (London: Weidenfeld and Nicolson, 1964), quotations 345, 350.

64. Foner, *The Story of American Freedom*, xiii, xiv.

65. Benedict R. Anderson, *Imagined Communities: Reflections on the Origin and Spread of Nationalism*, rev. and extended ed. (London: Verso, 1991), 224.

66. Karl Marx and Friedrich Engels, *The German Ideology*, http://www.marxists .org/archive/marx/works/1845/german-ideology/ch04a.htm See, e.g., vol. 2 on the "true socialism" of Hegel and Feuerbach: "They detach the communist systems, critical and polemical writings from the real movement, of which they are but the expression, and force them into an arbitrary connection with German philosophy. They detach the consciousness of certain historically conditioned spheres of life from these spheres and evaluate it in terms of true, absolute, i.e., German philosophical consciousness"; Perry Anderson, *The Indian Ideology* (Gurgaon: Three Essays Collective, 2012).

67. Paul V. Dutton, *Origins of the French Welfare State: The Struggle for Social Reform in France, 1914–1947* (New York: Cambridge University Press, 2002), 3.

68. John Carson, *The Measure of Merit: Talents, Intelligence, and Inequality in the French and American Republics, 1750–1940* (Princeton, N.J.: Princeton University Press, 2007), 107; Dutton, *Origins*, 7–11; Philip Nord, "The Welfare State in France, 1870–1914," *French Historical Studies* (1994): 821–38; Seth Koven and Sonya Michel, "Womanly Duties: Maternalist Politics and the Origins of Welfare States in France, Germany, Great Britain, and the United States, 1880–1920," *American Historical Review* 95 (October 1990): 1076–1108.

69. Nord, "Welfare State"; see also Nord, "Republicanism and Utopian Vision: French Freemasonry in the 1860s and 1870s," *Journal of Modern History* 63 (June 1991): 213–29.

70. Charles Ferguson, as cited in Fink, *Workingmen's Democracy*, 64.

71. Jonathan Levy, *Freaks of Fortune: The Emerging World of Capitalism and Risk in America* (Cambridge, Mass.: Harvard University Press, 2012), see esp. 191–230 on the replacement of mutual aid among workers by "industrial insurance."

72. See David R. Roediger, *The Wages of Whiteness: Race and the Making of the American Working Class* (New York: Verso, 1991), 65–92.

73. W. E. B. Du Bois, as quoted in Anthony Bogues, *Empire of Liberty: Power, Desire, and Freedom* (Hanover, N.H.: Dartmouth College Press, 2010), 59.

74. William H. Sewell, Jr., *Work and Revolution in France: The Language of Labor from the Old Regime to 1848* (New York: Cambridge University Press, 1980), 162.

Chapter 2. Great Strikes Revisited

Epigraph: As quoted in Joseph Frazier Wall, *Andrew Carnegie* (Pittsburgh: University of Pittsburgh Press, 1989 [1970]), 572.

1. Gerald Berk, *Alternative Tracks: The Constitution of American Industrial Order, 1865–1917* (Baltimore: Johns Hopkins University Press, 1994), ix–x. See also Richard R. John, *Network Nation: Inventing American Telecommunications* (Cambridge, Mass.: Harvard University Press, 2010).

2. See, e.g., Steve Fraser and Gary Gerstle, eds., *Ruling America: A History of Wealth and Power in a Democracy* (Cambridge, Mass.: Harvard University Press, 2005); Kim Phillips-Fein, *Invisible Hands: The Businessmen's Crusade Against The New Deal* (New York: Norton, 2009); Bethany Moreton, *To Serve God and Wal-Mart: The Making of Christian Free Enterprise* (Cambridge, Mass.: Harvard University Press, 2010); and Nelson Lichtenstein, *The Retail Revolution: How Wal-Mart Created a Brave New World of Business* (New York: Picador, 2010).

3. Richard White, *Railroaded: The Transcontinentals and the Making of Modern America* (New York: Norton, 2011), 516.

4. *The Hebrew Bible*, Samuel 2:27.

5. Lynn shoeworkers' strike http://www.massmoments.org/moment.cfm?mid = 60, accessed 8–30–11.

6. Almont Lindsey, *The Pullman Strike: The Story of a Unique Experiment and of a Great Labor Upheaval* (Chicago: University of Chicago Press, 1943), 93–94.

7. Robert J. Cornell, *The Anthracite Coal Strike of 1902* (New York: Russell & Russell, 1957), 41.

8. Chicago Garment Workers' Strike, Harvard University Library, Open Collections Program, http://ocp.hul.harvard.edu/ww/chicagostrike.html, accessed 8–30–11.

9. William Cahn, *Lawrence, 1912: The Bread And Roses Strike.* (New York: Pilgrim Press, 1980).

10. On American business and the crisis of labor productivity in the late nineteenth century, see James Livingston, "The Social Analysis of Economic History and Theory: Conjectures on Late Nineteenth-Century American Development," *AHR* 92 (February 1987): 69–95, esp. 70–79. See also Richard Schneirov, Shelton Stromquist, and Nick Salvatore, "Introduction" in same authors, eds., *The Pullman Strike and the Crisis of the 1890s* (Urbana: University of Illinois Press, 1999), 2–6.

11. Irving Bernstein, *The Lean Years: A History of the American Worker, 1920–1933* (Boston: Houghton Mifflin: 1960), 259–60, 318–19. Former Federal Reserve chairman Ben S. Bernanke thus wrote of "wage stickiness" that began in the late Hoover years. Ben S. Bernanke, "Nominal Wage Stickiness and Aggregate Supply in the Great Depression," *Quarterly Journal of Economics* 111, 3 (1996): 853–83; see also Jonathan D. Rose, "Hoover's Truce: Wage Rigidity in the Onset of the Great Depression," *Journal of Economic History* 70, 4 (2010): 843–70.

12. See, e.g., http://www.gaypatriot.net/2011/02/17, *comment by Ted B. (Charging Rhino)—February 17, 2011; Playgirl's Mechanical World, playgirl.livejournal.com/ 514577.html; Godlike Productions,* http://www.godlikeproductions.com/forum1/mes sage1366178/pg1, accessed 9–1-11.

13. David Brody, *Steelworkers in America: The Nonunion Era* (New York: Harper & Row, 1960), 60–68; Paul Krause, *The Battle for Homestead, 1880–1892: Politics, Culture, and Steel* (Pittsburgh: University of Pittsburgh Press, 1992), 19–20.

14. Joseph Frazier Wall, *Andrew Carnegie* (Pittsburgh: University of Pittsburgh Press, 1989 [1970], 579.

15. Kenneth Warren, *Triumphant Capitalism: Henry Clay Frick and the Industrial Transformation of America* (Pittsburgh: University of Pittsburgh Press, 1996), 77–84.

16. Krause, *The Battle for Homestead*, 4, 86, 358.

17. Carnegie, as quoted in Richard Krooth, *A Century Passing: Carnegie, Steel and the Fate of Homestead* (Lanham, Md.: University Press of America, 2004), 432.

18. Krause, *The Battle for Homestead*, 239, 350–51.

19. *Triumphant Democracy* selection, as reproduced in Carnegie, *Problems of Today: Wealth, Labor, Socialism* (Garden City, N.J.: Doubleday, 1933 [1908]), 43–46.

20. Wall, *Andrew Carnegie*, 27, 34, quotation 99.

21. A. S. Eisenstadt, *Carnegie's Model Republic: Triumphant Democracy and the British-American Relationship* (2007)

22. Wall, *Andrew Carnegie*, 439.

23. Interview in *Aberdeen Northern Daily News*, as quoted in Eisenstadt, *Carnegie's Model Republic*, 162.

24. Gerlach, *British Liberalism and the United States* (New York: Palgrave, 2001), 198. Historian Iain McLean surmises that Carnegie's donation derived from sympathy for a fellow Scot who, like himself, had risen from poverty to a prominent position in public life. Though crucial to Hardie's campaign, news from America embarrassed the newly elected Hardie into a like contribution to the Homestead strikers—an act he accomplished at some personal turmoil by raiding his wife's life savings. Iain McLean, *Keir Hardie* (New York: St. Martin's 1975), 38–40; Caroline Benn, *Keir Hardie* (London: Hutchinson, 1992), 91–92.

25. As quoted in Warren, *Triumphant Capitalism*, 69–71.

26. Eisenstadt, *Carnegie's Model Republic*, 161.

27. Quoted in ibid., 164–65.

28. Gerlach, *British Liberalism*, 187.

29. Warren, *Triumphant Capitalism*, 207–68.

30. Schwab (1935) quoted in Warren, *Triumphant Capitalism*, 94. Near the end of the strike, Frick had already batted down Carnegie's own Monday-morning doubts about the Pinkerton strategy: "If we had adopted the policy of sitting down and waiting, we would have still been sitting, waiting, and the fight would yet have to be made, and then we would have been accused of trying to starve our men into submission" (94).

31. Richard Krooth, *A Century Passing: Carnegie, Steel and the Fate of Homestead* (Lanham, Md.: 2004), 360–61.

32. *Autobiography of Andrew Carnegie* (Boston: Houghton Mifflin, 1920), v–vi, 235–39, quotation 237. This "autobiography" is really a series of memoir sketches completed before 1914, then published posthumously by Professor Van Dyke and Carnegie's widow, Louise Whitfield Carnegie. The racial and cultural connotations of McLuckie's "damned white" compliment likely deserve more scrutiny than is possible here. McLuckie likely meant it in the sense of "morally or spiritually pure or stainless," one of the colloquial uses of the word at the time (OED, 2nd ed., 1989). Perhaps

both protagonists recognized an unspoken "outsider' kinship in their Scottish roots or perhaps it was just Carnegie who translated a possibly more ambivalent message into undiluted unity with a former foe.

33. James Weinstein, *The Corporate Ideal in the Liberal State, 1900–1918* (Boston: Beacon, 1968), 16. Overturning contempt citations on a technicality dating to a 1906 metal polishers' boycott, the *Gompers v. Buck's Stove and Range Co.*, 221 U.S. 418 (1911) decision kept Gompers and other AFL leaders out of jail but ducked the issues of free speech vs. injunctive power that occasioned the confrontation.

34. Quotation in Wall, *Andrew Carnegie*, 694.

35. Wall, *Andrew Carnegie*, 1008, 1037; Wall notes that the last page of his 1914 autobiography was entitled "The Kaiser and World Peace" (1012).

36. Quoted in Krause, *The Battle for Homestead*, 334.

37. *Chicago Arbeiter-Zeitung,* July 25, 1892; *Die Fackel* (in effect, the Sunday edition of the *Arbeiter-Zeitung*), July 31, 1892.

38. Krause, *The Battle for Homestead*, 348–51, quotation 348.

39. Eric Leif Davin, *Crucible of Freedom: Workers' Democracy in the Industrial Heartland, 1914–1960* (Plymouth, Mass.: Lexington Books, 2010), 225.

40. Quoted in Warren, *Triumphant Capitalism*, 107.

41. See, e.g., Jeffrey R. Kerr-Ritchie, "Fugitive Slaves Across North America," in Leon Fink, ed., *Workers Across the Americas: The Transnational Turn in Labor History* (New York: Oxford University Press, 2011), 363–83.

42. For elaboration, see Fink, *Sweatshops at Sea: Merchant Seamen in the World's First Globalized Industry, from 1812 to the Present* (Chapel Hill: University of North Carolina Press, 2011), 119–28.

43. John S. Garner, *The Model Company Town: Urban Design Through Private Enterprise in Nineteenth-Century New England* (Amherst: University of Massachusetts Press, 1984).

44. Anthony Lukas, *Big Trouble: A Murder in a Small Western Town Sets Off a Struggle for the Soul of America* (New York: Simon & Schuster, 1997), 311.

45. Samuel Yellen, *American Labor Struggles* (New York: Harcourt Brace, 1936), 113–35; Lindsey, *Pullman Strike*, 122–46.

46. Ray Ginger, *The Bending Cross: A Biography of Eugene Victor Debs* (New Brunswick, N.J.: Rutgers University Press, 1949), 173–74, 192–93; Carl Smith, *Urban Disorder and the Shape of Belief: The Great Chicago Fire, the Haymarket Bomb, and the Model Town of Pullman* (Chicago: University of Chicago Press, 1995), 237.

47. Stanley Buder, *Pullman: An Experiment in Industrial Order and Community Planning* (New York: Oxford University Press, 1967), 43.

48. Garner, *Model Company Town*, 59–60.

49. Smith, *Urban Disorder*, 184–85, 194.

50. Ibid., 202.

51. Malcolm Elwin, *Charles Reade: A Biography* (London: Jonathan Cape, 1931), 202; In the aftermath of a defeated saw-grinders' strike in 1866, a violent faction of

strikers attacked blackleg workers, killing one in a house explosion, an act quickly dubbed the "Sheffield Outrages." Established trade unions blamed the violence on the lack of a legitimate structure of industrial relations, and a parliamentary inquiry, leading to legalization of trade unions and repeal of the Master and Servant Act, followed in 1871. "Sources for the Study of the Sheffield Outrages," www.sheffield.gov.uk/archives, accessed December 2, 2011.

52. Lindsey, *Pullman Strike*, 351–57

53. Buder, *Pullman*, 210.

54. Richard Slotkin, *The Fatal Environment: The Myth of the Frontier in the Age of Industrialization, 1800–1890* (New York: Atheneum, 1985), 481, 496.

55. Peter R. DeMontravel, *A Hero to His Fighting Men: Nelson A. Miles, 1839–1925* (Kent, Ohio: Kent State University Press, 1998), 214–15, 223; Gerald G. Eggert, *Richard Olney: Evolution of a Statesman* (State College: Pennsylvania State University Press, 1974), 142. Annoyed with Miles's seeming distaste for urban riot patrol, President Cleveland insisted that as commanding officer, Miles take full responsibility over how and when to use deadly force.

56. White, *Railroaded*, 417, 418.

57. Quoted in White, *Railroaded*, 431.

58. Eggert, *Richard Olney*, 132.

59. Ibid., 140–41. As Eggert summarizes: "From the announcement of the boycott in late June to the collapse of the strike in mid-July, Olney's primary objective was to crush the strike" (147).

60. Ibid., 129–30. As Eggert suggests, it is hard to intuit Olney's motive here: that is, not wanting to complicate government prosecution of the Commonwealers by strike intervention, commercial-derived animosity to the Great Northern's James J. Hill, or initial legal qualms about the constitutional proprieties involved?

61. Ibid., 157–59; note that the government's brief proved unavailing in the courts.

62. Lindsey, *Pullman Strike*, 351; Eggert, *Richard Olney*, 151–64, quotation 163.

63. Nick Salvatore, "Eugene V. Debs: From Trade Unionist to Socialist," in Melvyn Dubofsky and Warren Van Tine, eds., *Labor Leaders in America* (Urbana: University of Illinois Press, 1987), 101–2. An amendment to strike out the whites-only provision of the membership requirements failed by a 112–100 vote at the 1894 ARU convention. Ginger, *The Bending Cross*, 116.

64. White, *Railroaded*, 429.

65. Janice L. Reiff, "A Modern Lear and His Daughters: Gender in the Model Town of Pullman," in Schneirov, Stromquist, and Salvatore, *The Pullman Strike*, 79–80.

66. Rieff, 65–86.

67. Salvatore, "Eugene V. Debs," quotations 128–29; Ginger, *The Bending Cross*, 128.

68. Graham Adams, Jr., *Age of Industrial Violence, 1910–15: The Activities and Findings of the United States Commission on Industrial Relations* (New York: Columbia University Press, 1966).

69. Selig Perlman, *A History of Trade Unionism in the United States* (New York: Macmillan, 1923), 177.

70. Cornell, *Anthracite Coal Strike*, 170.

71. Craig Phelan, *Divided Loyalties: The Public and Private Life of Labor Leader John Mitchell* (Albany, N.Y.: SUNY Press, 1994), 168–74.

72. Elsie Gluck, *John Mitchell, Miner: Labor's Bargain with the Gilded Age* (New York: Greenwood, 1969), 115–16.

73. Cornell, *Anthracite Coal Strike*, 185–86; John A. Garraty, *Right-Hand Man: The Life of George W. Perkins* (New York: Harper, 1960), 154–56; Andrew Sinclair, *Corsair: The Life of J. Pierpont Morgan* (Boston: Little Brown, 1981), 151–55.

74. Cornell, *Anthracite Coal Strike*, 253–59; Joint conferences with direct negotiations between anthracite owners and the UMWA took place in 1916 and 1920. *Reports of the Department of Labor, 1920*, vol. 8 (Washington D.C.: GPO, 1921), 111–12.

75. Victor Greene, *The Slavic Community on Strike* (Notre Dame, Ind.: University of Notre Dame Press, 1968), 201–3. Alas, Mitchell himself continued to harbor a low opinion generally of non-English speaking immigrants. As historian Craig Phelan neatly summarizes, "As Mitchell's personal views indicate . . . union policy on race and ethnicity sprang from the nature of the industry, not the 'progressive' outlook of its president," *Divided Loyalties*, 146–47.

76. Andrew Roy, *A History of the Coal Miners of the United States* (Westport, Conn.: Greenwood, 1970 [1905]), 440; Phelan, *Divided Loyalties*, 182–90. Note that Phelan, *contra* my own interpretation here, argues that Mitchell "might well have spurned the offer to arbitrate and battled to achieve full recognition" (188).

77. Of the three, Mitchell enjoys the most thorough and compelling, if still under-recognized, biography (see Phelan).

78. Sidney Lens, *The Labor Wars* (New York: Doubleday, 1973), 140.

79. Bruno Ramirez, *The Politics of Industrial Relations in the Progressive Era, 1898–1916* (Westport, Conn.: Greenwood, 1978), 23.

80. Ibid., 34–35.

81. Alexander Trachtenberg, *The History of Legislation for the Protection of Coal Miners in Pennsylvania, 1824–1915* (New York: International, 1942), 134–41.

82. Perry K. Blatz, *Democratic Miners: Work and Labor Relations in the Anthracite Coal Industry, 1875–1925* (Albany, N.Y.: SUNY Press, 1994), 53.

83. Mitchell, as quoted in Cornell, *Anthracite Coal Strike*, 91.

84. Herbert Croly, *Marcus Alonzo Hanna: His Life and Work* (Hamden, Conn.: Archon, 1965 [1912], 91.

85. Ibid., 404; Lewis L. Gould, *The Presidency of William McKinley* (Lawrence, Kan.: Regents Press, 1980), 7; Margaret Leech, *In the Days of McKinley* (New York: Harper & Brothers, 1959), 53. Though McKinley's national reputation was made on

tariff protection and the gold standard (and ultimately robust interventionism abroad), as governor he backed a franchise tax on corporations, compensation for injured railroad and streetcar employees, an industrial commission, and a fine for employers who demanded a yellow-dog (i.e., an anti-union pledge) test for employment.

86. Ramirez, *Politics of Industrial Relations*, 54.

87. Marguerite Green, "The National Civic Federation and the American Labor Movement, 1900–1925" (Ph.D. dissertation, Catholic University of America, 1956), 126.

88. Croly, *Hanna*, 400.

89. Ibid., 400.

90. Garraty, *Right-Hand Man*, 114; On Perkins's role in the NCF and evolving worldview, see Jonathan Levy, *Freaks of Fortune: The Emerging World of Capitalism and Risk in America* (Cambridge, Mass.: Harvard University Press, 2012), 264–307.

91. Green, "National Civic Federation," 327, 426.

92. Cathie Jo Martin, "Sectional Parties, Divided Business," *Studies in American Political Development* 20 (Fall 2006): 160–84, esp. 160, 170–71; Albion Guilford Taylor, "Labor Policies of the National Association of Manufacturers," *University of Illinois Studies in the Social Sciences* 15 (March 1927): 14; Albert K. Steigerwalt, *The National Association of Manufacturers, 1895–1914* (Grand Rapids: Bureau of Business Research, University of Michigan, 1964), quotation 113.

93. See Phelan, *Divided Loyalties*, 314–60.

94. Croly, *Hanna*, xi; In offering his own, personalistic account of Hanna's career, the historian Thomas Beer allowed that Croly's account "sank . . . through a scum of tepid reviews." Beer, *Hanna* (New York: Knopf, 1929), viii. See also Clarence A. Stern, *Resurgent Republicanism: The Handiwork of Hanna* (Ann Arbor, Mich.: Edwards Brothers, 1963), 34–35, 84, who cites more dismissive assessments of Hanna's career in Matthew Josephson, *The Politicos, 1865–1896* (New York: Harcourt, Brace, 1938) and William Allen White, *Masks in a Pageant* (New York: Macmillan, 1928); and Edward A. Stettner, *Shaping Modern Liberalism: Herbert Croly and Progressive Thought* (Lawrence: University Press of Kansas, 1993).

95. While generally taking a dim view of Croly's Hanna project, David W. Levy, *Herbert Croly of the New Republic* (Princeton, N.J.: Princeton University Press, 1985) acknowledges ways the work fits "into the historical framework of *The Promise of American Life*," 146–50, quotation 149.

96. Croly, *Hanna*, 465–79.

97. Herbert Croly, *The Promise of American Life* (New York: Macmillan, 1909), 385–98.

98. Ibid., 405.

99. David Brody, *Steelworkers in America: The Nonunion Era* (New York: Harper & Row, 1960), 60–68; Green, 25–36; Croly, *Promise of American Life*, 391.

100. Morgan story, as cited in Meredith Tax, *The Rising of the Women: Feminist Solidarity and Class Conflict, 1880–1017* (New York: Monthly Review Press, 1980), 229–30.

101. Croly, *The Promise of American Life*, 407.

102. Robin Archer, *Why Is There No Labor Party in the United States?* (Princeton, N.J.: Princeton University Press, 2007), 106–7, 134–39, 237–38.

103. Weinstein, *The Corporate Ideal in the Liberal State.*

Chapter 3. The University and Industrial Reform

Epigraph: Merle Curti and Vernon Carstensen, *University of Wisconsin: A History* (Madison: University of Wisconsin Press, 1949), 1: 542.

1. S. Robert Wilson to Ely, Nov. 1, 1883, Richard T. Ely Papers, Wisconsin Historical Society (WHS).

2. Joseph Labadie to Ely, Aug. 8, 1885. In November 1885 August Spies, editor of the Chicago *Arbeiter-Zeitung*, also wrote Ely to correct the latter's underestimation of the impact of the Chicago International Working People's Association. Armed revolutionaries were organizing everywhere, Spies insisted: "secretly of course," "every day brings us more accessions." Ten months later, Spies wrote again—this time while awaiting his Haymarket trial—requesting Ely's latest book to review in the *AZ*.

3. Sidney Webb to Ely, Nov. 21, 1888.

4. Powderly to Ely, Jan. 1, 1891.

5. Frances Willard to Ely, April 17, 1890.

6. "Social economy was, in short, the ambulance wagon of industrial capitalism," Daniel T. Rodgers, *Atlantic Crossings: Social Politics in a Progressive Age* (Cambridge, Mass.: Harvard University Press, 1998), 12.

7. Ira Katznelson, "Knowledge About What: Policy Intellectuals and the New Liberalism," in Dietrich Rueschemeyer and Theda Skocpol, eds., *States, Social Knowledge, and the Origins of Modern Social Policies* (Princeton, N.J.: Princeton University Press. 1996), 17–18, 26–28.

8. See especially Daniel, *Atlantic Crossings*, 1–7, and also James T. Kloppenberg, *Uncertain Victory: Social Democracy and Progressivism in European and American Thought, 1870–1920* (New York: Oxford University Press, 1986)

9. If anything, the "second" generation of Verein leaders proved even more intellectually if not politically influential, including Werner Sombart, Ferdinand Tönnies, Max Weber, and Friedrich Naumann. Dietrich Reuschemeyer and Ronan Van Rossem, "The Verein and the Fabian Society," in Rueschemeyer and Skocpol, *States*, 121; Rodgers, *Atlantic Crossings*, 85–88. In the 1880s, some 2,000 Americans per year were studying in Germany. Walter P. Metzger, *Academic Freedom in the Age of the University* (New York: Columbia University Press, 1955), 93–94.

10. Axel R. Schäfer, *American Progressives and German Social Reform, 1875–1920* (Stuttgart: Franz Steiner, 2000), 45–46.

11. Howe, as quoted in ibid., 49.

12. Reuschemeyer and Van Rossem, "The Verein," 123; Fritz K. Ringer, *The Decline of the German Mandarins: The German Academic Community, 1890–1933* (Cambridge, Mass.: Harvard University Press, 1969), 143–62; David F. Lindenfeld, *The Practical Imagination: The German Sciences of State in the Nineteenth Century* (Chicago: University of Chicago Press, 1997), 223–39.

13. Reuschemeyer and Van Rossem, "The Verein," 149.

14. Walter P. Metzger, *Academic Freedom in the Age of the University* (New York: Columbia University Press, 1955), 114.

15. Erik Grimmer-Solem, "Imperialist Socialism of the Chair: Gustav Schmoller and German *Weltpolitik*, 1897–1905," in Geoff Eley and James Retallack, eds., *Wilhelminism and Its Legacies: German Modernities, Imperialism, and the Meanings of Reform, 1890–1930* (New York: Berghahn, 2003), 107–22.

16. Kevin Repp, *Reformers, Critics, and the Paths of German Modernity: Anti-Politics and the Search for Alternatives, 1890–1914* (Cambridge, Mass.: Harvard University Press, 2000), 80, 200–211.

17. Rueschemeyer and Van Rossem, "The Verein," 145.

18. Reba N. Soffer, *Discipline and Power: The University, History, and the Making of an English Elite, 1870–1930* (Stanford, Calif.: Stanford University Press, 1994); Radhika Desai, *Intellectuals and Socialism: "Social Democrats" and the Labour Party* (London: Lawrence and Wishart, 1994), 39–45.

19. No academics appear to have participated in the formative meetings of the society; rather, civil servants, teachers, writers, and assorted self-employed individuals defined the group's social sphere. By 1896 four "University Societies" had been added and these would only spread and grow over the next decade. Studies of the subject, however, suggest that even these Fabian redoubts were largely student-centered. As an early and influential Fabian presence, Oxford University philosopher Sidney Ball seems to stand out as the exception. See Norman MacKenzie and Jeanne MacKenzie, *The Fabians* (New York: Simon and Schuster, 1977), 16–29; A. M. McBriar, *Fabian Socialism and English Politics, 1884–1918* (Cambridge: Cambridge University Press, 1962), 167–69; Fabian Society (Great Britain), *Fabian Tracts*, Nos. 1–114 (London: Fabian Office, n.d.).

20. Webb, as quoted in Reuschemeyer and Van Rossem, "The Verein," 128.

21. Richard Bomford, "Just Good Friends: The Fabian Society's Relationship to the Labour Party," http://www.twfabians.co.uk/f&l.html.

22. See, e.g., Yosef Gorni, "Beatrice Webb's Views on Judaism and Zionism," *Jewish Social Studies* 40 (Spring 1978): 95–116.

23. Rodgers, *Atlantic Crossings*, 63–66.

24. Ibid., 65; Kathryn Kish Sklar, *Florence Kelley and the Nation's Work: The Rise of Women's Political Culture, 1830–1900* (New Haven, Conn.: Yale University Press, 1995), 289.

25. Thomas P. Jenkin, "The American Fabian Movement," *Western Political Quarterly* 1 (1948): 121–22.

26. David P. Thelen, *The New Citizenship: Origins of Progressivism in Wisconsin, 1885–1900* (Columbia: University of Missouri Press, 1972), 204–11; Charles Mc-Carthy, *The Wisconsin Idea* (New York: Macmillan, 1912, as quoted in Leon Fink, *Progressive Intellectuals and the Dilemmas of Democratic Commitment* (Cambridge, Mass.: Harvard University Press, 1997), 89. See also Fink, "A Hard Break with Wisconsin's Past," *Raleigh News and Observer*, February 27, 2011.

27. Note that a younger generation of Verein members, led by Max Weber and Friedrich Naumann, did attempt direct contacts with the burgeoning Social Democrats. As a close study of the radical intellectuals' relation to German politics indicates, "Anticipation reached its height in 1912, when Progressives, Social Democrats, and many National Liberals joined to support [August] Bebel's candidacy for Reichstag president." Repp, *Reformers, Critics,* 53–63, quotation 61.

28. Andrew Feffer, *The Chicago Pragmatists and American Progressivism* (Ithaca, N.Y.: Cornell University Press, 1993), 117.

29. Nicholas Murray Butler, *Scholarship and Service: The Policies and Ideals of a National University in a Modern Democracy* (Freeport, N.Y.: Scribner's, 1921), 11. While urging engagement with the community, Butler, to be sure, was equally determined Columbia students not give way to the contemporary "spirit of unrest" but rather hew to the "cornerstone" principles of "civil and industrial liberty, private property, and the inviolability of contract" (277–81).

30. W. Bruce Leslie, *Gentlemen and Scholars: Colleges and Community in the "Age of the University"* (New Brunswick, N.J.: Transaction, 2005 [1986]), 231–36.

31. Merle Curti and Vernon Carstensen, *The University of Wisconsin: A History 1848–1925* (Madison: University of Wisconsin Press, 1949), 1: 194–95, 288, and more broadly, 275–95.

32. Ibid., 1: 280–81, quotation 288; 2: 18–19; Maurice M. Vance, *Charles Richard Van Hise: Scientist Progressive* (Madison: Wisconsin Historical Society, 1960), 80.

33. Curti and Carstensen, *University of Wisconsin,* 1: 542.

34. Ibid., 545.

35. A recent assessment comparatively denigrates Ely the economist as "by any standard a thinker inferior to both [John Bates] Clark and [Henry Carter] Adams." Nancy Cohen, *The Reconstruction of American Liberalism, 1865–1914* (Chapel Hill: University of North Carolina Press, 2002), 164; Rodgers, *Atlantic Crossings,* 99.

36. On the origins of the AEA, see Mary O. Furner, *Advocacy and Objectivity: A Crisis in the Professionalization of American Social Science, 1865–1905* (Lexington: University Press of Kentucky, 1975), 69–80; and A. W. [Bob] Coats, *The Sociology and Professionalization of Economics: British and American Economic Essays* (New York: Routledge, 1993), 2: 205–24; Richard T. Ely, *French and German Socialism in Modern Times* (New York: Harper & Brothers, 1883), preface, 13–14. I have not been able to identify the original source of Ely's quotation of Marx, but note that it is also included in the *Encyclopedia Britannica* (1902) entry on "Communism." http://www.1902en cyclopedia.com/C/COM/communism.html.

37. John A. DeBrizzi, *Ideology and the Rise of Labor Theory in America* (Westport, Conn.: Greenwood, 1983), 31–34; Benjamin G. Rader, *The Academic Mind and Reform: The Influence of Richard T. Ely in American Life* (Louisville: University Press of Kentucky, 1966), 29–30.

38. Ely's influence was reportedly especially marked among the Methodist, United Brethren in Christ, and the Christian Social Union of the Protestant Episcopal churches. Rader, *Academic Mind*, 61.

39. Rader, *Academic Mind*, 22–23; Robert M. Crunden, *Ministers of Reform: The Progressives' Achievement in American Civilization 1889–1920* (New York: Basic, 1982), 16–63.

40. Richard T. Ely, *The Labor Movement in America* (New York: Thomas Crowell, 1886), 138.

41. Ibid., 6; Fink, *Progressive Intellectuals*, 54–59.

42. Ely, *Labor Movement in America*, 139.

43. Ibid., vii.

44. Richard T. Ely, *The Strengths and Weaknesses of Socialism* (New York: Chautauqua Press, 1894), 4.

45. Edward R. Bemis to Ely, Nov. 19, 1888.

46. Cohen, *Reconstruction of American Liberalism,* 168–76.

47. Julie A. Reuben, *The Making of the Modern University: Intellectual Transformation and the Marginalization of Morality* (Chicago: University of Chicago Press, 1996), 197; on the less common case of political manipulation of the social science faculty from the "left," see Scott M. Gelber, *The University and the People: Envisioning American Higher Education in an Era of Populist Protest* (Madison: University of Wisconsin Press, 2011), esp. 126–46.

48. Curti and Carstensen, *University of Wisconsin*, 1: 510.

49. Ibid., 508–26, quotations 509.

50. Pushback against Ely's religious-tinged moralism within the AEA was already apparent by the 1892 selection of conservative economist Charles Dunbar as association president. Crunden, *Ministers of Reform*, 70–71.

51. Fink, *Progressive Intellectuals*, 64; Curti and Carstensen, *University of Wisconsin*, 1: 508–27.

52. Rader, *Academic Mind*, 154–55.

53. Rodgers, *Atlantic Crossings*, 106; see also Furner, *Advocacy and Objectivity*, 156–59.

54. Ely's later writings include *Monopolies and Trusts* (1900), *Elementary Principles of Economics* (1904), *Property and Contract in Their Relation to the Distribution of Wealth* (1914), and *Elements of Land Economics* (1926).

55. As quoted in Rodgers, *Atlantic Crossings*, 137.

56. Rader, *Academic Mind*, 183–87, 190, 223–27.

57. Ibid., 204–13, quotation, 236. Under mounting outside criticism for his private funding sources, Ely moved himself and the Land Economics Institute (funded

by a variety of business associations) to Northwestern University in 1925; Furner, *Advocacy and Objectivity*, e.g., largely echoes Rader on this point: "in the events of the 1890s and in the changing expectations of academic social scientists were forces that actually restructured Ely's perceptions of his own role. Never again did he style himself as a reform leader. When Ely relinquished his claim to activism, he exchanged advocacy for acceptability" (162). To be sure, many Progressives to the left of Ely backed the technocratic Hoover in 1928, including Jane Addams. Ely to Jane Addams, Nov. 3, 1928; *Chicago Daily News*, October 17, 1928.

58. Furner, *Advocacy and Objectivity*, "Introduction to the Transaction Edition," xxvi.

59. Responding to an appeal from Henry Demarest Lloyd, Clarence Darrow indicated that he would "like to help" [Bemis], but "do not think I ought to use my money in that way." Still, wrote Darrow, he was "glad for Ely's interest in the matter." Darrow to Lloyd, Jan. 2, 1895 [letter forwarded to Ely], Ely Papers. See also Rader, *Academic Mind*, 167–71; on Bemis's subsequent career, see Shelton Stromquist, *Re-Inventing "The People": The Progressive Movement, the Class Problem, and the Origins of Modern Liberalism* (Urbana: University of Illinois Press, 2006) 29–31; Gelber, *University and the People*, 133–39, 167.

60. Barbara H. Fried, *The Progressive Assault on Laissez Faire: Robert Hale and the First Law and Economics Movement* (Cambridge, Mass.: Harvard University Press, 1998), 11, 29–30.

61. Rader, *Academic Mind*, 104.

62. Ely, *Property and Contract*, 1: 41, 359 n. 10.

63. This is not to say that the Wisconsin-bred investigators forsook all middle-class condescension and prejudice toward the poor or radical working-class agitators: see, e.g., Frank Tobias Higbie, *Indispensable Outcasts: Hobo Workers and Community in the American Midwest, 1880–1930* (Urbana: University of Illinois Press, 2003), 66–67, 82–90.

64. Richard T. Ely, *Ground Under Our Feet: An Autobiography* (New York: Macmillan, 1938), 186–88. When it came to the "look and see" method of social investigation, "no man," wrote Ely, "has been more successful than Professor Commons. . . . He kept in touch, on the one hand, with labor, and on the other, with the management of industry. He mingled with all classes of people. He introduced to his classes people such as W. F. Foster [the syndicalist leader] and Emma Goldman, who were regarded as very dangerous radicals. To him, these people were simply human representatives, whom his students should know face to face. On the other hand, he was just as eager to have his classes know capitalists and leaders of industry." Ely claimed Anna was "studying for her PhD." However, the record indicates she took an MA in economics at Madison (following her BA the previous year) in 1919, before pursuing a second Master of Science (field unspecified) in 1920, while Alice received her BA in 1919, http://search.ancestry.com/Browse/View.aspx?dbid = 2207&
path = Wisconsin.University + of + Wisconsin.1921.107.360. Always close to her

father, Anna married fellow economist Edward W. Morehouse (who collaborated with Ely at Wisconsin's Institute for Research in Land Economics) and published a revised version of Ezra Towne's *Social Problems: A Study of Present Day Social Conditions* (New York: Macmillan, 1934 [1931]); later she and her husband settled in Princeton, New Jersey, where she was known as a passionate advocate for racial justice. Rader, *Academic Mind*, 164–65, 206, 214; on Edward Morehouse, see http://www.classism.org/ward-morehouse. In 1931 (when he was supposedly well into a "retreat" from his former progressivism), Ely self-consciously applied a version of the same method in his prescription for unemployment relief in a book called *Hard Times—The Way in and the Way Out with a Special Consideration of the "Seen and the Unseen": A Program of Action Based on Research* (New York: Macmillan, 1932). Anticipating FDR's Civilian Conservation Corps, Ely's prime proposal was for a "peace-time army," a skeletal organization in normal times that would expand rapidly to meet the needs for employment at public works in hard times (96–114).

65. Rodgers, *Atlantic Crossings*, 236.

66. Ely to R. C. McCrae, Dec. 3, 1907; Papers of the American Association for Labor Legislation, 1905–1943 (Glen Rock, N.J.: Microfilming Corp. of America, 1974, originally at Cornell Labor-Management Documentation Center).

67. Harold L. Miller, ed., *Wisconsin Progressives: The Richard T. Ely Papers: Guide to a Microfilm Edition* (Madison: Wisconsin Historical Society, 1986).

68. Ely to Robert Hunter, April 25, 1903; Hunter to Ely, April 27, April 28, 1903; Addams to Ely, Dec. 21, 1903; Ely to Frederic Howe, March 16, 1904.

69. Edward A. Ross to Ely, Jan. 26, 1904. Though Ross found secure employment at Wisconsin following dismissal from Stanford for political advocacy in 1900, Bemis—contra Ross's rosy assessment—was not so fortunate; working as a "gypsy scholar" for several years, he had effectively been blacklisted from academia by 1900 in favor of municipal and federal administrative employment. See Furner, *Advocacy and Objectivity*, 192–98, 231–59.

70. Lloyd to Ely, Dec. 11, 1902; Ely to Lloyd, Jan. 2, 1903.

71. Ely to Lloyd, April 27, 1903.

72. Kathryn Kish Sklar, "Hull-House Maps and Papers: Social Science as Women's Work in the 1890s," in Helene Silverberg, ed., *Gender and American Social Science: The Formative Years* (Princeton, N.J.: Princeton University Press, 1998), 136.

73. Addams to Ely, Nov. 27, 1894; Kelley to Ely, Sept. 17, 1895.

74. Thus it was to Hull House that Ely successfully turned to place a Japanese Ph.D. student eager to earn his travel money home. Ely to Addams, Oct. 10, 1900; Addams to Ely, Oct. 14, 1900; In natural turn, Ely intervened with the president of the Macmillan Company not only to promote Addams' recent lectures but to prepare a special limited edition of Addams's newly published *Democracy and Social Ethics* according to the design of Hull House bookbinder Ellen Gates Starr. Ely to George P. Brett, Dec. 23, 1902.

75. Sklar, "Hull-house Maps," 132.

76. John R. Commons, David J. Saposs, Helen L. Sumner, E. B. Mittelman, H. E. Hoagland, John B. Andrews [and] Selig Perlman; with an introductory note by Henry W. Farnam, *History of Labour in the United States*, 4 vols. (New York, Macmillan, 1935–46); Nancy Folbre, "The 'Sphere of Women' in Early-Twentieth-Century Economics," in Silverberg, *Gender and American Social Science*, 42–43.

77. Robyn Muncy, *Creating a Female Dominion in American Reform, 1890–1935* (New York: Oxford University Press, 1991), 51.

78. Ely to Simons, Nov. 22, 1900; Simons to Ely, Dec. 28, 1896.

79. Ely to Robert La Follette, July 7, 1900; La Follette to Ely, July 12, July 16, 1900; Ely to La Follette, Aug. 9, 1900, March 28, 1901; Rader, 174; Curti and Carstensen, *University of Wisconsin*, 1: 88.

80. Robert M. La Follette to Ely, July 15, 1912, Ely Papers.

81. Ely to Francis McGovern, Jan. 8, 1914; Feb. 18, 1914; Jan. 29, 1915; McGovern to Ely, Jan. 2, 1915; Jan. 19, 1915, Ely papers. On the W. H. Allen Survey, see Curti and Carstensen, *University of Wisconsin*, 2: 267–83.

82. Charles McCarthy, *The Wisconsin Idea* (New York: Macmillan, 1912), 27.

83. 1915 Declaration of Principles on Academic Freedom and Academic Tenure, http://www.aaup.org/AAUP/pubsres/policydocs/contents/1915.htm; Metzger, *Academic Freedom*, 134.

84. John R. Commons, *Myself* (New York: Macmillan, 1934), 95.

85. Ibid., 65.

86. Richard A. Gonce, "John R. Commons 'Five Big Years': 1899–1904," *American Journal of Economics and Sociology* 61 (October 2002): 758–59; Clarence E. Wunderlin, Jr., *Visions of a New Industrial Order: Social Science and Labor Theory in America's Progressive Era* (New York: Columbia University Press, 1992).

87. Wunderlin, *Visions of a New Industrial Order*, 34–35, 45, 67. Commons, e.g., had dropped an earlier emphasis (borrowed in part from fellow economist Henry Carter Adams) on the worker's individual job rights and instead looked to powerful state commissions (preferably with the power of compulsory arbitration) to settle industrial conflicts. On Commons's borrowing from Adams, see also DeBrizzi, 47.

88. Malcolm Rutherford, "Wisconsin Institutionalism: John R. Commons and His Students," *Labor History* 47 (May 2006): 164; Commons, *Myself*, 131.

89. Fink, *Progressive Intellectuals*, 80–113.

90. Rutherford, "Wisconsin Institutionalism," 172–73; Roy Lubove, "Economic Security and Social Conflict in America: The Early Twentieth Century, Part II," *Journal of Social History* 1 (Summer 1968): 325–50; A recent account of Commons's influence alone lists Mt. Holyoke (Ethel Dietrich), Black Mountain (William Zeuch), University of Oklahoma (Leonard Logan and John Ewing), and University of California, Berkeley (Ira Cross, Paul Taylor), and Cornell University (Sumner Slichter), among others, that hired Commons's students. Rutherford, "Wisconsin Institutionalism," 161–88.

91. Commons, *Labor and Administration* 1913, 395–96; Industrial Commission of Wisconsin, *Report on Allied Functions, 1912–1914* (Madison, 1914): 68–74, 81–85.

92. William C. Haygood and Theron Schlabach interview with David Saposs, Sept. 8, 1964, David J. Saposs Papers, WHS.

93. Ibid.

94. Quoted in Fink, *Progressive Intellectuals*, 73; The distinction may have also reflected a division of labor in the Wisconsin curriculum: until 1918 Ely regularly offered the department's core theory courses, in which he exposed students to an eclectic mix of the newly dominant marginal utility and marginal productivity approaches alongside historicist and institutionalist writings that had shaped his own early intellectual development. Marginalist theory, as best represented in the United States by Columbia University economist John Bates Clark, himself a former historicist, tended to validate the classical doctrine of marketplace competition by measuring the value of a commodity on the basis of its utility to the potential consumer (as opposed to labor cost or cost of production). Emphasizing the "psychological relations between people and goods" rather than the "socioeconomic relations between classes of people," the marginalist revolution, as historian Mary O. Furner has explained, at once ushered in an age of more precise, mathematical modeling and a turn away from the "application of theory to practical problems." Precisely such problems concerned Commons and his students. Furner, *Advocacy and Objectivity*, 188.

95. Ely to Commons, March 19, 1904. Commons, *Proportional Representation* (New York: Thomas Y. Crowell, 1896); "Proportional Representation in Belgium," May 1900 in Articles, Speeches, and Miscellaneous Writings, reel 15, Commons Papers, WHS. Given the egos involved, perhaps not surprisingly within two years of Commons's appointment, a conflict had also broken out over the control of finances and attributions in the publication of the labor history documentary collection. Though the two principals ultimately made up, Saposs insinuates that there was a period when Ely tried to block Commons's students from getting their degrees. Rader, *Academic Mind*, 169–70; Commons, *Myself*, 136–38; Saposs interview; Rutherford, "Wisconsin Institutionalism," 164.

96. Commons, "Progressive Individualism," *American Magazine of Civics* (June 1895): 561–74, quotation 562–63. Commons's delimitations on the proper sphere of government regulation largely echoed the framework found in Henry Carter Adams's influential 1887 essay, "Relation of the State to Industrial Action"; Coats, "Henry Carter Adams: A Case Study in the Emergence of the Social Sciences in the United States, 1850–1900," in Coats, *On the History of Economic Thought: British and American Essays* (New York: Routledge, 1992), 1: 365–85; Furner, *Advocacy and Objectivity*, 131; see also Furner, "The Republican Tradition and the New Liberalism: Social Investigation, State Building, and Social Learning in the Gilded Age," in Michael J. Lacey and Mary O. Furner, eds., *The State and Social Investigation in Britain and the United States* (New York: Cambridge University Press, 1993), 237–41.

97. Commons, "Robert Marion La Follette," *North American Review* (1910): 672–77, quotation 672–73.

98. Saposs interview. The young radicals even advanced an "anti-fraternity" bill, limiting fraternity influence over campus organizations at the state house, but discovered to their chagrin that even progressive governor McGovern was a "fraternity man." David Saposs to William M. Leiserson, Jan. 28, 1913, William M. Leiserson Papers, WHS.

99. Fink, *Progressive Intellectuals*, 74–75; Saposs claimed regarding his own fainter "Jewishism" ("we were brought up with Judaism [but] religiously and culturally we were not really Jews") that Professor Commons and his wife treated him differently from Mittelman (and presumably Perlman): "they didn't know because we [the Saposs family] didn't feature it." Saposs interview.

100. Sumner Slichter to Leiserson, Jan. 19, 1915; Leiserson to Ira Cross, July 20, 1910, William L. Leiserson Papers, WHS.

101. Robert S. Maxwell, *La Follette and the Rise of the Progressives in Wisconsin* (Madison: WHS, 1956), 74–86, 153–72.

102. Commons, *Myself*, 152, Elmer Axel Beck, *The Sewer Socialists: A History of the Socialist Party of Wisconsin 1897–1940*, vol. 1, *The Socialist Trinity of the Party, the Unions, and the Press* (Fennimore, Wis.: Westburg Associates, 1982), 98.

103. Isserman, "'God Bless Our American Institutions': The Labor History of John R. Commons," *Labor History* 17 (Summer 1976), 310; Isserman's take, a reflection of the general "new labor history' revolt from Commons' School institutionalism, was regularly echoed by others. To take but one example: "the Wisconsin labor economist John Commons worked hand in glove with Milwaukee socialists on specific legislative measures but devoted his career to refuting the class struggle and finding a place within the capitalist marketplace for collective bargaining." Alan Dawley, *Struggles for Justice: Social Responsibility and the Liberal State* (Cambridge, Mass.: Harvard University Press, 1991), 101. See also Rosemary Feurer, "Interrogating the Wisconsin Idea," *H-Labor*, March 18, 2011; Norman Markowitz, "Interrogating the Wisconsin Idea," *H-Labor*, March 19, 2011. To be sure, the Wisconsin Idea also experienced a "left opposition" in its own day, most notably during the tensions that erupted between the Commons-McCarthy wing of the U.S. Commission on Industrial Relations and commission chairman Frank Walsh. Stromquist, *"Re-Inventing "The People"* recounts: Walsh relentlessly ridiculed the scientific and professional pretensions of those subscribing to the "Idea." They favored creating "what they call "large constructive programs," the proposed measures containing legal machinery which would provide for countless employees, experts, and the like, "of thorough scientific training," the very thought of which should throw the legal profession into spasms of delight, and the proletariat into hopeless despair. While this is going on, fundamentals remain practically untouched (183–84).

104. Republican stalwarts regained the state's legislative reins as early as 1914, and in 1939 in the form of the Employment Peace Act, passed a precedent-setting encroachment on union security, as established by the national Wagner Act; by 1959, however, Progressive Wisconsin again pioneered with a public employee bargaining

law. Elizabeth Tandy Shermer, *Sunbelt Capitalism: Phoenix and the Transformation of American Politics* (Philadelphia: University of Pennsylvania Press, 2013), 97–98.

105. See Desai, *Intellectuals and Socialism*, 49–54; Peter Gay, *Weimar Culture: The Outsider as Insider* (New York: Harper & Row, 1968), 38–45.

106. Paddy Riley, "Clark Kerr: From the Industrial to the Knowledge Economy," in Nelson Lichtenstein, ed., *American Capitalism; Social Thought and Political Economy in the Twentieth* Century (Philadelphia: University of Pennsylvania Press, 2006), 73–74.

107. Elizabeth A. Fones-Wolf, *Selling Free Enterprise: The Business Assault on Labor and Liberalism, 1945–60* (Urbana: University of Illinois Press, 1994), 73–86; Tobias Higbie, "Stirring the Pot and Adding Some Spice: Workers Education at the University of California, 1921–1962," Working Papers Series, UCLA: Institute for Research on Labor and Employment, retrieved from http://escholarship.org/uc/item/2d15z31p; "History of ILR School," http://www.ilr.cornell.edu/about/ILRhistory.html; Riley, 77–79; Michael Hillard, "The End of Collaboration: Industrial Relations' Re-engagement of the Labor Question and Progressive Labor Policy Activism," *Labor: Studies in Working-Class History of the Americas* 9, 4 (2012): 54–60, 54.

Chapter 4. Labor's Search for Legitimacy

Epigraph: U.S. Strike Commission, *Report on the Chicago Strike of June–July, 1894* (Washington, D.C.: GPO, 1895), http://books.google.com/books?id = KUopAAAAY AAJ&pg = PR9&source = gbs_toc_r&cad = 4#v = onepage&q&f = false.

1. For a careful deconstruction of the conversion narrative, see Nick Salvatore, *Eugene V. Debs: Citizen and Socialist* (Urbana: University of Illinois Press, 1982), 147–77. Debs sealed his own preferred version of the story some thirty years later in a tribute to German Social Democratic leader Karl Kautsky: "I was in jail . . . sitting in the darkness as it were, when your pamphlets first came into my hands and your influence first made itself felt in my life" (150). Although Pullman does seem to have marked a turning point in Debs's thought from industrial to political strategies for change, it took him two more years, and only after the defeat of Bryan and Populism in 1896, to declare himself a socialist (161).

2. Stanley Buder, *Pullman: An Experiment in Industrial Order and Community Planning* (New York: Oxford University Press, 1967), 187; Salvatore, *Eugene V. Debs*, 132–38; David Ray Papke, *The Pullman Case: The Clash of Labor and Capital in Industrial America* (Lawrence: University Press of Kansas, 1999), 20–38.

3. U.S. Strike Commission, *Report on the Chicago Strike*, 176–78.

4. While originally twinned with "arbitration" in many advocates' minds, legal "incorporation" of unions—perceived as a way to impose both standing and responsibility on labor actors—soon fell into disuse, particularly as the unions themselves saw little tangible benefit from the move. Nicholas Paine Gilman, *Methods of Industrial Peace* (Boston: Houghton, Mifflin, 1904), 149–97.

5. In New Zealand, compulsory arbitration was abolished (under a Labour government) in the private sector in 1984 and the public sector four years later. By 1991 the Employment Contract Act had also abolished compulsory trade union membership and minimum wage awards that buttressed the entire system. Melanie Nolan and Pat Walsh, "Labour's Leg-Iron? Assessing a Century of Trade Unionism Under the Arbitration System," in Walsh, ed., *Trade Unions, Work and Society: The Centenary of the Arbitration System* (Palmerston North: Dunmore Press, 1994), 9–37, appendices 199–204; Gordon Anderson and Michael Quinlan, "The Changing Role of the State: Regulating Work in Australia and New Zealand, 1788–2007" *Labour History* 95 (November 2008): 125–27; Chris Howell, *Trade Unions and the State: The Construction of Industrial Relations Institutions in Britain, 1890–2000* (Princeton, N.J.: Princeton University Press, 2005), 8.

6. On the "Cardinal's peace" in the dockworkers' strike and larger commitment to the arbitration of labor conflicts, see Robert Gray, *Cardinal Manning: A Biography* (New York: St. Martin's, 1985), 306–11; E. H. Hunt, *British Labour History, 1815–1914* (London: Wiedenfeld and Nicolson, 1981), 304–17, 393 n. 50, quotation 316; H. A. Clegg, Alan Fox, and A. F. Thompson, *A History of British Trade Unions Since 1889* (Oxford: Clarendon, 1964), 1: 388–406; Neville Kirk, *Comrades and Cousins: Globalization, Workers and Labour Movements in Britain, the USA and Australia from the 1880s to 1914* (London: Merlin Press, 2003), 45.

7. Clegg, Fox, and Thompson, *History of British Trade Unions*, 318–19, 393 n. 3.

8. Anderson and Quinlan, "The Changing Role of the State," 122–23; Francis Castles, *The Working Class and Welfare: Reflections on the Political Development of the Welfare State in Australia and New Zealand 1890–1980* (Sydney: Allen and Unwin, 1985), 103. For the restrictive racial assumptions behind Australian welfarism, see esp. Marilyn Lake, "Translating Needs into Rights: The Discursive Imperative of the Australian White Man, 1901–30," in Stefan Dudink, Karen Hagemann, and John Tosh, eds., *Masculinities in Politics and War: Gendering Modern History* (Manchester: Manchester University Press, 2004), 199–237.

9. David Hackett Fischer, *Fairness and Freedom: A History of Two Open Societies, New Zealand and the United States* (New York: Oxford University Press, 2012), 300–302.

10. Peter J. Coleman, *Progressivism and the World of Reform: New Zealand and the Origins of the American Welfare State* (Lawrence: University Press of Kansas, 1987), 130–51; Richard Mitchell, "State Systems of Conciliation and Arbitration: The Legal Origins of the Australasian Model," in Stuart Macintyre and Richard Mitchell, eds., *Foundations of Arbitration: The Origins and Effects of State Compulsory Arbitration, 1890–1914* (Oxford: Oxford University Press Australia, 1989), 85; Stuart Macintyre and Richard Mitchell, "Introduction," *Foundations of Arbitration*, 18. New Zealand's industrial system commanded continuing political support, as rising but generally modest gains in settlement awards conciliated both labor and business interests, if not without moments of friction. Following a strike-free first decade of operation,

packinghouse workers famously struck in defiance of an arbitration decision in 1907 and the Wobbly-like "Red Feds" stoked workplace militancy in the pre-World War I years. Coleman, *Progressivism and the World of Reform*, 145; Fischer, *Fairness and Freedom*, 389–90.

11. Brian Fitzpatrick and Rowan J. Cahill, *The Seamen's Union of Australia, 1872–1972: A History* (Sydney: Seamen's Union, 1981), 21.

12. Kirk, *Comrades and Cousins*, 104.

13. Greg Patmore, *Australian Labour History* (Melbourne: Longman Cheshire, 1991), 105–6; Mitchell, "State Systems," 81–83, 88–89.

14. That Australian state actors should take the lead in resolving civil conflict was perhaps not surprising given their already established role in the dominion's economic development: by the 1880s, an estimated 40 percent of investment capital in New South Wales and Victoria derived from government tariffs and preferential contracts to local industrialists, not to mention the assisted immigration programs that sustained the provincial labor force. Patmore, *Australian Labour History*, 51. Note that the Australian Harvester firm bore no relation to the American agricultural implements firm of the same name.

15. For example, the first defector from the Conciliation and Arbitration Act of 1904 was its chief intellectual author, minister for trade and customs Charles Kingston. Insisting that the wage codes mandated by court settlements include seamen on foreign vessels in the coastal trade (as a way of ensuring Australian-flag wage parity with international competitors), the advanced labor advocate resigned his ministry when the affected clause was stripped from the bill. Joe Isaac and Stuart Macintyre, eds., *The New Province for Law and Order 100 Years of Australian Industrial Conciliation and Arbitration* (Cambridge: Cambridge University Press, 2004), 20–21. Kingston had indeed anticipated a key labor issue in world commerce, as the same clause would "anchor" the La Follette Seamen's Act in the United States a decade later. See Fink, *Sweatshops at Sea: Merchant Seamen in the World's First Globalized Industry, from 1812 to the Present* (Chapel Hill: University of North Carolina Press, 2011), 93–116.

16. "By reconciling Australian employers to trade unionism, compulsory arbitration made pragmatists of non-Labor [Party] politicians. . . . [Even] political conservatives, until the 1980s, learned to accept trade unions." Tim Rowse, "Elusive Middle Ground: A Political History," in Joe Isaac and Stuart Macintyre, eds., *The New Province for Law and Order 100 Years of Australian Industrial Conciliation and Arbitration* (Cambridge: Cambridge University Press, 2004), 17, 53; Kirk, *Comrades and Cousins*, 101, similarly refers to the overall achievement of the Australian labor movement as a success "unmatched in other countries." See also Patmore, *Australian Labour History*, 103–4; Terry Irving and Allen Seager, "Labour and Politics in Canada and Australia: Towards a Comparative Approach to Developments to 1960," in Gregory S. Kealey and Greg Patmore, eds., *Canadian and Australian Labour History: Towards a Comparative Perspective* (Sydney: Australian Society for the Study of Labour History, and St. Johns: Committee on Canadian Labour History, 1990), 239–77.

17. Layton, *Labor and Capital*, 1: 23.

18. John J. O'Neill, "Arbitration," in George E. McNeill, *The Labor Movement: The Problem of Today* (Boston: A.M. Bridgman, 1887), 499, 502–3; Hunt, *British Labour History*, 282.

19. John McClelland testimony cited in Stuart B. Kaufman, ed., *The Samuel Gompers Papers* [SGP], vol. 1, *The Making of a Union Leader, 1850–86* (Urbana: University of Illinois Press, 1986), 1: 287–88. For a more general assessment of Knights of Labor views of the state, see Fink, "Class Conflict American Style," and "The New Labor History and the Powers of Historical Pessimism: Consensus, Hegemony, and the Case of the Knights of Labor," in Fink, *In Search of the Working Class: Essays in American Labor History and Political Culture* (Urbana: University of Illinois Press, 1994), 15–32, 89–143.

20. "Samuel Gompers Introduction to Socialist Thought," "A Translation of a Pamphlet by Carl Hillmann," in SGP, 1: 22, 37.

21. U.S. Senate, *Report of the Committee of the Senate upon the Relations Between Labor and Capital* (Washington D.C.: GPO, 1885), 1: 1177.

22. Ibid., 85. Throughout the Senate inquiry, both committee chairman William H. Blair (R-N.H.) and James Z. George (D-Miss., aka "Mississippi's Great Commoner") made clear, alongside the witnesses' own testimony, their sympathy for unspecified measures of compulsory arbitration as well as related measures like the incorporation of trade unions.

23. Thomas A. Bailey, *A Diplomatic History of the American People* (New York: Appleton-Century-Crofts, 1969), 77, 155, 207, 384, 440–41, 502.

24. Ian Tyrrell, *Woman's World/Woman's Empire: The Woman's Christian Temperance Union in International Perspective, 1880–1930* (Chapel Hill: University of North Carolina Press, 1991), 178; Chicago's Protective Agency for Women and Children (which became Chicago Legal Aid in 1905)—led by reformers equally touched by the Social Gospel—similarly embraced arbitration over adversarial prosecution in the settlement of civil disputes. Felice Batlan, "Constructing a Female Dominion of Legal Aid: The Chicago Experience," paper delivered to Newberry Seminar on Women and Gender, September 28, 2012.

25. SGP, 1: 349.

26. McGuire testimony, *Report . . . Labor and Capital*, 1: 322.

27. For a recent qualification and partial defense of the early AFL's "anti-government" message as well as vigorous discussion thereon, see Dorothy Sue Cobble, "Pure and Simple Radicalism: Putting the Progressive Era AFL in Its Time," with responses by Melvyn Dubofsky, Andrew Wender Cohen, Donna T. Haverty-Stacke, and Julie Greene, *Labor: Studies in Working-Class History of the Americas* 10 (Winter 2013): 89–116.

28. McGuire testimony, *Report . . . Labor and Capital*, 1: 339.

29. Laura M Westhoff, *A Fatal Drifting Apart: Democratic Social Knowledge and Chicago Reform* (Columbus: Ohio State University Press, 2007), 137–38; Andrew

Wender Cohen, *The Racketeer's Progress: Chicago and the Struggle for the Modern American Economy, 1900–1940* (New York: Cambridge University Press, 2004), 108–11, 123–39.

30. 25 Stat. 501. For the most thorough treatment of these events, see Gerald G. Eggert, *Railroad Labor Disputes: The Beginnings of Federal Strike Policy* (Ann Arbor: University of Michigan Press, 1967), 54–107.

31. Cong. Rec., House, 49th Cong, 1st sess., vol. 17, pt. 3, April 1, 1886, 3008–3009–3010.

32. Ibid., 3017–18.

33. Ibid., 3034. Foran, of course, was all too prescient in citing the federal mails as a potential source of government repression of railway strike activity—exactly what happened amid the Pullman Boycott of 1894 (though the Crain Act had nothing to do with state intervention in that case).

34. Gompers to George Iden, July 15, 1892, SGP, 3: 192.

35. McGuire, AFL Convention, 1892, SGP, 3: 258–59.

36. Gompers testimony to Pullman Strike Commission, August 1894, SGP, 3: 575–76.

37. Edwin E. Witte, *Historical Survey of Labor Arbitration* (Philadelphia: University of Pennsylvania Press, 1952), 9–10.

38. Gompers Address to National Civic Federation Conference on Industrial Arbitration, December 17, 1900, SGP, 5: 300.

39. *John Swinton's Paper*, June 6, June 13, 1886.

40. Maude, as cited in James Cracraft, *Two Shining Souls: Jane Addams, Leo Tolstoy, and the Quest for Global Peace* (Lanham, Md.: Lexington, 2012), 65, and more generally, 25–69.

41. Tyrrell, *Woman's World/Woman's Empire*, 178.

42. Civic Federation of Chicago, *Report on Congress on Industrial Conciliation and Arbitration*. Chicago, Novemner 13–14, 1894 (Chicago: Wm. C. Hollister & Bro, 1894), 50.

43. Ibid., 31

44. Howard S. Kaltenborn, *Governmental Adjustment of Labor Disputes* (Chicago: Foundation Press, 1933), 37; Lloyd's continuing interest in the subject would lead to an extended visit to New Zealand, eventuating in a dreamy tribute, *A Country Without Strikes: A Visit to the Compulsory Arbitration Court of New Zealand* (New York: Doubleday, Page, 1900).

45. Westhoff, *A Fatal Drifting Apart*, 152.

46. U.S. Strike Commission, *Report on the Chicago Strike*, "Conclusions and Recommendations," xlvii.

47. Ibid., xlviii.

48. Ibid., lii–liv.

49. Ibid., xlvi–xlvii.

50. Salvatore, *Eugene V. Debs*, 134, 136. Unsurprisingly, therefore, Debs publicly applauded the recommendations of the Strike Commission. Almont Lindsey, *The Pullman Strike: The Story of a Unique Experiment and of a Great Labor Upheaval* (Chicago: University of Chicago Press, 1942), 357–58.

51. Witte, *Historical Survey of Labor Arbitration*, 17; The Newlands Act of 1913, built on the general principles of Erdman, permitted faster investigatory intervention by a government Board of Mediation. The Adamson Act of 1916 further extended mediation procedures while guaranteeing the running trades an eight-hour day. Following nationalization of the railroads in World War I, a Railway Labor Board (RLB) was established under the Transportation Act of 1920 with the authority to make nonbinding proposals (backed by the political authority of the government) for the resolution of disputes. Unhappy experience among the unionized railroad brotherhoods with government intervention during the bitter railroad shopcraft strike of 1922 doomed the RLB. In its place emerged the Railway Labor Act of 1926 (amended in 1934 and 1936 to include airline industry workers)—again an "exceptional" example of tripartite cooperation (business-labor-government) substituting strong mediation and implicit union recognition for strikes or arbitration. Elwin Wilber Sigmund, "Federal Laws Concerning Railroad Labor Disputes: A Legislative and Legal History, 1877–1934" (Ph.D. dissertation, University of Illinois, 1961).

52. Clarence E. Wunderlin, Jr., *Visions of a New Industrial Order: Social Science and Labor Theory in America's Progressive Era* (New York: Columbia University Press, 1992) offers the definitive account of USIC operations, 27–45, 64–68. On Jenks see also Mary O. Furner, "The Republican Tradition and the New Liberalism: Social Investigation, State Building, and Social Learning in the Gilded Age," in Michael J. Lacey and Furner, eds., *The State and Social Investigation in Britain and the United States* (Washington D.C.: Woodrow Wilson Center Press, 1993), 230–31.

53. "Industrial Arbitration," *Hull-House Bulletin*, April 1896 (reference courtesy of Shana Bernstein); Jane Addams, *Twenty Years at Hull House* (Boston: Bedford, 1999 [1910]), 128–29.

54. Addams, *Newer Ideals of Peace* (New York: Macmillan, 1907), 133.

55. Richard A. Greenwald, *The Triangle Fire, the Protocols of Peace, and Industrial Democracy in Progressive Era New York* (Philadelphia: Temple University Press, 2005), 14, 57, 68, 73–74.

56. Jo Ann E. Argersinger, *Making the Amalgamated: Gender, Ethnicity, and Class in the Baltimore Clothing Industry, 1899-1939* (Baltimore: Johns Hopkins University Press, 1999), 43–44, 122.

57. Philippa Strum, *Brandeis: Beyond Progressivism* (Lawrence: University Press of Kansas, 1993), 27, 34.

58. Greenwald, *The Triangle Fire*, 214–22.

59. Brandeis, as quoted in Strum, *Brandeis*, 24–25.

60. On the unions' repeated attempts to secure legislative relief from injunctions, see Fink, "Labor, Liberty, and the Law: Trade Unionism and the Problem of the American Constitutional Order," in *In Search of the Working Class: Essays in American Labor History and Political Culture* (Urbana: University of Illinois Press, 1994), 155–56.

61. Harry A. Millis and Royal E. Montgomery, *Organized Labor* (New York: McGraw-Hill, 1945), 505–6, 630–31.

62. Melvyn Dubofsky, "The Federal Judiciary, Free Labor, and Equal Rights" in Richard Schneirov, Shelton Stromquist, and Nick Salvatore, eds., *The Pullman Strike and the Crisis of the 1890s* (Urbana: University of Illinois Press, 1999), 163, 165.

63. Clayton Antitrust Act, Sec. 6 (codified at 15 U.S.C. § 17).

64. Dallas L. Jones, "The Enigma of the Clayton Act," *Industrial and Labor Relations Review* 10 (January 1957): 214; David Brody, "Free Labor, Law, and American Trade Unionism," in Stanley Engerman, ed., *Terms of Labor: Slavery, Serfdom, and Free Labor* (Stanford, Calif.: Stanford University Press, 1999), 227–28. Yet, even the more politically effective Norris-LaGuardia Act (1932) and Wagner Act (1935)—that buttressed labor's legitimacy in later years—never escaped, according to Brody, the core ideological and legal confinement of collective worker behavior embedded in an "insurmountable case law." As Brody demonstrates, despite the legislative presumption under the Norris-LaGuardia Anti-Injunction Act (1932) and the Wagner Act (1935) that organized workers could best exercise "actual freedom of contract," core legal doctrines of individual property rights, subsequently confirmed and underlined by the Taft-Hartley Act (1947), privileged the rights of non-association as well as the employer's right to at-will decisions of hiring and firing, 236–44, quotations, 237, 241.

65. Marilyn Lake, "'This Great America': H. B. Higgins and Transnational Progressivism," *Australian Historical Studies* 44, 2 (2013): 172–88, quotation 174.

66. Interacting with its internal policy differences, the commission was divided by a series of personal and political conflicts, narrated previously in Fink, *Progressive Intellectuals and the Dilemmas of Intellectual Commitment* (Cambridge, Mass.: Harvard University Press, 1997), 80–113.

67. U.S. Commission on Industrial Relations, Final Report of the Commission on Industrial Relations, including the report of Basil M. Manly, director of research and investigation, and the individual reports and statements of the several commissioners (1916), http://archive.org/details/finalreportofcom00unitiala, 310–404.

68. Fink, *Progressive Intellectuals*, 105.

69. Joseph A. McCartin, *Labor's Great War: The Struggle for Industrial Democracy and the Origins of Modern American Labor Relations, 1912–1921* (Chapel Hill: University of North Carolina Press, 1997), 90, quotation 175.

70. Barry D. Karl, *The Uneasy State: The United States from 1915 to 1945* (Chicago: University of Chicago Press, 1983), 43.

71. R. Todd Laugen, *The Gospel of Progressivism: Moral Reform and Labor War in Colorado, 1900–1930* (Boulder: University Press of Colorado, 2010), 97–98.

72. The justificatory language for state intervention in Kansas—"clothed with a public interest"—was drawn directly from the *Munn v. Illinois* (1877) Supreme Court decision, permitting government regulation of railroad rates. John Hugh Bowers, *The Kansas Court of Industrial Relations: The Philosophy and History of the Court* (Chicago: McClurg, 1922), 39–45; Court of Industrial Relations http://www.kshs.org/kansapedia/court-of-industrial-relations/12017 stet.

73. *Chas. Wolff Packing Co. v. Court of Industrial Relations of Kansas*, 262 (U.S. 522 (1923).

74. Laugen, *The Gospel of Progressivism*, 116–22, quotation 118.

75. Ibid., 120–24.

76. Charles Delgadillo, "'The Balance Wheel": William Allen White, the Kansas Industrial Court, and the Progressive Approach to the Labor Question, 1914–1925," *Labor: Studies in Working-Class History of the Americas* 10 (Spring 2013): 81–98; Bowers, *The Kansas Court*, 48–50.

77. Delgadillo, "The Balance Wheel," 94–97.

78. Larry G. Gerber, "The United States and Canadian National Industrial Conferences of 1919: A Comparative Analysis," *Labor History* 32 (1991): 42–65.

79. "Arbitration—Compulsory or Voluntary," *New Republic* 22 (May 26, 1920): 396–98.

80. Ibid., quotation from W. Jett Lauck, 61; McCartin, *Labor's Great War*, 194.

81. On the Taft-Walsh trajectory across the war years, see esp. Valerie Jean Conner, *The National War Labor Board: Stability, Social Justice, and the Voluntary State in World War I* (Chapel Hill: University of North Carolina Press, 1983), 173–86.

82. Conner, *The National War Labor Board*, 176.

83. Howell, *Trade Unions and the State*, 47–58, 61–69, quotations 13, 16.

84. While hewing to the general principle of anti-statism or "voluntarism," the AFL, especially at the local level, engaged heavily in the politics of governmental regulation. Michael Rogin, "Voluntarism: The Political Functions of an Anti-Political Doctrine," *Industrial and Labor Relations Review* 15 (July 1962): 534–35; Julie Greene, *Pure and Simple Politics: The American Federation of Labor and political activism, 1881–1917* (Urbana: University of Illinois Press, 1988).

85. Current-day union density rates offer only a crude measure of union "presence" and legitimacy, but still they provide an overall comparative sense of strength in a time of generally downward pressures on workers. The latest (2011) OECD figures list the U.S. at 11.3 percent as one of the world's lowest union density rates (Korea is next at 9.7 percent), well below New Zealand (20.8) and Australia 18.0, the latter down considerably from its 1999 standing at 24.9. The highest rates pertain to countries with strong state support (via long-governing Social-Democratic parties) for industry-wide collective-bargaining agreements: e.g., Sweden 67.7 and Norway 54.6. OECD StatEx tracts, "Trade-Union Density," http://stats.oecd.org/Index.aspx?DatasetCode = UN _DEN; see also Walter Galenson, *The World's Strongest Trade Unions: The Scandinavian Labor Movement* (Westport, Conn.: Quorum Books, 1998), and for industrial

relations systems by country, see the European Industrial Relations Observatory online, http://www.eurofound.europa.eu/eiro/country_index.htm.

86. Sanford M. Jacoby, "American Exceptionalism Revisited: The Importance of Management," in Jacoby, ed., *Masters to Managers: Historical and Comparative Perspectives on American Employers* (New York: Columbia University Press, 1991), 173–200, esp. 178–79; Cathie Jo Martin, "Sectional Parties, Divided Business," *Studies in American Political Development* 20 Fall 2006): 174, 181; Albert K. Steigerwalt, *The National Association of Manufacturers, 1895–1914: A Study in Business Leadership* (Grand Rapids: Bureau of Business Research, University of Michigan, 1964), 114.

87. The best overall text here is probably Nelson Lichtenstein, *State of the Union: A Century of American Labor* (Princeton, N.J.: Princeton University Press, 1982). See also Jefferson Cowie and Nick Salvatore, "The Long Exception: Rethinking the Place of the New Deal in American History," *ILWCH* 74 (September 2004): 3–32. On post-1970s developments, and especially a sure-handed comparison of U.S. and Australian developments, see David Brody, "A Tale of Two Labor Laws," *Dissent* 57 (Spring 2010): 63–68.

88. M. K. Gandhi, *An Autobiography: The Story of My Experiments with Truth* (Ahmedabad: Navajivan Publishing House, 1927), 63–64; Cracraft, *Two Shining Souls*, 73.

89. Erik H. Erikson, *Gandhi's Truth: On the Origins of Militant Nonviolence* (New York: Norton, 1969), 255–95.

90. The twists and turns of Indian industrial relations, resulting in a bureaucratic system that reportedly stifles business innovation on the one hand and independent trade unionism on the other, requires a careful treatment of its own. See, e.g., Rohini Hensman, *Workers, Unions and Global Capitalism: Lessons from India* (New Delhi: Tulika Books, 2011).

Chapter 5. Coming of Age in Internationalist Times

Epigraph: Sally M. Miller, *From Prairie to Prison: The Life of Social Activist Kate Richards O'Hare* (Columbia: University of Missouri Press, 1993), 26.

1. "Triangle Fire: Biography: Pauline Newman," *American Experience*, 2011.

2. Charles Elbert Zaretz, *The Amalgamated Clothing Workers of America: A Study in Progressive Trades: Unionism* (New York: Ancon, 1934), 94.

3. "Internationalism as applied to socialism meant not only the international organization that brought national socialist parties together at regular intervals before World War I in the Second International and its International Socialist Bureau, but also the broad congruity of individual national socialist ideologies and policies that were in symbiotic (and sometimes even dialectical) relationship with the International through debates and policymaking. Further, internationalism was a key expression of the socialist belief that workers had more in common with one another across national boundaries than they did with their own national employers." Stephen Burwood, "Debsian Socialism Through a Transnational Lens," *JGAPE* 2 (July 2003): 255.

4. Daniel Bell, "Marxian Socialism in the United States," in Donald Drew Egbert and Stow Persons, eds., *Socialism and American Life*, vol. 1 (Princeton, N.J.: Princeton University Press, 1952), 267.

5. Ibid., 283, quotation 267.

6. To be sure, by common contemporary measure, the concept of "socialist identity politics" is an oxymoron. Thus, even as "socialism" invokes a modernist, universalizing ideology that stresses material political-economic egalitarianism, "identity politics"—as associated with late twentieth-century social movements including second wave feminism, Black Power, and gay and lesbian liberation—self-consciously rejects universalism in order to combat the marginalization of particular groups with a strategy of "recognition, "self-awareness," and close examination of community "experience." "Identity Politics," *Stanford Encyclopedia of Philosophy* (July 2002, rev. February 2012), http://plato.stanford.edu/entries/identity-politics/.

7. Bell, "Marxian Socialism in the United States," 217–18.

8. See, e.g., David A. Shannon, review of Egbert and Parsons, eds., *Socialism and American Life*, *Pennsylvania History* 19 (October 1952): 511–13. For two works of genuine subtlety that probe the question of comparative outcomes outside Bell's framework, see Seymour Martin Lipset and Gary W. Marks, *It Didn't Happen Here: Why Socialism Failed in the United States* (New York: Norton, 2000); and Robin Archer, *Why Is There No Labor Party in the United States?* (Princeton, N.J.: Princeton University Press, 2007).

9. Kathryn Kish Sklar, *Florence Kelley and the Nation's Work: The Rise of Women's Political Culture, 1830–1900* (New Haven, Conn.: Yale University Press, 1995), 86.

10. Upton Sinclair to Floyd Dell, May 1, 1912, Floyd Dell Papers, Newberry Library Special Collections, Box 4, Folder 153.

11. Ira Kipnis, *The American Socialist Movement, 1897–1912* (New York; Columbia University Press, 1952), 81–106.

12. Algie Martin Simons, *Social Forces in American History* (New York: Macmillan, 1911), 317.

13. Kipnis, *American Socialist Movement*, 125–27; Shannon, *Socialist Party*, 16–17.

14. *ISR* 1 (Feb. 1, Dec. 1, 1900).

15. *Milwaukee Leader*, January 24, 1912. The reference was to the socialist jump to the single largest party delegation, as led by Karl Liebknicht, in the Reichstag.

16. Howard H. Quint, *The Forging of American Socialism: Origins of the Modern Movement* (Columbia: University of South Carolina Press, 1853), 28–30, 72–102.

17. Salvatore Salerno, *Red November, Black November: Culture and Community in the Industrial Workers of the World* (Albany, N.Y.: SUNY Press, 1989), 49–52; Marian J. Morton, *Emma Goldman and the American Left: "Nowhere at Home"* (New York: Twayne, 1992), 55–57.

18. James R. Green, *Grass-Roots Socialism: Radical Movements in the Southwest, 1895–1943* (Baton Rouge: Louisiana State University Press, 1978), 12–52.

19. Kent Kreuter and Gretchen Kreuter, *An American Dissenter: The Life of Algie Martin Simons 1870–1950* (Lexington: University Press of Kentucky, 1969), 72.

20. Kreuter and Kreuter, *An American Dissenter*, 56, 69–70, 93–94, 144–45, 152–55, 159–62. On the SPA's so-called Right, Victor Berger's Milwaukee (along with several other city-based socialist machines) effectively embraced a more incremental, "revisionist," or "gradualist" path most fully articulated in Germany by Eduard Bernstein and in France by Jean Jaurès. Rejecting the revolutionism of the Communist Manifesto, Berger, like Bernstein, embraced socialism as a process that was advancing "every day" and serving the interests not only of the "working class" but of "all mankind." Even in self-consciously accommodating themselves to American electoral realities, however, the Wisconsin socialists carefully nursed their European bona fides. Responding to criticism in more orthodox quarters for publishing a "municipal program," Berger lieutenant Carl Thompson lashed out at those he deprecated as "impossibilists." Notwithstanding the fierceness of factional conflict on both sides of the Atlantic, Milwaukee socialists happily welcomed German left-winger Karl Liebknecht (son of SPD founder Wilhelm) as part of a speaking tour on behalf of SPA electoral candidates in 1910. Kipnis, *American Socialist Movement*, 118–21; Carl D. Thompson, "Wisconsin and Her Critics," *ISR* 6 (July 1905): 21.

21. Melvyn Dubofsky, *"Big Bill" Haywood* (Manchester: Manchester University Press, 1987), 10–23.

22. Ibid., 33.

23. Salerno, *Red November, Black November*, 75.

24. Bell, "Marxian Socialism in the United States," 286.

25. Salerno, *Red November, Black November*, 60, 94.

26. James R. Barrett, *William Z. Foster and the Tragedy of American Radicalism* (Urbana: University of Illinois Press, 1999), 48–49.

27. Fraina biographer Paul M. Buhle goes so far to as to suggest that he "might have been the [American] Communists' Antonio Gramsci, if not likely their Lenin," *A Dreamer's Paradise Lost: Louis C. Fraina/Lewis Corey (1892–1953) and the Decline of Radicalism in the United States* (Atlantic Highlands, N.J.: Humanities Press, 1995), 54–57.

28. Wayne Thorpe, *"The Workers Themselves": Revolutionary Syndicalism and International Labor, 1913–1923* (Amsterdam: International Institute of Social History, 1989), 1–28, quotation, 1; Salerno, *Red November, Black November*, 36–37.

29. James R. Green, *Death in the Haymarket, A Story of Chicago, the First Labor Movement, and the Bombing That Divided Gilded Age America* (New York: Pantheon, 2006), 128–32.

30. Morton, *Emma Goldman and the American Left*, 11; On Chernyshevsky and the Russian *narodnik* vision of a peasant-based socialism, see Lindemann, *History of European* Socialism, 168–69.

31. Failing to concoct an effective bomb, Berkman fired three shots from a revolver and jumped Frick with a knife to no avail. Berkman, whose silence protected

Goldman from prosecution, received a twenty-two-year sentence, later commuted to fourteen.

32. Berkman's *Prison Memoirs*, as quoted in Vivian Gornick, *Emma Goldman: Revolution as a Way of Life* (New Haven, Conn.: Yale University Press, 2011), 23.

33. Emma Goldman, *Living My Life*, vol. 1 (New York: Dover, 1970 [1931]), 3.

34. Helen C. Camp, *Iron in Her Soul: Elizabeth Gurley Flynn and the American Left* (Pullman: Washington State University Press, 1995), 3–18.

35. Ibid., 53.

36. "Biography," Inventory of the Ralph Korngold Papers, Newberry Library; *Chicago Daily Socialist*, Letter to Editor, Dec. 4, 1909, Ralph Korngold Papers, note from Piri Ozer Korngold, n.d. Box 8, folder 186.

37. For an enduring account of this shift, see James R. Green, *Grass-Roots Socialism: Radical Movements in the Southwest, 1895–1943* (Baton Rouge: Louisiana State University Press, 1978), 12–52.

38. Ibid., 20.

39. Ibid., 157.

40. This characterization is a distillation from Elliott Shore, *Talkin' Socialism: J. A. Wayland and the Role of the Press in American Radicalism, 1890–1912* (Lawrence: University of Kansas Press, 1988).

41. Ibid., 196.

42. Ibid., 34–37.

43. Burwood, "Debsian Socialism Through a Transnational Lens," 280.

44. Sally M. Miller, *From Prairie to Prison: The Life of Social Activist Kate Richards O'Hare* (Columbia: University of Missouri Press, 1993), quotation 26; see also 17, 21–44.

45. Debs, *Social Democrat*, as quoted in Nick Salvatore, *Eugene V. Debs: Citizen and Socialist* (Urbana: University of Illinois Press, 1982), 165.

46. Ibid.

47. Ray Ginger, *The Bending Cross: A Biography of Eugene Victor Debs* (New Brunswick, N.J.: Rutgers University Press, 1949), 26–27, 63, 80.

48. In separating the nineteenth- and twentieth-century European socialist tradition from its more ancient and medieval precedents, Albert S. Lindemann summarizes: "Modern socialists have normally been secular, basing their theories on human rationality, on specifically human feelings of solidarity, and on natural law, as distinguished from such mystical concepts as divine inspiration, brotherhood in Christ, or divine law. This is not to ignore that many socialists, even those who became militantly anti-Christian, emerged from a Christian background [etc.]. . . . Yet on balance modern socialism has been an enemy of organized religion and of theological approaches to social problems," *A History of European Socialism* (New Haven, Conn.: Yale University Press, 1983), xii.

49. Mark Pittenger, *American Socialists and Evolutionary Thought, 1870–1920* (Madison: University of Wisconsin Press, 1993), 89–90.

50. Floyd Dell, *Homecoming: An Autobiography* (Port Washington, N.Y.: Kennikat Press, 1961 [1933]), 68, 73, 192.

51. Tony Michels, *A Fire in Their Hearts: Yiddish Socialists in New York* (Cambridge, Mass.: Harvard University Press, 2005), 179.

52. Harry Rogoff, *An East Side Epic: The Life and Work of Meyer London* (New York: Vanguard, 1930), 8–12.

53. Pittenger, 103–10.

54. Cahanas quoted in Michels, 80.

55. Pittenger, 40, 101–2.

56. L. Glen Seretan, *Daniel DeLeon: The Odyssey of an American Marxist* (Cambridge, Mass.: Harvard University Press, 1979), 78–81; Carl Reeve, *The Life and Times of Daniel De Leon* (New York: Humanities Press, 1972), 6.

57. As Ira Kipnis fairly noted, the pre-World War I Socialist Party—despite a rhetorical stand for racial equality—"made virtually no effort to use the Party in a struggle for Negro rights," while tolerating separate racial party locals in the South as well as openly racist stands by party leaders like Victor Berger, 131, 133–34; Similarly, see Shannon, *The Socialist Party of America* (Chicago: Quadrangle Books, 1967 [1955]), 50–53, though the latter also notes the exceptional work of racial liberals like William English Walling and Charles Edward Russell. On Debs's own progressive racial convictions, see William P. Jones, " 'Nothing Special to Offer the Negro': Revisiting the 'Debsian View' of the Negro Question," *ILWCH* 7 (2008): 212–22.

58. David Levering Lewis, *W. E. B. Du Bois: Biography of a Race, 1868–1919* (New York: Henry Holt, 1993), 186, 313, 338.

59. Ibid., 65.

60. Ibid., 117–49.

61. Axel R. Schäfer, "W. E. B. Du Bois, German Social Thought, and the Racial Divide in American Progressivism, 1892–1909," *JAH* 88 (Dec. 2001); 925–49, quotations 947, 937.

62. Du Bois as quoted in Lewis, 313, 420–22.

63. Ibid., 423, 526.

64. Jeffrey P. Perry, *Hubert Harrison: The Voice of Harlem Radicalism, 1883–1918* (New York: Columbia University Press, 2009), 4–10, 57, 83–87, 115, 137, 147.

65. Ibid., 8, 277, 289–91; Judith Stein, *The World of Marcus Garvey: Race and Class in Modern Society* (Baton Rouge: Louisiana State University Press, 1986), 43–48, 50–51.

66. Hillquit, as quoted in Gerald Sorin, *The Prophetic Minority: American Jewish Immigrant Radicals, 1880–1920* (Bloomington: Indiana University Press, 1985), 115.

67. Sorin, *The Prophetic Minority*, quotation 3, 61–62.

68. Carl D. Thompson, "The Principles and Program of Socialism," *Wayland's Monthly* 44 (December 1903): 9.

69. For a useful overview, see Dan McKanan, "The Implicit Religion of Radicalism: Socialist Party Theology, 1900–1934," *Journal of the American Academy of Religion*

78 (September 2010): 750–89. For an excellent account of cross-over tendencies in the Plains states between Pentecostalism and socialism, see Jarod Roll, *Spirit of Rebellion Labor and Religion in the New Cotton South* (Urbana: University of Illinois Press, 2010), 27–51.

70. Wicker pamphlet, as promoted on cover of *Wayland's Monthly* 44 (Dec. 1903), J. A. Wayland, Girard, Kansaa.

71. Walling famously (and with characteristic vituperative exaggeration) accused A. M. Simons and other National Executive Committee members of plotting to seize control of the party and turn it into a "labor party." See, e.g., John Spargo to Simons, Nov. 29, 1909; Spargo to J. G. Phelps Stokes, Dec. 3, 1909; Victor Berger to Simons, Dec. 6, 1909, Records of the Socialist Party of America, ProQuest microfilm edition, reel 4 (1903–1913). See also Shannon, *Socialist Party*, 60–68.

72. George M. Marsden, *Fundamentalism and American Culture* (New York: Oxford University Press, 2006), 104–5, quotations 149, 159.

73. Gary Dorrien, *The Making of American Liberal Theology: Idealism, Realism, and Modernity, 1900–1950* (Louisville, Ky.: Westminster John Knox Press, 2003), 24–26.

74. Ibid., 77.

75. Walter Rauschenbusch, *Christianity and the Social Crisis in the 21st Century: The Classic that Woke up the Church*, ed. Paul B. Rauschenbush (New York: Harper-One, 2007), 2, 8, 31.

76. *Christianizing the Social Order* as quoted in Dorrien, *Making of American Liberal Theology*, 114.

77. Marilyn Howley Smith, "Vida Scudder and Social Reform: A Theology of Hope" (Ph.D. dissertation, St. Louis University, 1996), 1–15, 199–200; Dorrien, 128–38.

78. Robert D. Reynolds, Jr., "Millionaire Socialist and Omnist Episcopalian: J. G. Phelps Stokes's Political and Spiritual Search for the 'All'," in Jacob H. Dorn, ed., *Socialism and Christianity in Early Twentieth Century America* (Westport, Conn.: Greenwood Press, 1998), 199–222, quotation 204.

79. Herron as quoted in Quint, *Forging of American Socialism*, 133–34.

80. Mitchell Pirie Briggs, *George D. Herron and the European Settlement*, Stanford University Publications University Series, History, Economics, and Political Science 3, 2 (New York: AMS Press 1971 [1932]), 11–12.

81. Bebel, as quoted in Mari Jo Buhle, *Women and American Socialism, 1870–1920* (Urbana: University of Illinois Press, 1981), 27, 180–81.

82. Buhle, *Women and American Socialism*, 248–49.

83. O'Hare as quoted in Shore, *Talkin' Socialism*, 152.

84. Buhle, *Women and American Socialism*, 125.

85. Sally M. Ward, "Social Democratic Millennium: Visions of Gender," in Peter H. Buckingham, ed., *Expectations for the Millennium: American Socialist Visions of the Future* (Westport, Conn.: Greenwood, 2002), 65.

86. Shore, *Talkin' Socialism*, 156.

87. Kreuter and Kreuter, *An American Dissenter*, 120; Miller, "Social Democratic Millennium: Visions of Gender,"in Peter H. Buckingham, ed., *Expectations for the Millenium: American Socialist Visions of the Future* (Westport, Conn.: Greenwood, 2002), 66.

88. "The Simplification of Life," n.d., May Walden Papers, Box 6, folder 154, Newberry Library Special Collections.

89. Christine Stansell, *American Moderns: Bohemian New York and the Creation of a New Century* (New York: Metropolitan Books, 2000), 227.

90. Goldman as quoted in Candace Falk, *Love, Anarchy, and Emma Goldman* (New York: Holt, Rinehart and Winston, 1984), 115–16.

91. May Walden Papers, Box 6, folder 155.

92. Stokes and Strunsky as quoted in Leon Fink, *Progressive Intellectuals and the Dilemmas of Democratic Commitment* (Cambridge, Mass.: Harvard University Press, 1997), 158–59; for an extended account of the Strunsky-Walling relationship, see 147–83.

93. Margaret Sanger, *U.S. History*, http://www.u-s-history.com/pages/h1676.html. On the larger relations of feminism to sex education, see Nancy F. Cott, *The Grounding of Modern Feminism* (New Haven, Conn.: Yale University Press, 1987), 145–74.

94. Ibid., 66; on Goldman's public image, see Stansell, *American Moderns*, 120–44.

95. Walden, "Anticipate the Best Women," 1913 Walden Papers, Box 6, folder 152. In a note scrawled at the end of her typed manuscript, Walden wrote, ""'This was written in 1913 and rejected because of its sentiment in underlined line 1, this page. They [presumably *Daily Socialist*] would accept it if I would agree to change that line. But I refused." The line in question reads, "Every weapon we can grasp we must make use of to further our Cause, which is the Cause of ALL Humanity."

96. Recent accounts agree on this point. Compare Michael Kazin, "The springtime of the left ended abruptly in the spring of 1917"; Michael Kazin, *American Dreamers: How the Left Changed a Nation* (New York: Vintage, 2011), 146; and John Patrick Diggins who describes how the socialist intellectuals he calls the Lyrical Left became "hopelessly divided by the war," *The Rise and Fall of the American Left* (New York: Norton, 1992), 104.

97. Kazin, *American Dreamers*, 146–54; Shannon, *Socialist Party*, 126–49.

98. Miller, *From Prairie to Prison*, 185.

99. Green, *Grass-Roots Socialism*, 381–82.

100. F. M. Goodhue, "History of Commonwealth College [1924–1931]," ms. copy (145–46) in Richard W. St. John Collection, Commonwealth College Papers, University of Arkansas, Fayetteville, Arkansas, reference courtesy of Thomas Alter.

101. Miller, *From Prairie to Prison*, 166, 192–237, quotation 217–18.

102. For an example of transnational organizational breakdown (and this among seamen, the most international of labor forces), see Fink, *Sweatshops at Sea: Merchant*

Seamen in the World's First Globalized Industry, from 1812 to the Present (Chapel Hill: University of North Carolina Press, 2011), 135–41.

103. Joseph Schlossberg, *The Workers and the Their World: Aspects of the Workers' Struggle at Home and Abroad* (New York: A.L.P. Committee, 1935), 160.

104. Goldman and Reitman, as quoted in Falk, *Love, Anarchy, and Emma Goldman*, 135–36. Stansell notes of the contemporary experiments in "sexual modernism" that "few . . . were as successful as the participants billed them. . . . The persistence, even the consolidation, of men's privileges within an egalitarian framework would prove a defining feature of twentieth-century American society" (227).

105. Dell, as quoted in Frank A. Stricker, "Socialism, Feminism, and the New Morality: The Separate Freedoms of Max Eastman, William English Walling, and Floyd Dell, 1910–1930" (Ph.D. dissertation, Princeton University, 1974), 134, 159; Dell, *Homecoming*, 199.

106. May Walden Papers, Box 7, folder 186.

Epilogue

1. Steve Fraser, "The Two Gilded Ages," *TomDispatch*, April 22, 2008, http://www.tomdispatch.com/post/174922.

2. Jefferson Cowie and Nick Salvatore, "The Long Exception: Rethinking the Place of the New Deal in American History," *International Labor and Working-Class History* 74 (Fall 2008): 3–32. See, e.g., "Our founding mythos of individualism has structured our collective life, created much of value, and become so intimately intertwined with the very essence of the nation itself that its limitations become most difficult to perceive and discuss," 25–26.

3. Ira Katznelson, *Fear Itself: The New Deal and the Origins of Our Time* (New York: Norton, 2013).

4. Rodgers, *Atlantic Crossings: Social Politics in a Progressive Age* (Cambridge, Mass.: Harvard University Press, 1998), 409–46.

5. For the reform push, see, e.g., Mary L. Dudziak, *Cold War Civil Rights: Race and the Image of American Democracy* (Princeton, N.J.: Princeton University Press, 2000).

6. Victoria De Grazia, *Irresistible Empire: America's Advance Through Twentieth-Century Europe* (Cambridge, Mass: Harvard University Press, 2005); Charles S. Maier, "'Malaise': The Crisis of Capitalism in the 1970s," in Niall Ferguson et al., eds., *The Shock of the Global: The 1970s in Perspective* (Cambridge, Mass.: Belknap Press of Harvard University Press, 2010), 25–48; Elizabeth Tandy Shermer, "The South's No. 1 Salesman; Luther Hodges and the Transatlantic Origins of the Global Nueva South," in Andrew Preston and Doug Rossinow, eds., *American Politics, World Politics* (London: Oxford University Press: forthcoming).

7. Steve Fraser, "Dress Rehearsal for the New Deal: Shop-Floor Insurgents, Political Elites, and Industrial Democracy in the Amalgamated Clothing Workers," in Michael H. Frisch and Daniel J. Walkowitz, eds., *Working-Class America: Essays on Labor, Community, and American Society* (Urbana: University of Illinois Press, 1983),

212–55; Steven Fraser, *Labor Will Rule: Sidney Hillman and the Rise of American Labor* (New York: Free Press, 1991), 324–48; David M. Kennedy, *Freedom from Fear: The American People in Depression and War, 1929–1945* (New York: Oxford University Press, 1999), 120–24.

8. Ronald W. Schatz, "The National War Labor Board of World War II: A Re-Interpretation," Paper presented to University of Pennsylvania Economic History Forum, October 28, 2012 http://www.history.upenn.edu/economichistoryforum/docs/schatz_13a.pdf.

9. Nelson Lichtenstein, *State of the Union: A Century of American Labor*, rev. ed. (Princeton, N.J.: Princeton University Press, 2013), xii–xiii, 114–18, 120–22.

10. Jordan A. Schwarz, *The New Dealers: Power Politics in the Age of Roosevelt* (New York: Vintage, 1994), 123–37.

11. Jack Temple Kirby, *Rural Worlds Lost: The American South, 1920–1960* (Baton Rouge: Louisiana State University Press, 1987), 82, 226–27; Jonathan Scott Holloway, *Confronting The Veil: Abram Harris, Jr., E. Franklin Frazier, and Ralph Bunche, 1919–1941* (Chapel Hill: University of North Carolina Press, 2002).

12. Michael Denning, *The Cultural Front: The Laboring of American Culture in the Twentieth Century* (London: Verso, 1996), 68–69.

13. Howard Brick, *Transcending Capitalism: Visions of a New Society in Modern American Thought* (Ithaca, N.Y.: Cornell University Press, 2006), 12–13; http://www.irle.berkeley.edu/events/fall03/kerr.html; http://www.nytimes.com/2003/12/02/national/02KERR.html.

14. Steven Greenhouse, "VW Workers in Tennessee to Vote on Union," *New York Times*, February 3, 2014.

15. On Stern and political partnering, see Leon Fink and Brian Greenberg, *Upheaval in the Quiet Zone: 1199SEIU and the Politics of Health Care Unionism* (Urbana: University of Illinois Press, 2009), 275–80. To be sure, Stern's entrepreneurialism as well as autocratic governing style (both, incidentally also in the tradition of John Mitchell) drew sharp criticism. See, e.g., Steve Early, *The Civil Wars in U.S. Labor: Birth of a New Workers' Movement or Death Throes of the Old?* (Chicago: Haymarket, 2011)

16. See, e.g., Ruth Milkman, *L.A. Story: Immigrant Workers and the Future of the U.S. Labor Movement* (New York: Russell Sage, 2006).

Index

Abramowitz, Bessie, 107
Academic freedom, 80–81
Adams, Charles Francis, 28
Adams, Charles Kendall, 75
Adams, Graham, 53
Adams, Henry Carter, 66, 74, 103, 174n87
Adamson Act of 1916, 182n51
Addams, Jane, 69, 102, 103, 125, 137,
    172n57; on industrial relations, 53, 106–7,
    118; and Richard Ely, 78, 79, 173n74
AFL-CIO, 117
African Americans, 24, 33, 44, 135–36, 151;
    and socialism, 124, 135–36; and unions,
    19, 26, 52, 73
Alabama, 24
Allen, Henry J., 112, 113
Amalgamated Association of Iron and Steel
    Workers (AAISW), 38, 42, 44, 60. See also
    Homestead Strike of 1892
Amalgamated Clothing Workers (ACW),
    107–8, 150
Amana Society, 84–85
American Association for Labor Legislation,
    77–78
American Association of University Profes-
    sors, 80–81
American Economics Association (AEA), 72,
    75, 76, 79, 80, 171n50
American Exceptionalism, 6, 8, 9, 54, 149,
    153; and Homestead Strike of 1892, 44;
    and Pullman strike and boycott, 47, 49
American Fabian League, 69
American Federation of Labor (AFL), 4, 43,
    59, 61, 152, 184n84; and industrial arbitra-
    tion, 10, 98–99, 101, 106, 109, 115; labor
    radicals and, 127, 128; and Pullman strike,
    90, 105; in World War I, 111. See also
    Gompers, Samuel

"American Plan," 16. See also Open shop
American Railway Union (ARU), 52, 91, 105;
    in Pullman strike and boycott, 47, 51–53,
    61; and race, 52, 165n63
American Revolution, 15
Ameringer, Oscar, 126, 131
Anarchism, 124, 129
Anderson, Benedict, 31
Anderson, John A., 100
Anderson, Perry, 31
Andrews, John, 78, 83
Andrews, Thomas G., 15
Anthracite Coal Commission, 78–79, 105
Anthracite miners, 28, 36, 152. See also
    Anthracite strikes
Anthracite strikes, 28; 1900, 54–55, 58, 60;
    1902, 16, 35–36, 54, 55–57, 58, 60, 102,
    117; John Mitchell and, 9, 36, 53, 54, 55,
    56, 57, 61; Mark Hanna and, 55–58, 60
Anti-Semitism, 21–22, 67, 85
Appeal to Reason, 80, 131, 132, 137, 140
Arbeiter-Zeitung, 44–45
Arbitration, between nations, 43, 90, 97–98.
    See also Industrial arbitration
Arbitration Act of 1888, 99
Archer, Robin, 61
Armour, Philip, 3
"Auburn system," 23
"Australasian road," 92, 93–94, 95–96, 118;
    and industrial arbitration, 92, 96, 112, 116;
    limited influence in U.S., 112, 116, 117.
    See also Australia; New Zealand
Australia, 92, 94–95, 112; industrial relations
    in, 10, 92, 95, 112; labor politics in, 61, 95.
    See also Australasian road
Austria, 106, 124

Baer, George T., 35–36, 54, 55
Baker, Ray Stannard, 16

Bakunin, Mikhail, 124
Bascom, John A., 71, 82
Bebel, August, 123, 141
Belgium, 106, 125–27
Bell, Daniel, 121–22, 145
Bellamy, Edward, 69, 94, 124
Belmont, Alva, 60
Belmont, August, Jr., 58
Bemis, Edward R., 73–74, 76, 78, 103,
    173n69
Bender, Thomas, 5
Berger, Victor, 83, 86, 126, 133, 140, 187n20.
    See also *Milwaukee Leader*
Berkman, Alexander, 39, 124, 126, 129,
    187–88n31
Berle, Adolf, 151
Berlin, Ira, 4
Besant, Annie, 68
Bill of Rights, 150
Birge, Edward, 71
Blaine, James G., 21
Bliss, W. D. P., 69
Blissert, Robert, 21
Bloomfield, Meyer, 108
Bolshevik Revolution, 143
Brandeis, Louis D., 28, 107–10, 118
Brentano, Lujo, 66
Britain, 46, 48, 53, 97–99, 115–16, 164–
    65n51; Andrew Carnegie and, 39–41, 43–
    44, 46; "collective laissez-faire" in, 92, 115,
    118, 151; industrial arbitration in, 96, 114;
    intellectuals in, 67–68, 88; Labour Party
    in, 68, 88, 93, 127; Trade Disputes Act in,
    92, 93, 110, 115. See also Fabian Society
Brockhausen, Frederick, 87
Brody, David, 28, 110
Brotherhood of Locomotive Firemen, 18, 52
Brotherhood of Railway Trainmen, 51
Brown, David S., 6–7
Bryan, William Jennings, 43, 132
Buck's Stove and Range case. See *Gompers v.
    Buck's Stove and Range*
Buhle, Mari Jo, 141
Building trades, 62, 99, 113, 116
Burlington strike of 1888, 52, 99
Burns, John, 40, 46
Bush, George H. W., 1, 155n1
Butler, Nicholas Murray, 70, 170n29

Cahan, Abraham, 126, 134
Camp, Helen C., 130

Canada, 10, 92, 95, 111, 112, 114
Carnegie, Andrew, 3, 38, 122; and Britain,
    39–41, 43–44, 46, 163n24; and Homestead
    Strike, 9, 34, 35, 36, 38–39, 41–42, 46, 49,
    61, 163n24; as reformer, 39–41, 42–44, 58,
    117
Carnegie Endowment for International
    Peace, 43
Case, Theresa A., 26–27
Castles, Francis, 94
Chamberlin, Thomas, 63, 71
Chernyshevsky, Nikolai, 129
Chicago, 3, 129; building trades in, 99; strikes
    in, 36, 47, 49, 106–7. See also Civic Federa-
    tion of Chicago
Chicago Daily Socialist, 130, 142
Child labor, 23, 25
Chinese workers, 20–21, 26, 33
Christian pacifists, 102, 137
Christian socialism, 69, 124, 137–40
Civic Federation of Chicago, 52–53, 102–3
Civil Rights Act of 1964, 150
Clark, John Bates, 78, 175n94
Clayton Antitrust Act (1914), 109–10
Cleveland, Grover, 49; and Pullman strike,
    47, 49, 50, 51, 165n55; and U.S. Strike
    Commission, 91, 105
Closed shop, 18, 106, 108, 109, 116
Coal industry, 15, 24, 25, 28; immigrants in,
    3, 26, 56–57, 152, 166n75. See also Anthra-
    cite strikes; United Mine Workers of
    America
Coeur d'Alene coal strike (1892), 36
Cole, G. D. H., 93
"Collective laissez-faire," 109; in Britain, 92,
    115, 118, 151
Colorado Fuel and Iron Company, 15, 111
Colorado Industrial Commission, 111–12,
    113
Columbia University, 7, 72, 76, 134, 151. See
    also Butler, Nicholas Murray
Coming Nation, 131, 132, 141
Commission on Industrial Relations (1912–
    1915), 82, 102, 110–12
Common law, 10, 14, 68, 92, 108–9
Commons, John R., 81–82, 84–85; and
    Commission on Industrial Relations, 110,
    111; and Richard Ely, 76–81, 83–84, 88,
    172n64, 175n95; and socialism, 86; on
    state mechanisms for conflict resolution,

106, 109, 110, 111, 118; at University of
Wisconsin, 76, 78, 79, 81–84, 87, 88, 89;
and U.S. Industrial Commission, 106
Commons, Nell D., 85
Commonwealth College, 144
Commonwealth Colony, 140–41
Commonwealth v. Hunt (1842), 13
Communist International (Comintern), 144
Communist Manifesto, 123
Company stores, 25, 30, 57
Company towns, 35, 48, 49. *See also* Pull-
man, Illinois
Confédération Génerale du Travail (CGT),
128
Conger, Josephine, 126, 142
Congress of Industrial Organizations (CIO),
45, 152
Contingency, role of, 35–36, 53, 61–62
Contract labor, 20–21, 22–23, 32
Convict labor, 23–24, 26, 30, 32, 33, 144
Corey, Lewis. *See* Fraina, Louis
Cornell University, 74, 88
Cottenham, Green, 24
Craft unions, 18–19, 97, 98, 100, 159n45. *See
also* Building trades; Railroad
brotherhoods
Crain, William H., 99–101
Croly, Herbert, 59–61, 62
Cross, Ira B., 83, 86
Crownhart, C. H., 82
Currey, Margery, 134

Deakin, Alfred, 95
Debs, Eugene V., 18, 51–53, 125, 126, 133,
145; conversion of, to socialism, 47, 90,
132–33, 177n1; imprisonment of, 35, 47,
49, 51, 90–91; and industrial arbitration,
52, 53, 91, 105; and IWW, 127, 130; as
presidential candidate, 121, 125, 135; and
Pullman strike, 9, 35, 47, 51–53, 55, 90–
91, 105; and religion, 133; and Socialist
Party of America, 121, 123, 131–33, 135
Declaration of Independence, 15
Degler, Carl, 3
De Leon, Daniel, 126, 127, 128, 130, 134–35
Dell, Floyd, 122, 126, 133–35, 146
Democratic Party, 7, 45, 51
Depression of 1870s, 5
Depression of 1890s, 5, 36, 69, 76, 91–92
Dilke, Charles, 40

Dockworker unions, 46
Domestic workers, 23, 153
Du Bois, W. E. B., 33, 126, 135–36
Dunbar, Charles, 171n50
Dunlop, John, 89
Durand, E. Dana, 106

Easley, Ralph, 55, 58, 103
Eastman, Max, 126, 144
Eggert, Gerald G., 51
Eisenstadt, A. S., 40
Ely, Anna, 77, 172–73n64
Ely, Richard T., 63–64, 71–81, 89; and Amer-
ican Economics Association, 72, 75, 76, 79,
171n50; extensive contacts of, 63–64, 69,
78, 79–81; and Jane Addams, 78, 79,
173n74; and John R. Commons, 76–81,
83–84, 88, 172n64, 175n95; in post-World
War I era, 75, 172n57, 173n69; and reli-
gion, 72–73, 171n38; and University of
Wisconsin, 71–72, 74–75, 76–78, 82–84
Emerson, Ralph Waldo, 102
Emmerson, Charles, 5
Engels, Friedrich, 31, 123, 161n66
"Equal pay for equal work," 25
Erdman Act (1898), 51, 105
Ethnic nationalisms, 124

Fabian Society, 66, 67–69, 70, 87; and British
academia, 68, 169n19; and Labour Party,
68, 88; overseas influence of, 69, 94. *See
also* Webb, Sidney
Fahy, John, 57
"Fair wage," 30
Feminism, 79, 124, 141–43
Feuerbach, Ludwig, 31, 161n66
Field, Stephen A., 16, 19
Filene, Lincoln A., 108
First International, 15, 128
Flynn, Elizabeth Gurley, 126, 129–30, 144
Foner, Eric, 16
Foran, Martin, 100–101
Foran Act (1885), 22–23
Ford, Henry, 115
Foster, Frank, 97, 98
Foster, W. H., 97
Foster, William Z., 126, 128, 144
Fraina, Louis (Lewis Corey), 126, 128, 144
France, 9, 12–13, 31–32, 33, 157n2; indus-
trial relations in, 13, 19, 33, 48, 95, 106;
syndicalism in, 128

Frankfurter, Felix, 110, 150, 151
Fraser, Steve, 148, 150
"Free-labor" ideology, 9, 13–14, 30–33; conservative tilt of, 9, 13–14, 15–16; and contract workers, 19–25, 26; and women's wage labor, 18–19; workers' use of, 14–15, 16–19, 20–21, 24–25, 26–28
French Revolution, 157n2
Frick, Henry Clay, 35, 41; and Homestead Strike, 38, 39, 41, 44, 45, 61; shooting of, 39, 124, 129
Furner, Mary, 76
Furuseth, Andrew, 29

Gage, Lyman, 52–53, 102–3
Gandhi, Mohandas K., 13, 118–19
Garment industry, 107–8, 116, 150; mechanisms in, for conflict resolution, 28–29, 107–8, 116; strikes in, 29, 107; sweatshops in, 21–22
Garrison, William Lloyd, 102
Gates, George A., 140
George, Henry, 94
Germany: industrial relations in, 48, 79, 97; intellectual movements in, 66–68, 70, 87, 88, 138; socialism in, 123, 124, 135, 141–42, 170n27; universities in, 66–68, 70, 71, 72, 76–77, 122, 135, 168n9
Gibson, Eustace, 99–100
Gilman, Daniel Coit, 71
Gladden, Washington, 102–3, 139
Gladstone, William, 40, 46
Goldman, Emma, 126, 129, 142, 143, 144, 145–46, 187–88n31
Goldmark, Josephine, 110
Gompers v. Buck's Stove and Range, 43, 164n33
Gompers, Samuel, 43, 61, 78, 90, 102, 110, 164n33; and industrial arbitration, 97, 98, 101; and National Civic Federation, 58, 60, 61, 81, 101
Gordon, Colin, 29
Gould, Jay, 18, 26, 27. See also Great Southwest Strike of 1886
Graham, Frank Porter, 151
Great Depression, 37, 149
Great Northern Strike of 1893, 51, 52, 53, 105
Great Southwest Strike of 1886, 26–27
Green, James R., 7

Gronlund, Lawrence, 124
Gutman, Herbert, 4, 7, 15, 16

Hagerty, Thomas J., 126, 128
Haldeman-Julius, Emanuel, 126, 142, 143
Haldeman-Julius, Marcet, 126, 142
Hale, Robert, 76
Hall, Covington, 126, 144
Hanna, Mark, 9, 58–61, 62, 117, 152; and anthracite strikes, 55, 56, 57, 58, 60; death of, 58, 106, 117; and National Civic Federation, 58–59, 60, 102
Hardie, Kier, 40, 46, 163n24
Harper, William Rainey, 70, 74
Harper's Weekly, 51
Harrison, Hubert, 126, 136
Hay, John, 43
Haymarket affair (1886), 74, 129
Haywood, William "Big Bill," 126, 127–28, 129, 144
Hegel, G. W. F., 31, 161n66
Hemchandran, Narayan, 118
Herron, Carrie Rand, 141
Herron, George, 126, 140–41
Higgins, Henry Bourne, 95, 110
Hill, James J., 3, 52. See also Great Northern Strike of 1888
Hillman, Sidney, 107, 150
Hillquit, Morris, 123, 126, 137
Hobsbawm, E. J., 1, 2, 30
Hodges, Luther, 149
Hofstadter, Richard, 7
Homestead Strike of 1892, 38–39, 41–42, 44–48, 61, 108; aftermath of, 35, 41–43, 45–46, 129; Andrew Carnegie and, 9, 34, 35, 36, 38–39, 41–42, 46, 49, 61, 163n24; Henry Clay Frick and, 38, 39, 41, 44, 45, 61; strikebreakers in, 38, 41–42; trigger for, 36, 38
Hoover, Herbert, 75
Howat, Alexander, 113
Howe, Frederic, 67, 78
Howell, Chris, 115
Howells, William Dean, 69
Hoxie, R. M., 27
Hull House, 79, 102, 106
Hunter, Robert, 78

immigrant workers, 3–4, 6–7, 20–23, 137; Chinese, 20–21, 26, 33; in coal mining, 3,

26, 56–57, 152, 166n75; in garment trades, 21–22; racialized views regarding, 20–22, 41; restrictive legislation on, 21, 22–23, 145; in Socialist Party, 11, 137, 144; in twenty-first century, 152–53. *See also* Contract workers
India, 31, 118–19, 136
Industrial arbitration, 45, 83, 91; in Australia and New Zealand, 10, 92, 93–94, 95–96, 110, 112, 116; in coal industry, 54, 55, 58; in France, 13; in garment industry, 107, 108; proposals for, in Gilded Age U.S., 91, 96–97, 99–100, 102–4, 105–9, 110, 118; and railroad industry, 27, 49, 51, 52, 53; states' experimentation with, 105, 106, 111–14; union attitudes toward, 98–99, 100–101, 105, 109, 117; in World War I, 111, 114
"Industrial democracy," 108
"Industrial pluralism," 118, 151. *See also* "Collective laissez-faire"
Industrial Workers of the World (IWW), 120–21, 127–28, 129–30, 143
Ingersoll, Robert, 133
Injunctions, 16, 27, 109; limiting of, in Britain, 92; in railroad strikes, 27, 47, 52
Intercollegiate Socialist Society, 136, 140
International Ladies' Garment Workers Union (ILGWU), 22, 107
International Socialist Review, 80, 124, 127, 146
International Women's Day, 142
Irish, 20–21, 26, 33
Irons, Martin, 26, 27, 126, 131
Isserman, Maurice, 87

James, Edmund, 66
Jenks, Jeremiah, 106
Jews, 6–7, 21–22, 85, 130, 134, 137
Johns Hopkins University, 71, 72, 74, 81
Joint Board of Sanitary Control, 22
Jones, Mary "Mother," 54, 57, 125, 126, 127, 129

Kansas Court of Industrial Relations, 112–14
Katznelson, Ira, 65, 149
Kautsky, Karl, 123
Kearney, Dennis, 21
Keefe, Daniel, 58
Kelley, Florence, 66, 69, 78, 79, 122, 126

Kellor, Frances, 23
Kendrick, John W., 50
Kennedy, Thomas, 45
Kerr, Charles, 126, 127, 132, 142, 143, 146
Kerr, Clark, 88–89, 151–52
Kessler-Harris, Alice, 18–19
Keyserling, Leon, 150
King, MacKenzie, 111
Kingston, Charles Cameron, 94, 95, 179n15
Knies, Karl, 72
Knights of Labor (KOL), 4, 17, 21, 32, 159n45; left intellectuals and, 69, 73; legislation supported by, 17, 22, 24–25, 64, 96, 101–2; and industrial arbitration, 96, 97, 101–2; and race, 26, 73; strikes by, 18, 26, 27, 99; and wage system, 17, 25
Knox, Philander C., 45
Korngold, Piri, 130
Korngold, Ralph, 126, 130
Krause, Paul, 45
Kropotkin, Peter, 124

Labadie, Joseph, 63–64
"Labor republicanism," 7, 96
Labour Party (Britain), 68, 88, 93, 115
La Follette, Robert M., 71, 75, 82; as governor, 69, 82; and Richard Ely, 75, 80
La Follette Act. *See* Merchant Seamen's Act of 1915
La Pietra Report, 4–5
Lauck, Jett, 114
Laugen, Todd R., 113
Lawrence textile strike of 1912, 36–37
Layton, Robert, 96
Leiserson, William M., 82, 83, 85–86, 150
Lenroot, Katharine, 79
Leo XIII, 102
Lewis, David Levering, 135
Lewis, John L., 113
Lichtenstein, Nelson, 150
Liebknecht, Wilhelm, 123
Lilienthal, David, 151
Lincoln, Abraham, 12, 14, 16
Lloyd, Henry Demorest, 69, 78–79, 103, 118
Lodge, Oliver, 68
London, Meyer, 126, 134
London School of Economics, 68, 94
Los Angeles Times bombing (1910), 102
Lovejoy, Arthur, 81

Ludlow Massacre (1914), 111
Lundberg, Emma O., 79

MacDonald, Ramsey, 68
Macy, V. Everitt, 78
Magee, Christopher L., 44
Manly, Basil, 115
Manning, Henry Edward, 93, 118
Marshall, Louis, 108
Marx, Karl, 31, 72, 84, 123, 134, 143, 161n66
Master and servant laws, 16, 25, 92
Maude, Aylmer, 102
Maurer, James H., 123, 126
Mauss, Marcel, 39
May, Vanessa H., 23
Mayo, Elton, 88
McBride, John, 61
McCarthy, Charles, 69, 80, 82, 86–87, 110
McClelland, John, 96
McCormick, Stanley, 78, 79
McDonnell, Joseph P., 15
McGovern, Francis, 69, 80
McGuire, P. J., 98–99, 101
McIlyar, J. J., 45–46
McKeen, William Riley, 18
McKinley, William, 54–55, 57–58, 105,
    166–67n85
McLuckie, John, 38–39, 42, 163–64n32
McNeill, George E., 17, 25
Mechanics' lien legislation, 24–25
Meitzen, E. R., 126, 144
Merchant seamen, 29–30, 32
Merchant Seamen's Act of 1915 (La Follette
    Act), 29–30,
Miles, Nelson A., 47, 49–50, 165n55
Militia, state. See National Guard
Miller, Sally M., 144
Mills, Walter Thomas, 126, 132, 144
Milwaukee Leader, 124, 127
Minimum wage laws, 152
Mitchell, John, 56, 59, 62, 152, 193n15; and
    anthracite strikes, 9, 36, 53, 54, 55, 56, 57,
    61; background of, 56; and immigrant
    workers, 56, 152, 166n75; and National
    Civic Federation, 55, 58, 59, 102
Mittelman, E. B., 83, 85
M'Lachlan, Daniel, 15
Moley, Raymond, 151
Morgan, Anne, 60

Morgan, J. P., 3, 36, 60, 115, 117; and anthra-
    cite strikes, 55, 56, 60
Morgan, Lewis Henry, 134
Morley, John, 40, 41
Moses, Jacob, 108
Most, Johann, 124, 129
Moyer, Charles, 127
Muncy, Robyn, 79
Mundella, A. J., 96

National Association of Manufacturers
    (NAM), 58–59, 117
National Civic Federation, 58–59, 60–61, 81,
    117, 152; Andrew Carnegie and, 43, 117;
    John Mitchell and, 55, 58, 59, 102; Marc
    Hanna and, 58–59, 60, 102; origins of, 52,
    58, 102–3; retreat of, from early views, 60,
    62; Samuel Gompers and, 58, 60, 61, 81,
    101
National Guard, 27, 57, 101, 113; in Home-
    stead Strike, 38, 44–45
National Industrial Conferences (1919), 114
National Industrial Recovery Act (1933), 150
National Labor Reform Party, 23
National Labor Relations Act (Wagner Act),
    148, 150
National Labor Union, 21
National Municipal League, 23
Native Americans, 49–50
New Deal, 45, 82, 145, 148–50, 151, 153
New Llano Cooperative Colony, 144
Newman, Pauline, 120, 126
New Republic, 59, 114
New York State School of Industrial and
    Labor Relations, 88
New Zealand, 10, 92, 93–94, 104, 110, 112,
    178n5. See also "Australasian road"
Nord, Philip, 32
Novak, William J., 14

Occupy Wall Street, 152
O'Donnell, Hugh, 44
Odum, Howard W., 151
O'Hare, Frank, 126, 132, 144
O'Hare, Kate Richards, 120, 126, 132, 141,
    144, 145
Olivier, Sydney, 68
Olney, Richard T., 35, 47, 49, 50–51, 52
O'Neill, John J., 96, 99
Open shop, 16, 58, 106, 117

Organization of American Historians, 4–5
Owen, Chandler, 126, 136

Pacifists. *See* Christian pacifists
Palmer, William J., 15
Pannekoek, Anton, 128
Parry, David M., 58–59
Parsons, Albert, 21, 129
Parsons, Lucy, 126, 127
Parsons, Kans., 26, 27
Paterson silk workers' strike of 1913, 130
Patten, Simon, 66
Pattison, Robert E., 44
Paxson, Edward, 45
Peck, Gunther, 23
People's Party (Populists), 17, 50
Perkins, Charles Elliott, 51
Perkins, George, 55, 58
Perlman, Selig, 54, 83–84, 85
Phelps Stokes, J. G., 126, 139–40
Picketing, 16, 93, 113
Pillsbury, Charles A., 102
Pinkerton, Alan, 15.
Pinkerton agents, 38, 39, 45
Pittsburgh Survey, 82
Populists (People's Party), 17, 50
Potter-Webb, Beatrice, 68, 69
Pouget, Émile, 128
Pound, Roscoe, 81
Powderly, Terence, 27, 64
"Preferential shop," 107, 108
Public-sector workers, 37
Pullman, George, 35, 38, 46–47, 48–49; and 1894 conflict, 35, 36, 47, 49, 61
Pullman, Illinois, 46–47, 48
Pullman Commission. *See* U.S. Strike Commission
Pullman strike and boycott (1894), 35, 46–47, 60; and arbitration proposals, 53, 102, 103, 106; aftermath of, 49, 51; background to, 47–49; Debs and, 9, 35, 47, 51–53, 55, 90–91, 105; trigger for, 36, 47; union strategy in, 51–53, 55, 105

Radical America, 7
Railroad brotherhoods, 18, 19, 27, 51, 52, 99, 109
Railroad industry, 3, 18, 20, 182n51; and anthracite strikes, 55, 56, 99; dispute resolution mechanisms in, 51, 105; unions in,

28. *See also* American Railway Union; Railroad brotherhoods; Railroad strikes
Railroad strikes, 18, 50, 113. *See also* Great Northern Strike of 1893; Great Southwest Strike of 1893; Pullman strike and boycott
Railway Labor Act of 1926, 182n51
Rand, Mrs. Carrie D., 140, 141
Randolph, A. Philip, 126, 136
Rand School, 141
Rauschenbush, Walter, 126, 138–39
Raushenbush, Elizabeth Brandeis, 83
Reade, Charles, 48–49
Reddy, William, 19
Reed, John, 126, 130, 144
Reeves, William Pember, 94
"Regulatory unionism," 29
Reitman, Ben, 126, 145–46
Religion, 133–34, 137–41. *See also* Christian pacifists; Christian socialism; Social Gospel movement
Republican Party, 57, 89, 136
Rerum Novarum, 102
Research universities, 88–89, 151–52; German influence on, 71, 76–77; rise of, 10, 71–72; shifting focus of, 88–89; significance of, 3, 10, 64–65
Reuschemeyer, Dietrich, 67
Richberg, Donald, 151
Ricker, A. W., 137–38
"Right to work," 16, 150. *See also* Open shop
Ritschl, Albrecht, 138, 139
Rockefeller, John D., 3
Rockefeller, John D., Jr., 111, 115, 117
Rodgers, Daniel T., 5, 10, 72, 149
Roosevelt, Franklin D., 57, 150
Roosevelt, Theodore, 55, 58, 117
Root, Elihu, 55
Ross, Edward A., 74, 76, 78, 173n69
Roy, Andrew, 56
Ruskin, John, 132, 139
Ruskin College, 127
Ryan, John A., 103

St. Louis Post-Dispatch, 41
Salvatore, Nick, 53, 132
Sandburg, Carl, 130
Sanger, Margaret, 126, 143
Saposs, David, 83, 85, 150
Schäfer, Axel R., 135
Schiff, Jacob, 108

Schlossberg, Joseph, 120, 126, 145
Schmoller, Gustav von, 66, 67, 135
Schwab, Charles, 41–42
Scudder, Vida, 126, 139
Second International, 123, 124, 127, 128, 137; and women, 141, 142
Sedalia, Missouri, 26
Seidel, Emil, 130
Seligman, E. R. A., 81
Senate Committee on the Relations Between Labor and Capital, 96, 97, 98–99
Sewell, William H., Jr., 33
Shaw, George Bernard, 68
Shaw, Lemuel, 13
Sherman Anti-Trust Act, 47, 109
Shirtwaist strike of 1909, 29, 60
Shore, Elliott, 131
Simons, Algie M., 125–27, 143; and Richard Ely, 78, 80; and Socialist Party, 80, 123, 124, 127, 130, 143
Simons, May Wood, 125, 126, 127, 142, 144
Sinclair, Upton, 122–23, 125, 126, 145
Slichter, Sumner, 83, 85–86, 89
Slotkin, Richard, 49
Social Darwinism, 16, 34, 148
Social Democracy of America, 133
Social Gospel movement, 68–69, 70, 72, 139, 140–41
Socialist Labor Party (SLP), 80, 125, 127, 130, 140
Socialist Party of America (SPA), 128, 144, 145; African Americans in, 135–36, 189n7; Debs and, 121, 123, 131–33, 135; factions in, 130, 144; founding of, 127; immigrants in, 11, 137, 144; and internationalism, 10–11, 121–24, 132; in Milwaukee, 86, 127, 137, 187n20; and Populist legacy, 131; and religion, 133, 137; and World War I, 80, 127, 143–44; youthful age profile of, 120–21, 125, 126, 130
Sombart, Werner, 6, 67
Sorin, Gerald, 137
Spargo, John, 126, 130, 143, 144
Spencer, Herbert, 76, 134
Stanford University, 74, 86, 106
Stansell, Christine, 142
Steel strike of 1919, 115
Stern, Andy, 152, 193n15
Steward, Ira, 17, 19, 25
Stokes, Rose Pastor, 126, 139, 140, 144

Stolberg, Benjamin, 29
Strikebreakers, 15, 41–42, 44
Strong, Josiah, 139
Studies on the Left, 7
Subcontracting, 21–22
Sumner, Helen, 79, 83
Sumner, William Graham, 16, 148
Sweatshops, 21–22, 120
Swedberg, Richard, 12
Swift, Gustavus, 3
Sylvis, William, 21
Syndicalism, 128–29

Taff Vale judgment (1901, Britain), 93
Taft, William Howard, 109, 111, 112–13, 114; as president, 82, 110
Taft-Hartley Act (1947), 150
Tawney, James A., 103
Taylor, Graham, 78
Taylor, Paul S., 88, 152
Tennessee Coal, Iron & Railroad Company, 24
Thomas, Norman, 126, 137
Thompson, Carl D., 126, 137, 187n20
Thoreau, Henry David, 102
Tocqueville, Alexis de, 12–13, 157n2
Tolstoy, Leo, 102, 118
Tomlins, Christopher, 14
Trade Disputes Act (1906, Britain), 92, 93, 110, 115
Trautmann, William, 126, 128
Trevellick, Richard, 21
Tugwell, Rexford, 151
Tuley, Murray F., 99
Turner, Frederick Jackson, 71, 82, 125
Twain, Mark, 2

United Garment Workers, 107
United Kingdom. See Britain
United Mine Workers of America (UMWA), 15, 45, 58, 59, 61, 113. See also Anthracite strikes; Mitchell, John
Universities. See Research universities; specific institutions
University of California, 88, 151–52
University of Chicago, 70, 74
University of North Carolina at Chapel Hill, 151
University of Wisconsin at Madison, 7, 10, 64; presidents of, 71–72, 75, 80, 82, 150;

progressive policy intellectuals at, 10, 69–70, 71–72, 74–75, 76, 79, 80, 82–89; and "Wisconsin Idea," 69–70, 71, 75–76. *See also* Commons, John R.; Ely, Richard
U.S. army, 47, 49–50
U.S. Bureau of Labor Statistics, 79
U.S. Chamber of Commerce, 117
U.S. Children's Bureau, 79
U.S. Constitution, 14, 100, 103, 110, 112, 150
U.S. Industrial Commission (1898–1902), 81, 105–6
U.S. Steel Corporation, 38, 45, 60
U.S. Strike Commission ("Pullman Commission"), 49, 51, 90, 91, 101, 103–4, 105
U.S. Supreme Court, 9, 19, 28, 47, 112–13, 114

Vagrancy laws, 24, 25, 113
Valesh, Eva McDonald, 21
Van Devanter, Willis, 112
Van Dyke, John C., 42
Van Hise, Alice, 77
Van Hise, Charles, 71, 77, 78, 80, 150
Van Rossem, Ronan, 67
Verein für Socialpolitik, 66–67, 68, 70, 87, 168n9, 170n27

Wachman, Marvin, 86
Wage cuts, 15, 26, 36–37, 94–95
"Wage slavery," 14, 17
Wagner, Adolph, 66, 67, 135
Wagner, Robert F., 150. *See also* National Labor Relations Act
Walden, May, 126, 142, 143, 146
Waldman, Louis, 126, 137
Wall, Joseph, 40
Wallas, Graham, 68, 78
Walling, Anna Strunsky, 126, 142–43
Walling, William English, 125, 126, 138
Walsh, Frank, 110–11, 113, 114–15, 176n3
War Labor Conference Board (World War I), 111, 114
War Labor Conference Board (World War II), 150
Warner, Charles Dudley, 2
Wayland, Julius A., 126, 131–32, 140, 142
Webb, Sidney, 64, 68, 69, 78, 84, 93

Weber, Max, 121
Weeks, James D., 103
Weinstein, James, 62
Wells, H. G., 68
Wells, Oliver E., 75
Western Federation of Miners (WFM), 127
West Virginia, 28
White, Richard, 35, 50
White, William Allen, 112, 113
Whitley, J. H., 114
Whitman, Walt, 143
Wildcat strikes, 108, 113
Willard, Frances, 64, 69
Wilson, Woodrow, 115, 117, 141
Wilson v. New (1917), 112–13
"Wisconsin Idea," 69–70, 71, 76, 80, 86–87, 89, 176n103; origins of, 71–72, 75–76; Richard Ely and, 75–76, 80. *See also* Wisconsin Industrial Commission
Wisconsin Industrial Commission, 82–83, 86
Witte, Edwin, 82, 83, 150
Wolff Packing Co. cases (1923, 1925), 112–13
Women, 18–19, 36, 159n45; in garment industry, 21, 36, 60, 108; in higher education, 77, 79; and socialism, 124, 125, 141–43. *See also* Women's Christian Temperance Union
Women's Christian Temperance Union (WCTU), 64, 69, 98, 102, 141
Women's Trade Union League, 60 (no WTUL)
Woods, Robert A., 69
Woolf, Leonard, 68
Woolf, Virginia, 68
World War I, 75, 143–44; industrial relations during, 102, 111, 114, 117; socialists and, 80, 127, 137, 140, 141, 143–44
World War II, 114, 148, 150
Worthington, Nicholas, 91
Wounded Knee massacre, 50
Wright, Carroll R., 91, 103, 106
Wunderlin, Clarence E., Jr., 106

Yellen, Samuel, 61
Yellow-dog contracts, 38

Zangwell, Israel, 40
Zetkin, Clara, 142

Acknowledgments

Like my previous effort, this book largely grew up within the inviting environs, physical and social, of the Newberry Library. The additional facilitator this time was the Newberry's Lloyd Lewis Fellowship in 2012–2013, for which I am of course most grateful. A stellar group of fellows and residential scholars under the direction of Daniel Greene and Liesl Olson added stimulus as well as good cheer to the fellowship year: I particularly enjoyed wide-ranging discussions with Robert Hellyer, Michelle Dowd, and Michael Goode. In addition, I benefitted enormously from the specific ministrations of librarians Jill Gage and Lisa Schoblasky as well as Scholl Center dynamos Christopher Cantwell and Carmen Jaramillo. I also gratefully acknowledge the continuing support of colleagues, graduate students, and administrators at my University of Illinois at Chicago home. In the final stretch, Alison Anderson proved a most helpful copy editor, while Jim O'Brien and Jenny Schwartzberg served as exceptional proofreaders.

In the course of my research and rough chapter drafts, I reached out to a number of experts in the field and was always rewarded with a judicious mixture of selective criticism and positive reinforcement. Sven Beckert helped get the whole project rolling and kindly invited me to offer a chapter to his history of capitalism seminar, where I also received useful commentary from Alexander Keyssar. Others who provided thorough chapter readings include David Brody, Eric Foner, Gerald Friedman, Robert Johnston, Scott Nelson, Axel Schäfer, Jean-Christian Vinel, and Jeffrey Sklansky. In addition, Nelson Lichtenstein helped steer me to a sharper set of conclusions.

From start to finish, four people made signal accomplishments that deserve special recognition. As usual, Susan Levine viewed everything in its early, molten state, helpfully distinguishing between themes worth developing and those better left to another project. Elizabeth Tandy Shermer took the lead in recruiting my developing manuscript to the University of Pennsylvania Press. As I revised, she injected a contagious enthusiasm and a nearly endless spray of valuable references and questions on multiple drafts that pushed the project forward. Eric Arnesen also answered the call of a friend in need: his merciless reading is like an airport scanner that unfailingly identifies every ill-fitting or overused expression and undocumented assertion. As the book neared completion, editor Bob Lockhart took up the argument from afar and shrewdly cut away the brush to clear the main path. The dedication is to my grandchildren, who provided some of my happiest moments during the preparation of this book.